"Unputdownable . . . I have re[...] with high admiration, but none of them can match this story, for its sheer oddity . . . By telling the story of the brazen theft of a cookbook, and the fate of its title long after the war, Urbach has also retold the tragic Holocaust story in quite unforgettable lines" A.N. WILSON

"A remarkable and important story" BBC Radio 4 *Woman's Hour*

"Unlike Nazi art theft, about which there are many excellent books, there has been surprisingly little research into the Nazi theft of Jewish authorship . . . As this engaging memoir, smoothly translated by Jamie Bulloch, makes clear, the theft of the cookbook remained for Alice's entire life the symbol of everything that had been stolen from her"
CAROLINE MOOREHEAD, *Times Literary Supplement*

"In a remarkable new book, Alice's granddaughter Karina, a noted historian, has traced what happened to her family but also what happened to the cookbook" DANIEL FINKELSTEIN

"What the historian has brought to light is perfect film material – persecution, murder, fraud, imprisonment, escape, rescue, friendship, secret service activities, rise, fall and a new beginning . . . And Urbach's writing is exciting, cinematic" SUSANNE KIPPENBERGER, *Tagesspiegel*

"This new book is an important act of reclamation"
Prospect Magazine Books of the Year 2022

"A gripping piece of 20th-century family history but also something much more original: a rare insight into the 'Aryanisation' of Jewish-authored books during the Nazi regime. Urbach has meticulously pieced together everything she could find about how and why Alice's publishers were able to deny her authorship for more than 80 years . . . It's impossible to read this moving and clear-eyed book without admiring Alice's fiercely optimistic spirit" BEE WILSON, *Financial Times*

KARINA URBACH

ALICE'S BOOK

How the Nazis Stole
my Grandmother's Cookbook

Translated from the German by
Jamie Bulloch

MACLEHOSE PRESS
QUERCUS · LONDON

First published as *Das Buch Alice: Wie die Nazis das Kochbuch meiner Großmutter raubten* by
Propyläen/Ullstein Buchverlage, Berlin, in 2020

First published in Great Britain in 2022 by MacLehose Press
This paperback edition published in 2023 by

MacLehose Press
An imprint of Quercus Editions Limited
Carmelite House
50 Victoria Embankment
London EC4Y 0DZ

An Hachette UK company

A CIP catalogue record for this book is available
from the British Library.

ISBN (MMP) 978 1 52941 632 9
ISBN (Ebook) 978 1 52941 633 6

10 9 8 7 6 5 4 3 2 1

Designed and typeset in Albertina by Libanus Press Ltd
Printed and bound in Great Britain by Clays Ltd, Elcograf S.p.A.

For Wera and Otto

CONTENTS

PREFACE
THE BOOK OF AN UNKNOWN WOMAN

I can't cook, which is probably why it took me so long to realise that we had two cookbooks on our shelf at home with the same title: *So kocht man in Wien!* (Cooking the Viennese Way!). The text and colour photographs in both books were identical; the only difference was in the name on the cover. The 1938 edition was attributed to Alice Urbach, whereas the 1939 one claimed Rudolf Rösch as its author.

Alice Urbach was my grandmother. I hardly ever saw her because she lived in America and I grew up in Germany. She died while I was still a child and my memories of her are hazy. I knew from family lore that she had been a famous cook in 1930s Vienna and that her culinary skills had saved her life. But why and exactly how this had happened remained unclear.

When, many years after her death, I became a historian, it never crossed my mind to write about her.

But, one day, my American cousin Katrina (a single "t" is the difference between our names) gave me a box with family letters and old cassettes. Katrina is a dedicated paediatrician and a pragmatist. She thought it only natural that I, a historian, should explore our grandmother's story. As so often is the case, my family members had a wealth of anecdotes and few facts. But when I started reading the letters and listening to Alice's voice on tape, I began to get an idea of what she had been through. From that moment on, all I wanted to do was tell her story.

The research took me from Vienna to New York via London. And as the geographical scope of my investigation widened, so did the group of protagonists. Alice was part of a complex family history, which began in a ghetto and then continued in Viennese millionaire circles. Famous individuals such as Anna Freud and the physicist Lise Meitner played a role in Alice's life, as did many others whose names are unknown to history. These included an American secret agent by the name of Cordelia Dodson, a Munich publisher, and twenty-four Jewish children whom Alice looked after in the Lake District during the Second World War. The story of Alice's own children – her sons Otto and Karl – was remarkable too. While Otto led an adventurous life in China, back in Vienna Karl believed for a long time that he was safe from the Nazis.

This book is also an indictment of theft. Alice was a cookery writer who saw her work appropriated by an "Aryan". What happened to her was part of a large-scale fraud that German publishers continued to practise after the war. Alice's case meant that this fraud was first made public in autumn 2020, leading to some surprising revelations. They are discussed for the first time in this new edition.

Although Alice fought for her book to the bitter end, she would have hated being thought of as a female Job. She wanted to be remembered for her "adventures and actions". Her son Otto also strove to avoid sentimentality. When he tried to get Karl out of Vienna in 1938, he wrote to his brother, "I beg you to do without maudlin sentiment . . . It's completely unnecessary to gush with gratitude in your letters."[1]

This book will attempt to avoid maudlin sentiment.

Karina Urbach
Cambridge, November 2021

1: THE VIENNA STATE OPERA, 1938

"Red-white-red unto death!"
Cornelia Dodson, 2003[1]

On Friday 11 March Cordelia, Elizabeth and Daniel Dodson bought tickets for the Vienna State Opera. They'd been in Vienna for some time and knew their way around the city. All the same, no-one would have taken them for locals. The three siblings looked exactly as you'd imagine young Americans from a well-to-do family to look: tall, sporty and casually dressed, in an expensive way. Cordelia was the eldest and the undoubted leader of the group. The twenty-five-year-old decided their programme and that evening she had scheduled a visit to the opera.

If Cordelia's later comments are to be believed, she resolved to change her life after the events of 11 March.[2] Until then she had led an extremely sheltered existence. Like many American college students of her generation, Cordelia was accustomed to a life of security. Her father, William Dodson, was the chairman of the chamber of commerce in Portland, Oregon.[3] He had financed an expensive university education for all his children, but Cordelia was his great hope. It was no coincidence that he'd named her after one of Shakespeare's heroines. And like King Lear's daughter, in the end Cordelia Dodson would not fail to meet her father's expectations.

The reason for Cordelia's coming to Vienna in 1938 lay a few years in the past. As a schoolgirl she had become enthused by *Sturm-und-Drang* writers and decided to study German literature. It was pure chance that she enrolled at Reed College in Portland as a literature student, as was the fact that she met the Austrian exchange student Otto Urbach there. Nothing else of the story was chance, however. Cordelia went to Vienna on Otto's recommendation. She met his mother Alice and his brother Karl, and ultimately their friendship would save the lives of several people.

Cordelia had no inkling of this future mission and her role in it when she went to the opera with her siblings on the night of 11 March 1938. Playing was Tchaikovsky's *Eugene Onegin*, and the performance began at 7 p.m. *Eugene Onegin* is not light entertainment. It's about a Russian aristocrat who rejects the advances of Tatyana and not long afterwards shoots dead a friend of his for completely trivial reasons. What is interesting about the character of Onegin is that he's unable to show empathy. A similar phenomenon – an utter lack of empathy – would soon engulf the whole of Vienna, including the staff at the State Opera. Not only the Jewish conductor that evening, Karl Alwin, but also the singer in the role of Tatyana, Jarmila Novotná, would soon lose their careers and the sympathy of others.

We still don't know why Cordelia and her siblings went to see *Eugene Onegin* that evening rather than Wagner's *Tristan and Isolde* the following day. Perhaps the Wagner was already sold out or she didn't like his music. Or maybe she didn't have much of a clue about opera and merely did what tourists still do to this day – buy the first opera tickets they can get hold of and book a table somewhere for afterwards. So although there was nothing unusual about Cordelia's opera visit, the atmosphere in which it played out was anything but usual. The city had been gripped by a tension for days. On 9 March, the Austrian chancellor Kurt Schuschnigg had announced a referendum, in which all Austrians would be asked to declare their support for a "free, German, independent, social, Christian and united Austria". On 10 March the National Socialists succeeded in having the plebiscite cancelled. Now everybody was waiting for the next move.

At 7.47 p.m., while Cordelia and her siblings were still watching the first act of *Onegin*, Chancellor Schuschnigg broadcast a speech on the radio. He informed the country that he was yielding to force and announced his resignation with immediate effect, clearing the way for the Austrian Nazis. A few hours later, Hitler's man Arthur Seyss-Inquart took over as chancellor.

Maybe the Dodsons heard about Schuschnigg's speech in the interval after the first act. If they hadn't, they would have realised that something serious had happened when they left the State Opera at 10 p.m. Their Viennese friend Karl Urbach was waiting for them at the exit. The expression on his face was clear; they would have to forgo their planned restaurant visit.

Until then Cordelia's passion for *Sturm-und-Drang* literature had been purely theoretical. She was interested in human emotion, so much so that she had also attended a psychology seminar at Reed College. But what she witnessed over the coming days in Vienna was an explosion of feeling that went beyond the boundaries of any psychology course.

On the morning of 12 March 1938 the first German troops crossed the Austrian border, reaching Vienna the following day. The city, which Karl had proudly shown his American guests around over the past few weeks, was transformed into a sea of Nazi flags. It was an orgy of jubilation and hatred. With her own eyes Cordelia saw both ecstatic triumph and utter despair, and what surprised her was the extraordinary speed of this change: "Things just happened so fast. All of our civilian rights, the police system, certain protections that everyone took for granted were just gone . . . I learned to hate the Nazis from that time on. They were so arrogant, so merciless." Without mentioning Alice's or Karl's name, she said of the scenes on the streets: "The persecution of the Jews was inhumane."[4] Determined to help her new Jewish friends, Cordelia took a decision that would change the course of her life. Although she did not yet know what she could do, she was willing to take serious risks.

During the Second World War this naïve college student would turn into a steely member of the Office of Strategic Services (OSS), the most elite of the American intelligence agencies. This was partly a result of her meeting with a short, rotund woman by the name of Alice Urbach.

2: A BLIND FATHER AND A POOR
CARD-PLAYER

"When I look at the Jews,
It gives me little joy.
But when I see the others,
I'm happy to be a Jew."
Albert Einstein[1]

It was a long, narrow alley. The houses stood close together and every square centimetre of living space was precious. The shops were on the ground floor, stuffed with fabrics, and one storey higher were the living quarters, stuffed with people. Around 5,000 people lived here, even though the official number was far lower. Not everybody wished to be registered and some lived illegally with friends and relatives. Alice's story began in Judengasse in the Pressburg (now Bratislava) ghetto, sixty kilometres to the east of Vienna. It was where her grandfather Salomon Mayer (1798–1883) had grown up. According to family legend, when he was seven he stood with his parents at the window of the small apartment and watched world history being made. As the story goes, his mother pointed outside and told him, "Look down at the street my son, and all your life remember that little man riding on a white horse down there. He is the man before whom the whole world trembles. His name is Napoleon."[2]

As is so often the case with family anecdotes, this one isn't particularly reliable. Although the Peace of Pressburg was concluded in December 1805 not far from Judengasse, the signatories to the treaty were Napoleon's foreign minister, Talleyrand, and Johann Joseph Prince Liechtenstein, representing the Habsburgs. Napoleon himself didn't come to Pressburg until four years later. Maybe they had simply got the year wrong and Salomon was eleven when he caught sight of the French emperor. The colour of the steed isn't quite right either, however; Napoleon's war horse was a light-grey Arabian called Marengo. It is perfectly possible, of course, that Salomon's mother assumed the horse was just dirty from the last battle and actually white in colour.[3] Using your imagination was important in the ghetto, as a way of blocking out the greyness of everyday life. A white horse sounded much more romantic than a grey one.

Whether or not Salomon did see Napoleon and his horse in 1809, the key reason for the significance of the episode to him and the other Jews of Pressburg is omitted from the anecdote. It didn't need saying as everybody knew it at the time. Napoleon embodied the French Revolution, and for many Jews, France was now the Promised Land. Since 1791 the Jewish population of that country had been made up of free French citizens who – theoretically, at least – differed from the rest of the population only by dint of their religion. In the eyes of the Pressburg Jews, Napoleon carried this idea with him throughout Europe. Which explains why in their family memory the Mayers placed themselves at the window and saw what they wanted to see. Ultimately, the precise year and the colour of the horse were insignificant; all that mattered was the hope for a future without fear. It was a sort of founding myth for the Mayers, and later Alice's brother Felix even toyed with the idea of writing a family history with the title "From Napoleon to Hitler". He compiled a little statistic for this which established that amongst his relatives there had been very few divorces or cases of cancer, but two suicides. No Mayer – according to Felix's records – had ever become a criminal,[4] but countless family members fell victim to the most heinous crime of the century. In the end Felix could not bring himself to write about this crime and his book project came to nothing.

Thus the family history begins with Salomon Mayer at the window. Salomon was also an important figure for his descendants because he always made the right decisions in life. This included marrying a clever woman with whom he could forge something extraordinary: Antonia (Tony) Frankl (1806–95), who became part of the family legend.[5] At the time there were thirty textile wholesalers in the Pressburg ghetto and, thanks to Tony's good taste, the Mayers were one of the most successful.[6] Not only did Tony work incredibly hard, she also gave birth to sixteen children, of whom only nine survived. For the time this was not unusual. Children died with predictable regularity, from whooping cough, typhus, diarrhoea, scarlet fever, measles, and so on. The infant mortality rate in the ghetto, furthermore, appears to have been higher than average. Alice's father Sigmund blamed the premature deaths of his siblings on poor hygiene. In his memoir he describes the primitive living conditions in the ghetto:

> Wooden, wobbly and pitch-black steps led up to the apartments, which at the rear could not be anything but damp and dark because they were right up against the hillside. The sewerage was pitiful, the tiny courtyards meant that the circulation of fresh air was wholly inadequate and the atmosphere was heavy and stifling. Not a single building had a well. The entire population had to draw bad, barely drinkable water from two communal wells.[7]

But there were other reasons why Sigmund hated the ghetto. He swore that he and his siblings never laughed. Nor could he recall a single child ever having played in Judengasse. Only one feeling existed here: fear. If you had to live in the ghetto you were closed in, literally so. Every evening "the city police shut off the street with heavy iron railings".[8] Officially these railings were to protect the Christians from the "dangerous" Jews. In reality they were put up to protect the Jews from acts of violence. And the violence could occur at any moment. Although the citizens of Pressburg came to the Jewish shops during the day to buy goods cheaply, the mood could rapidly turn. Someone who in the morning had purchased silk, haberdashery, linen, brushes, buttons and combs from a Jewish shop might get irate about the price that same evening. Sigmund recalled a Catholic merchant by the name of Philipp Scherz, whom the family had to deal with and who used to say, "You cannot appreciate Jews and pigs until they're dead."[9]

They also lived in fear of landlords, who could turn them out into the street at a moment's notice. Even if you had saved enough money, as a Jew you weren't permitted to buy property in Judengasse. This was only possible indirectly, by having a Christian third party buy the house and then negotiating a usufruct or long-term lease with them.[10]

The parents' fear that they might lose everything at any moment spread to the children. They were regularly beaten up by Christian children of their age and weren't allowed to complain, let alone fight back. But it wasn't just the outside world that was threatening; conflict existed inside the ghetto too. Jewish schoolteachers took out their aggression on the children and their educational methods were brutal. In this, of course, they differed only marginally from their non-Jewish counterparts, but life was torture for the children, knowing that they weren't safe from physical harm either at school or in the street. The constant feeling that they were at the mercy of everything and everyone made inhabitants of the ghetto become at worst resigned, and at best sarcastic. For Sigmund this behaviour was the key to understanding the works of the great Jewish authors: "Only those who have lived and suffered alongside these prisoners in Judengasse can understand Ludwig Börnes' grim disdain, Heine's cynicism, and appreciate why . . . Ferdinand Lassalle and Karl Marx were Jews." [11]

You could take yourself out of the ghetto, but never take the ghetto out of yourself. In his memoir Sigmund paints such a desperate picture of Judengasse that it is easy to forget how early he was able to get away from there. He was eleven when the Pressburg ghetto was opened in 1842 and the Mayers moved to a better house, thereby increasing the survival prospects of Sigmund and his later siblings. They escaped the worst hygiene conditions and grew up more healthily.[12]

When in 1917 Sigmund Mayer published his book *Die Wiener Juden*, he was convinced he was describing a sad state of affairs that belonged firmly in the past: "Very few of those alive today will have known a real . . . ghetto."[13] It was quite clear as far as he was concerned that this horror would never return. He was not alive to see three of his children thrust from their middle-class existence back into a ghetto in 1942. His daughter Alice escaped this fate; ironically this was due to the fact that she had always been overlooked in the family.

Alice admired and feared her father. She had good reason to do both: "My father was a remarkable personality. He was of a very short build and was bothered by his appearance all his life. He turned his physical shortcomings into spiritual assets. From his mother, my grandmother [. . .] he inherited a brilliant brain, a strong will, a good sense of humour and a full amount of superiority."[14]

With a dream of entering the legal profession, Sigmund studied law in Prague and Vienna. An infection left him partially blinded, however, and as nobody would have hired a lawyer with limited vision, he had no option but to enter the family business. This, at least, he intended to make a great success. Over the next few decades, with his siblings Albert and Regine, he built up the international textile firm A. Mayer & Co. and expanded into the Levant.[15] In 1882 the firm's headquarters was in Alexandria, with several regional offices including Constantinople, Smyrna and Vienna.[16] The tireless efforts of the Mayer siblings eventually paid off: in 1910 they found themselves on the list of the thousand richest Viennese and Lower Austrians.[17]

Whereas his siblings were content with this, Sigmund pursued another goal – he became involved with Vienna city council, where his chief adversary was the anti-Semite Karl Lueger.

Adolf Hitler would later feel inspired by Lueger in many ways, but "handsome Karl" had not always been anti-Semitic. Sigmund even thought that Lueger only turned into a Jew-hater so he could become mayor of Vienna: "Lueger's anti-Semitic stance was never anything but a sham. In particular there was no way you could accuse him of racial hatred against the Jews. Earlier he had not merely enjoyed the company of Jews, but preferred it [. . .] In the house of deputies I said to him, 'I don't reproach you for being an anti-Semite, but for the fact that in truth you *aren't* one.'"

Whether it was feigned or genuine, the effect was ultimately the same. Lueger made anti-Semitism respectable in Vienna. Sigmund received threatening letters and challenges to duels, which he countered with the words, "When someone is nothing anymore, then he's an anti-Semite."[18]

As a local politician and a regular columnist for the *Neue Freie Presse*, Sigmund didn't only wrangle with anti-Semites.[19] He also got into a dispute with the Zionist Theodor Herzl. Whereas

Herzl believed that Jews had to establish their own "Jewish state" in reaction to anti-Semitism, Sigmund rejected Zionism outright, putting his faith in assimilation instead. Alice later wrote that her father and Herzl would have heated discussions.[20] These arguments came to an abrupt end in 1897, however, when Sigmund published a sarcastic attack on Herzl. The reason for this was the convocation of the first Zionist Congress in Basel, a "city without Jews", as Sigmund smugly observed. He described the initiators of the congress as "two ingenious columnists, Herr Herzl in Vienna and Herr Nordau in Paris, both of whom have suddenly turned from Jews by accident of birth into Jews by profession." Their notion of a Jewish state in Palestine would result in

> the Jews gaining a homeland of highly questionable value and in return genuinely becoming a guest people in all European countries! Is this what the best of our people fought two millennia to achieve? ... We believe, therefore, that the danger of the Jewish state coming into being is zero and barely worth mention in a serious newspaper. Herr Herzl, however, represents a very serious social danger for the Jews and their key interests.[21]

We can assume that the two men never spoke to each other again. In the end, however, they were both buried in the same place: the Jewish section of Döbling cemetery in Vienna.[22]

As well as fighting on numerous fronts professionally, at times Sigmund faced a battlefield in his private life. Alice owed her existence to the fact that Sigmund's first wife Henriette cheated on him. In the early 1870s, when he was often away in Cairo on business, Henriette took a lover and became pregnant. Without hesitation Sigmund decided to divorce his wife and keep little Gabriele. Henriette was given a financial settlement which included a ticket to the provincial backwater she had come from. The severity with which Sigmund punished her was in line with his tough character, but it was also typical of the time. In 1856 Gustave Flaubert had described the fate that awaited an "adulteress" like Madame Bovary, in 1878 Leo Tolstoy's Anna Karenina threw herself under a train, and in 1894 Theodor Fontane's unfaithful Effi Briest ended up in adversity. We don't know if Sigmund, who loved novels, ever read *Madame Bovary* or *Anna Karenina*, but this wouldn't have changed much. The deep humiliation he felt from his wife's actions resulted in him bringing up four children on his own for ten years.[23] But in the end he did marry again. His second wife, Pauline Gutmann, was twenty years younger and readily played the role of subservient wife.[24] He had a further three children with her: Felix (b. 1884), Alice (b. 1886) and Helene, known as Mutzi (b. 1894).

Alice had blue eyes and fair hair. People thought she was a pretty child, but for her father the far more important question was: Did she have a particular talent, something they could be proud of?

Almost all Jewish families longed to produce a wunderkind. A prodigy could raise the social status of the entire family and act as proof that you had arrived in society. There was no differentiating between boys and girls when it came to bringing a prodigy into the world; any child could be one. Maybe they had the potential to become a mathematical genius or a great pianist? Of course, a little help was in order. Entire companies of private tutors and French governesses were employed for this very purpose, and even families for whom money was tight invested their savings in improving the next generation. Decades later Alice could still name the Viennese families who had produced the most successful children. Top of the list was Sigmund Freud's daughter, Anna, closely followed by the children of the lawyer, Dr Meitner:

> [He] brought three of his daughters into our newly acquired home [. . .] I was very much impressed that one of the young girls was studying at the university. Little did I know that this graceful young girl [Lise Meitner], dressed in white [. . .] would later on have a much less innocent occupation and work on the atomic bomb! [. . .] The children were all gifted. One was a woman doctor, one a pianist (she was the mother of Otto Robert Frisch).[25]

Then there were all the literary prodigies. Alice's mother was friends with Alfred Polgar's mother, and of course everyone admired the Schnitzler family who had managed to produce two successful sons – the doctor, Julius, and the writer, Arthur. Frau Schnitzler was simply unable to assume the obligatory modesty. When asked how her "famous son" was, she'd reply, "Which one?"[26]

Alice dreamed of similar success. As a seven-year-old she hoped to become a famous singer, which caused her parents great embarrassment. In 1893 the whole family travelled to the

Altausee for their annual summer break. As usual, Alice was bored during their walk along the promenade, but when she noticed Johannes Brahms strolling past she broke into song. It can't have been a particularly good performance, for Alice was swiftly dragged off the promenade by her mother. "That was the end of my dream of a 'wunderkind'."[27]

In the internal sibling hierarchy Alice occupied a place near the bottom. Her four older half-siblings were regarded as intelligent, her brother Felix was a hard worker and later took a position in the family firm. Her younger sister Helene would fulfil her father's dream and complete a PhD in law. Alice, on the other hand, suffered her whole life from never gaining any educational qualifications, admitting that she was lazy and had to pay for this later.[28]

Until Alice was eleven the family lived at 32 Obere Augartenstrasse in the Viennese district of Leopoldstadt, which had a large Jewish population. The shop was at street level, Tony, Alice's grandmother from Pressburg, lived on the first floor, Sigmund's family on the second, and his brother Albert on the third. The Mayers harboured upper-middle-class ambitions, which Alice described in detail:

Seldom did a "lady" go shopping herself, "women" did. Ladies had their cooks do it [. . .] One had, of course, to go [grocery] shopping every day as there was no refrigerator [. . .] to keep a bigger amount of food fresh [. . .] "Ladies" did not cook, the cook did it [. . .] They did not look after their babies, the nurse did it. They did not supervise their older children, the governess did it. Shopping, going for walks, visiting and needlework was all there was to fill their days [. . .] The mid-day meal brought home all the family members [. . .] There was always a bouillon, and consequently boiled beef [. . .] The crown of every meal [. . .] – dessert! Most characteristic for Viennese cookery the boiled, sweet regiments of dumplings ("Knödel") filled with plums, cherries or apricots, according to the season [. . .] After lunch, everyone had a rest (and you needed it after such a heavy meal). The children had school again until four p.m., and the men mostly worked the whole afternoon. All the women had a coffee-break about four or five p.m., and this was also the social hour for friends to meet and gossip.[29]

Being a lady, Alice's mother paid only the odd visit to the kitchen, but for Alice it became the most important place in the house. The smells were wonderful and there were sweets in the pantry. Even as a small child she was allowed to sit on a stool and watch the kitchen helpers. Not only did they prepare interesting dishes, they also spoke about exciting things – amorous adventures at the *Heuriger* (wine tavern), or the latest murder reports in the *Kronenzeitung*. Alice's father might be in charge in the drawing room, but in the kitchen the cook called the shots. She was a staff-sergeant and everyone put up with her moods because much depended on her creativity. An accomplished cook could catapult a family up the social ladder and families were permanently worried about losing theirs to a rival hostess.[30] It wasn't only Hotel Sacher and Café Demel who tried to poach the best pastry chefs from each other; private houses too feared hostile takeovers at any moment. To keep the cook happy, the lady of the house worked with her in close cooperation. They would devise the menus together so that each course arriving at the table was a "culinary masterpiece". And of course every hostess dreamed of serving a dish at a large dinner party which was based on a secret recipe. In *Tante Jolesch* Friedrich Torberg shows how dogged this struggle for secret recipes was. His aunt was renowned for her *Krautfleckerln* (pasta squares with cabbage). As she lay on her deathbed, her niece made one last attempt to squeeze the recipe out of her:

> "Auntie – you can't take the recipe to the grave with you. Won't you leave it behind for us? Won't you finally tell us why your *Krautfleckerln* were always so good?" Summoning the last of her strength Aunt Jolesch sat up a little and said, "Because I never made enough of them . . ."
>
> Having said this, she smiled and passed away.[31]

Aunt Jolesch was decades ahead of marketing strategies. Dishes had to taste wonderful and look enticing, but most of all they had to be scarce. Even as a child Alice dreamed that one day she would cook really special things: "My father, in addition to his high intellectual standards, was a great gourmet! It was a joy [. . .] when I was barely old enough to reach the top of the kitchen table, to win a smile from his stern face, with some dish of his liking!"[32]

That Alice should learn to cook to please her father may sound like crude kitchen-sink psychology. In fact it was her only way of being noticed by him at all:

[My father] seldom spoke to us, we saw him at mealtimes when no talking was allowed! If spoken to, we answered politely – that was all! I cannot remember that, before I was twenty, my father took me – alone – for a walk. He went out by himself or with my mother [. . .] We children led a separate life from that of our parents.[33]

The kitchen was a link to the adult world. Here Alice learned something that everyone needed. And of course through cooking she hoped to gain the respect of those around her. It worked only partially. Sigmund appreciated Alice's food, which became increasingly refined over the years, but if someone had predicted that his dreamy daughter would write a bestselling cookbook, he would have been surprised. Perhaps he would have been pleased that she had finally woken up and made something of her life. But the circumstances that led to Alice's "awakening" would have horrified him.

Endless clichés exist about Alice's generation of Viennese women, for which Gustav Klimt's paintings and Arthur Schnitzler's plays are in part responsible. In Schnitzler's work the woman is often the "sweet girl" from the Viennese suburbs who truly loves her aristocratic admirer, but from the beginning suspects that she'll have to marry the dull porter. Her antagonist is the sophisticated upper-class wife who is anything but "sweet" and routinely cheats on her husband. None of these clichés applied to Alice. She was scared of sex, a fear widespread in her generation. Stefan Zweig, born like Alice into an affluent Jewish family in the 1880s, put down in words what she would

Alice (seated) with her sister Helene Eissler

never have been able to express – how dismal the love lives of that generation were. In Zweig's eyes they had no chance of normal sexual experiences: "The young girls were hermetically sealed from life and controlled by their family, hindered in their free physical and intellectual development, while the boys were driven to secrecy and deviousness by a morality that, in essence, nobody believed in or observed."[34]

This moral corset meant that most young men had their first sexual experiences with prostitutes. These "sad birds of paradise", as Zweig called them, stood on many Viennese street corners and their short "careers" usually ended in hospital. Men of all social classes used them, whether in a porch or one of Vienna's better brothels. It was never without risk. One of the major and very real fears that accompanied every sexual encounter was venereal disease. Syphilis was widespread in big cities and no cure yet existed. Arthur Schnitzler's father Johann, who taught medicine at the University of Vienna, was so worried that his son might become infected that he forced open his desk and read his secret diary. In this the sixteen-year-old Arthur had detailed all his – real and imaginary – experiences with "Greek goddesses". Reading the diary almost gave Johann a heart attack and he forced his son to study a medical textbook on syphilis and skin diseases.[35] The extreme illustrations had the desired effect; Arthur put an end to his visits to Greek goddesses for the time being. But he was unable to withstand this torture for long.

Sexual relations were, therefore, a lottery, and a young "hermetically sealed" virgin like Alice could only hope that her future husband was not infected before she married him. It was not unlikely.

*

There were a number of ruptures in Alice's life, the first of which came when she married. Until then her life had been comfortable.[36] Everything was in abundance, including fine clothes. "There's no such thing as ugly women, only badly dressed ones," they used to say in Vienna, and Alice agreed. Like many Viennese women of the pre-war generation she loved colourful material, large hats and extravagant ribbons. As she came from a family that had made its money through textiles, she never had to worry about supplies. There were also plenty of staff, and the affluent Jewish bourgeoisie had copied from the nobility the custom of having services performed "at home". Tailors, dressmakers and even the barber came to the house.[37] If you weren't giving a masked ball or a dinner you would go to a concert, the opera or the Burgtheater. Alice liked to go out and she wasn't unattractive. Her "dumpling figure" with an ample décolleté was considered very desirable before the First World War. Although she had fairly large feet – a feature said to be common amongst Viennese women at the time[38] – she could certainly have been successful on the marriage market. But Alice herself showed little interest. Her older half-sisters Sidonie (Sida) and Karoline (Karla) were already married and neither seemed particularly happy. Sidonie's husband Julius Rosenberg was a charming Hungarian who regularly chopped and changed jobs, and had to fall back on his wife's fortune.[39] Karoline did not fare much better. She was married to the bookseller Richard Löwit, of whom her father had been particularly fond. Sigmund Mayer was a passionate collector of books and he provided much financial help to support his son-in-law as a publisher.[40]

For Karoline the arrangement proved less than ideal; she blossomed again only after her husband died.[41]

Witnessing the generally negative experiences of her sisters, Alice did not believe that marriage would improve her life. Staying single, on the other hand, had many advantages: she could attend a language school, continue to take singing lessons and, most important of all, refine her culinary prowess. It was her dream to become a second Anna Sacher,[42] or at least to open a small restaurant:

I was interested in business, but for heaven's sake – how could a girl from a nice family run a tea room or coffee shop or anything like that? [...] I would have liked to have been a real apprentice in one of the good confectioneries of which Vienna is famously rich! No girls were admitted to that profession [...] When I was about eighteen years old my chance came. A lady near my home opened a very select, snobbish cookery school, and added as a final touch lessons by a French pâtissier employed in the finest Ringstrasse hotel [...] I attended this school, and these lessons – not so very numerous – were a turning point in my life. I had not the slightest idea what an important part this was to play in my life [...] It laid the foundation of knowledge which later on proved to be my "lifeboat" in the stormy sea of events. I learned from that man the art of confectionery. I still treasure his recipes. At the time, however, I never realized what this hobby was going to mean to me some day. I did not use my newly acquired knowledge for anything but pleasure. The parties in my parents' home had a few more fanciful desserts and the Christmas baskets or the boxes for birthday presents and other gifts were filled with homemade sweets, petits-fours, fantastic cakes and candies instead of the usual bought candies.[43]

Sigmund didn't see a future in confectionery. He took the decisions about which careers his children should aim for and whom they should marry. Although Alice managed to avoid marriage for as long as possible, her period of grace finally came to an end in 1912. She was twenty-six, "an old maid", when she submitted to Sigmund's will. She married the wrong man for the wrong reason: to make her parents happy and comply with society's expectations. In December 1912 Alice became Dr Maximilian Urbach's wife in the synagogue of the 19th district of Vienna.

At first glance Max Urbach was a good catch. He came from a leading family that had produced businesspeople, doctors and lawyers. On 1 July 1908 he earned his PhD in Prague, becoming a "doctor of general medicine" specialising in paediatrics.[44] Alice later wrote that Max had been interested in her because "[I was] a pretty, rich girl from a good family – and he was just starting a practice . . ."[45]

She never explained how they had met, but it's not unlikely that Sigmund resorted to the final option available to a concerned Jewish father and hired a "schadchen", a marriage broker who would be paid handsomely if it were a success. For upper middle-class families like the Mayers, a schadchen – who could be a man or a woman – would seek out lawyers and doctors. Nobody, after all, wanted their daughter to marry below her station. The future husband could earn well from such a marriage. Alice's dowry came to 80,000 crowns, an enormous sum of money at that time (a maid earned between 100 and 300 crowns a year; a university professor between 8,000 and 16,000).[46] If Alice's marriage did come about through the services of a broker, the family would have had every reason to demand their commission back. For Max Urbach wasn't the respectable son-in-law he pretended to be. He was a gambler and had many affairs.

In later years Alice wrote two versions of her memoir – a more detailed one for the family and a very short one for herself.[47] In the official version she deals with her marriage in just a few sentences: "After a marriage of seven years my husband passed away. I will not describe my feelings! This story is devoted to my actions, to my adventures, not to my sentiments!"[48] The unofficial version makes clear why she didn't go into more detail. She says about her wedding with Max, "I really do have the 6th sense and when I sat down to the wedding dinner I only had one thought – Oh God, what have I done!" The realisation came a few hours too late. Their wedding night was to be the first in a long line of marital catastrophes: "My husband did not know how to treat an innocent virgin [. . .] He took me for a few moments, never kissed me or fondled me, and when he was finished left me alone, smoked a last cigarette and went to sleep. I thought, I had to do my duty – but hated it."[49]

Neither in her secret nor official version could Alice bring herself to call Max by his first name, always keeping her distance and referring to him formally as "my husband". She never had a pet name for him, and for good reason. Her marriage to Max was not only a disappointment sexually, it turned out to be a major social step downwards.

When she was eleven Alice moved out of Leopoldstadt with her parents to the elegant district of Döbling.[50] It was considered to be the most beautiful residential area in the city, with affluent businesspeople and famous artists living nearby. In 1910 Arthur Schnitzler bought a villa at 71 Sternwartestrasse, while Schnitzler's friend Felix Salten, the author of *Bambi*, lived at 37 Cottagegasse (Salten would later advise Alice's young son on how to look after his rabbit).[51] Alice loved the new house, a villa painted a rich yellow like that of Schönbrunn palace.[52] The rooms were bright and in the garden apple trees blossomed, beneath which you could settle down with a book.

After the wedding Alice had to move to Ottakring, a part of the city she did not know except by name. Only a Viennese can understand what it must have meant to move from Döbling to Ottakring in 1912. Although the two districts are not far apart geographically, the social gulf between them appears unbridgeable even today.

Ottakring was a congested working-class neighbourhood with dark, stuffy apartments. Here there were no yellow houses or park-like gardens; instead the dominant hue was a sad grey. Nobody planted apple trees — there was no space for them in the asphalt jungle. In 1911 – the year before Alice's wedding – the rise in rents and food prices had led to serious unrest in Ottakring. Since then the district had been regarded as a hotbed of social problems, certainly not the ideal home for an upper middle-class lady like Alice. Even though her new apartment looked large and comfortable, the move must have been a considerable shock.

Alice had not expected to move into a house in Döbling, of course. She was marrying a doctor who had to start at the bottom and build up his practice. But she had not realised how low that starting point would be. Max's patients had barely enough money to cover their rent, let alone their doctor's bills. But Ottakring opened Alice's eyes. She saw how hard the lives of working-class women were:

They never had more than one room and a kitchen for a whole family! The room mostly faced towards the street – and what an ugly, dirty, noisy one – but the kitchen never had a window [. . .] In those dark places, without any proper daylight, the housewife cooked, washed her laundry, did all her housework, surrounded by her children. Sometimes, if the family was very poor and out of work, they had a boarder who slept in the kitchen while father, mother, children [. . .] healthy and sick, all slept in one room [. . .] Of course there was no bathroom and no private toilets [only seven per cent of all apartments had running water]. Many families shared the toilets in the hallways or sometimes downstairs in the backyard! Many violent quarrels between women and fights between the men had their roots in these *shared inconveniences*. It is no wonder that tuberculosis, called "white death", flourished in Vienna.[53]

*

Although Alice lived in a much nicer apartment, she was depressed by the gloominess of Ottakring. Her only joy during this time was the birth of her first child. "I was pregnant instantly and loved the little boy, who was dangerously ill but recovered [. . .] He was a charming little fellow – and a wonderful son."[54]

Otto was born in September 1913, ten months before the outbreak of the First World War. His first year would be one of the few periods of peace he experienced. Wars and uprisings – in Vienna, in China, as a soldier in the Second World War and in the long Cold War – would accompany him until his death. Even in his childhood home the atmosphere was one of permanent tension. In her secret memoir Alice writes:

> The first two years of my marriage were not unhappy. Then, when the war took all the opportunity of cooking food, my husband developed the habit, to go every evening in a little pub, where food was to be had, drank too much and played cards [. . .] I sat at home alone, evening after evening, playing proud and talked to the nursemaid. I had never seen such behaviour by a Jewish man. I was so ashamed at having made such a bad match that I never talked to anyone about it! To whom could I turn? My parents were old – one did not speak freely about what happened in the bedroom![55]

Worse than the problems in the bedroom was Max's gambling addiction. According to a famous witticism by Alfred Polgar there are two types of gambler: "One plays for fun, the other

Otto as a small boy

because he needs money. After some time the first type inevitably becomes the second."[56] Being married to Max meant that Alice had to share her life with an addict who was gradually leading them to financial ruin. The war didn't make the situation any better. While Alice's brother Felix, like all young men in the Mayer family, went to the front, Max was assigned to the Landsturm (reserve militia) as a regimental doctor.[57] This meant that he served in Vienna rather than at some distant front. Alice would have preferred him to be as far away as possible:

> I can't remember how [. . .] I got pregnant again. I always avoided him because I was afraid of an alcohol deformed child. Anyway, when I got pregnant [. . .] my husband wanted me to get rid of him and it was the first time that he told me he was a sick man. Then of course I could not think of a divorce. We lived a separate life. It was a terrible time.[58]

Alice never found out exactly which venereal disease Max was suffering from, or whether he had contracted it before they married and had concealed it from her. Only in one respect was she lucky: neither she nor her baby was infected. Her second son Karl was born healthy in November 1917. "Karli" became the very opposite of his father: a lovely, helpful boy who tried to make the people around him happy. The time in which he was born, however, could not have been less happy.

In November 1917 the Russian Revolution broke out, and in Vienna too social unrest became ever more heightened. Hunger and sickness were rampant and people were exhausted by the war. The new emperor, Karl, tried to secretly negotiate a peace with the Entente, behind the back of his German ally. His efforts failed and could not prevent the dissolution of the Habsburg Empire.[59]

Although everyone had longed for the war to end, defeat ultimately came as a shock. All the certainties that Alice's generation had known suddenly disappeared. Her cousin Lily Bader wrote, "For days rumours and commotion were rife in Vienna, and yet the emperor's departure on 11 November was unexpected. It was hard to imagine Austria without the Habsburgs who had ruled the country for more than 600 years. For us this event was as strange as the moon suddenly disappearing from its place in the sky."[60]

Her sons' first names remained Alice's only souvenirs of the Monarchy: the older one was named after Otto von Habsburg, the younger after the hapless emperor Karl. Both would become anything but monarchists and even Alice lost interest in fairy-tale Sissi[61] stories after 1918. She had experienced the reality of Ottakring.

Although the emperor lost his authority overnight, in Jewish families hierarchies survived despite the revolution, as is shown by the following anecdote about Paul and Egon Erwin Kisch. On 12 November 1918 the furious reporter and ardent communist Egon Erwin Kisch tried, with the Red Guard, to storm the editorial offices of the *Neue Freie Presse*. In the stairwell he came across his brother Paul, the paper's business editor. Paul blocked Egon's way with the words:

"What are you doing here, Egon?"

"Can't you see? We're occupying your offices."

"Who is 'we'?"

"The Red Guard."

"And why do you want to occupy the *Presse*?"

"Because it's a stronghold of capitalism."

"Stop being so ridiculous and get out of here."

"Paul, you're not seeing how serious this is. In the name of the revolution I insist you get out of the way. Otherwise ... !"

"Alright, Egon. I'll yield to force. But let me tell you: tonight I'm going to write to Mama in Prague about this."[62]

In the face of such a terrifying threat, Egon Erwin Kisch backed down. Doubt exists as to the authenticity of this story, although the *Neue Freie Presse* was indeed occupied by the Red Guard for a short time. Contemporaries who knew Mama Ernestina Kisch personally swear that the anecdote is true.[63]

The collapse of the Habsburg Monarchy also meant the loss of cheap wheat imports from Hungary and coal from Bohemia. The Viennese now had to barter with farmers. In her official memoir Alice wrote:

[My children] had never tasted fresh milk, did not know what an orange looked like or how chocolate tasted or how to buy bread without a ration card [. . .] In the years following the First World War, there was at first a terrible struggle for food! One still lived officially entirely on rations. Those who could not afford the black-market prices starved on allotted portions or tried to get across the border to exchange all their valuable possessions for a little food – a fur coat for a few pounds of butter, a camera for some potatoes. The farmers did not accept money any longer because they had more than they could use, but stocked their houses with things they had never seen before: a piano they could not play, evening clothes and dresses they could not wear, precious books they could neither read nor understand.[64]

During the first winter after the war, Viennese children learned that America represented a rich alternative world. US aid organisations supplied them with an "American soup kitchen".[65] The actor Leon Askin was one of these children. Later he would describe the manic-depressive atmosphere prevalent in Vienna at the time. Schools had to close because they could not be heated. Children hung around the streets, playing football for hours to avoid freezing. Nobody had a proper ball anymore, so they would roll up old scraps of cloth, wrap a wire around them and play with that.

Although Askin came from a very poor Jewish family he could continue to enjoy cultural life in Vienna. Food may have been unaffordable in Austria, but culture was cheap. To save on light, the theatres switched their performances to the afternoons and the curtain would fall at half past seven.[66] But nobody minded. Most important was to be able to escape everyday reality. Like Leon Askin, Otto loved these escapes too, and both particularly enjoyed ballet. At the State Opera they could marvel at *Le Petit Chaperon rouge* or Hans Christian

Andersen's *The Red Shoes* and for a few hours forget about the world outside.

The adults too would flee to the theatre and scrape together enough money for an evening at the coffee house afterwards. For Alice such excursions with her friends were crucial:

When I was a child [. . .] it was not popular with ["ladies"] to frequent a café without their husbands [. . .] The war, with its terrible shortage of fuel, electricity and food drove the women into the relative warmth and the light of the "coffee-houses" where they chatted or played bridge, and had a cup of "Ersatzkaffee" (coffee substitute) with saccharine or sugar, and if they wanted a roll, a ration card was punched [. . .] This habit of the female – the invasion of the coffee-house – [. . .] happened maybe to the regret of some of the men who thought that this institution should have stayed in their own domain![67]

For her part, Alice just wanted to get away from her husband as often as she could. All that still linked the two of them was disaster: "One day my husband lost a big sum in card games and forced me to sell my beautiful diamond bracelet, to pay his debts. This was the last straw – after that went I don't think he lived more than a week, because when he died I still had some of this money left!"[68]

It would not last long.

3: HUNGRY TIMES

"Enjoy these post-war times.
For it'll be pre-war times again soon."
Wolfgang Neuss and Wolfgang Müller
in *Wir Wunderkinder*[1]

When someone dies in Germany the will goes to a probate court. In Austria probate records are called *"Verlassenschaftsakten"*. The term has a slightly dramatic quality to it as *"verlassen"* in German can mean left or abandoned, which is usually a painful experience. When Max died at the Löw sanatorium in Vienna on 1 April 1920, aged forty-four, Alice was relieved to be rid of him. She would not have been able to play the part of satisfied wife for much longer. Max's death was a liberation for Alice, but her relief was short-lived. The reading of his will showed her that there was an even greater disparity between façade and reality than she had feared.

The will is still at the Stadt- und Landesarchiv in Vienna. It is a document running to more than fifty pages; from its length one might surmise that there was something to pass down. That presumption is wrong.

In the relatively short period of seven years of marriage, Max had managed to gamble away Alice's dowry of 80,000 crowns. According to the inventory he left behind only the following objects:

1. Clothes and linen worth 1,960 crowns, including a "dark, damaged winter coat for 150 crowns, a top hat (50 crowns), a tail coat (100 crowns)".
2. A gold watch (1,000 crowns).
3. Cash (300 crowns).
4. Medical instruments (dental forceps, tweezers etc.), various obstetric devices, a large and small examination table, wash stand, steriliser with console, desk.

Max owed debts to Sepp Bruckner (15 crowns), the Koet family (30 crowns) and Café Stadt Museum (115 crowns). Alice was left some Hungarian securities and a policy with Germania life insurance.[2]

Her father Sigmund died seven months later. He was buried in an elaborate family plot in the Jewish section of Döbling cemetery, several metres tall and semi-circular, with his name carved into the white stone on the right.[3] Beside his grave was sufficient place for his children, who were also to be buried here one day (nobody at the time could imagine that they would all die far from Vienna). The monument oozes upper-middle-class prosperity, and Sigmund's obituaries too celebrated a successful life. The *Neue Freie Presse* remembered the "short, half-blind man [. . .] who had an important influence on public life in Vienna [. . .] and made the leading theoretical economists sit up and listen."[4] When his will was read out, Sigmund made his family sit up and listen as well.

Although the great Mayer business empire collapsed with the Habsburg Monarchy at the end of the war, Sigmund – unlike Max – still had some possessions to bequeath in 1920. They too were listed precisely and included, besides the usual precious items, the villa in Döbling, a large library with first editions, as well as some securities.[5] The first version of Sigmund's will had been written in 1914, at which time his fortune ran to about 400,000 crowns, corresponding to around two million euros in today's money. By 1920 it had shrunk to 190,000 crowns, which because of inflation would only be worth 17,556 euros today. This money was to be distributed unequally to his wife Pauline, his son Felix and daughters Helene, Sidonie and Karoline. It was the will of a strict patriarch giving the greatest reward to the most obedient child.

Of Alice, it said: "When she married, my daughter Alice received a dowry of eighty thousand crowns and a furniture allowance of five thousand crowns. In addition I gave her five thousand crowns towards her wedding. I state, therefore, that she will gain nothing further from my estate except for what is earmarked for her under IIIA."[6]

Sigmund's eldest son from his first marriage was penalised too. Dr Arnold Mayer had become a Germanist and librarian at the Vienna University Library, which ought to have appealed to the bibliophile Sigmund. According to Felix's memoir, however, Arnold suffered from "Jewish self-hate" and had converted.

For Sigmund this seemed to herald the end of his love for his eldest son.[7] Arnold received no more than his obligatory share, while Helene, Sigmund's youngest child, got the most generous inheritance. It was with her that he had discussed his manuscripts and articles; she was the clever prodigy he had always wanted. For this reason he left her a special souvenir as well as money: "To my daughter Helene I bequeath as a keepsake my wedding ring for her future husband. May it bring her luck."[8]

Although several of his children received a sizeable inheritance, the money was soon worth very little. After Sigmund's death inflation in Austria accelerated ever faster. In 1914 one crown corresponded to 5.12 euros today. In 1923, however, 10,000 crowns were worth 4.37 euros. When Sigmund's heirs were finally paid their money in 1922, his cash assets were worth a meagre 193 euros.[9] Inflation had eaten it all up.

The will confirmed what Alice already knew, of course. Sigmund did not love her, and her financial situation remained catastrophic. Her social decline now seemed unavoidable. She was a thirty-four-year-old widow with no money. No man of sound mind would saddle himself with a penniless woman with two young sons. Alice had to find a way to feed her children, but she lacked confidence: "I had not learned anything (so I thought) to earn money [...] I had had singing and piano lessons. I travelled a lot with my parents and learned art and geography in this very pleasant way. The usual education of girls in first-class families, not having any particular talents."[10]

Alice benefited temporarily from a post-war problem: the critical housing shortage. She could take in lodgers "to whom

I had turned over the big drawing room, unused, as I didn't do any entertaining by then. They [. . .] paid in their own currency (Czech crowns, much more valuable than Austrian crowns or schillings). Some of the girls, I usually had three or four, all friends who shared the huge room, were interested in cookery. I taught them how to bake cakes for their birthdays and cookies for their parties!"[11] Baking with others helped Alice; cooking always gave her a feeling of security.

Further security came in the form of her brother-in-law, Ignaz Urbach. Assigned legal guardianship of Otto and Karl, he took his job seriously. Ignaz seemed to be the opposite of Max in every respect: he strove to give his family a good life and he wasn't interested in playing cards or having dalliances with other women. His wife Marie was a Viennese Catholic and he made every effort to spoil her and their children.[12] The family lived in an elegant house at 7 Sensengasse. From there it was not far to Ignaz's bank near Heldenplatz.[13] Since the start of the inflation he had been working especially hard, but still he paid regular visits to Alice to offer his help. She was pleased that Ignaz assumed some of the paternal role for Otto and Karl, although as so often in Alice's life this fortune did not last long.

In spring 1924 Alice noted a change in Ignaz that she could not explain. He was no longer the jovial relative who admired her culinary skills and played with Otto and Karl. Although only fifty-nine, Ignaz appeared to be ageing rapidly, and Alice couldn't understand why. On 5 July 1924, the reason became clear when she learned of his death in a newspaper. Several Viennese papers devoted a big spread to the story: the *Kronenzeitung* gave it a front-page headline, while *Der Tag* printed a long article on page five. Under the headline DEATH OF BANKER URBACH – ACCIDENT OR SUICIDE?" it read:

> Police are investigating a peculiar case. Ignaz Urbach, director of the bank Urbach und Co., was found yesterday at 8 a.m. on the second floor of 23 Gonzagagasse with a large wound to the back of his head. Five minutes later the rescue service was on the scene and an hour and a half later the police investigation commission arrived. The rescue service and police were only able to establish the time of death. It remains unclear whether the banker took his own life or, suddenly feeling unwell, fell outside the door of his lawyer Dr Zeisl on the second floor, thereby sustaining his injuries, or – ?[14]

The dramatically positioned question mark pointed to darker motives. The *Kronenzeitung* began by explaining to its readers who the dead man was. Until that fateful day in July 1924, it said, Ignaz Urbach

> [enjoyed] a good reputation on account of his integrity. A regular at the stock exchange for 35 years, he performed all his duties conscientiously. For the past fortnight, however, word had gone around that Ignaz Urbach's bank was in financial difficulties. It was known that clients had abandoned the firm and that Urbach was struggling to meet his obligations. On Thursday afternoon Urbach had gone to see his lawyer Dr Zeisl, accompanied by his son [Robert Urbach] who also worked for the bank.[15]

Dr Zeisl had not been much help, however. He advised Ignaz to see Dr Kantor, the representative of the banking association, whose office was next door to Dr Zeisl's on the second floor. Ignaz refused: "Urbach replied that this was pointless. He had already tried going down that route and had met with a rebuff."[16] According to the *Tag* reporter, Urbach returned to his bank after this discussion and "immediately ordered all his clerks to establish the precise status of the bank, a task which took most of the employees all night. At 6.45 the following morning a telegram arrived from Prague which caused Urbach great alarm. He hurriedly put on his hat, slipped the business report drawn up by his clerks into his bag, grabbed a few good cigars and . . ."[17] Nobody discovered what was in the mysterious telegram from Prague. What is certain is that after receiving the telegram that morning Ignaz headed off to his lawyer, Dr Zeisl. When he arrived at 23 Gonzagagasse, however, he didn't ring at either Zeisl's or Kantor's door, continued past their offices, and climbed another flight of stairs to the third floor. There he took off his hat and put down his stick. Perhaps he wanted to demonstrate how he had been let down by Zeisl and Kantor. Whatever the exact reason for his action, a few minutes later, at 8 a.m., Ignaz Urbach was found dead by the caretaker at Gonzagagasse:

His feet were by the window, pointing upwards, and his head lay in a pool of blood right outside the doors of the lawyers Dr Kantor and Dr Zeisl . . . Evidence pointing towards suicide include the difficulties facing Herr Ignaz Urbach and his bank, the mysterious telegram from

Prague and a letter found with the body and addressed to Frau Urbach. In the letter, dated 27th May and written in shaky handwriting, Urbach said he was at the end of his tether and that the initiation of settlement proceedings would be unavoidable. Beneath the signature is an addendum with the words: Forgive me, I beg you to have me cremated. The addendum is undated and it is possible that this message was written by Urbach just before he committed suicide.[18]

The newspapers speculated as to who might bear some responsibility for Ignaz's death. The *Kronenzeitung* believed it knew who was to blame. Under the headline ABANDONED BY INTERVENTION COMMITTEE it read:

Only last week banker Urbach appeared before the so-called bailout committee and asked for credit to be able to meet his obligations. Over the past few weeks a number of once-thriving companies and banks have had to approach the bailout committee. Many have been helped, but many more of those applying for credit have been turned down. Banker Urbach explained to the committee that his obligations ran to 1 billion and 300 million crowns. He had succeeded in obtaining some money from a different source but he needed another 650 million crowns, which he was claiming from the intervention committee as a credit. As security Urbach was offering his family's jewellery, two motorcars and securities with a total value of one billion crowns.

Yesterday at the stock exchange it was being said that Dr Bloch from the firm Kux, Bloch and Co., who has a lot of say on the intervention committee, had voiced his opposition to providing credit.[19]

To all the insiders it seemed clear that with this move Bloch had eliminated an unwelcome competitor. They believed that, by failing to help out, he certainly shared some of the responsibility for Ignaz's death along with Dr Kantor and Dr Zeisl. This was of little comfort to his family, however. For Alice it meant just one thing: her last male protector had gone. He had died in the most shocking way and was the subject of gossip throughout Vienna. Alice now decided once and for all never to rely on men again. Her father had not been able to cope with the collapse of the Habsburg Monarchy, her husband Max had sought refuge in his gambling addiction after the war, and even the dependable Ignaz had left his family in miserable circumstances.[20] In her memoir Alice writes: "I was brought up to look with respect and awe on the 'head of the family', and when this older brother-in-law died [. . .] only then did I realize I was completely alone."[21]

Alice resolved to work only with women, and in this she was proved right; over the coming years it was women who would help her achieve great professional success.

To have an appreciation for the atmosphere of 1920s Vienna you can read Stefan Zweig, Franz Werfel or Karl Kraus. Or you can browse Ludwig Hirschfeld's long-forgotten 1927 travel guide *Was nicht im Baedeker steht* (What you won't find in

Baedeker). Before the First World War Hirschfeld had published stories about the city of his birth in the *Neue Freie Presse*, but he couldn't use a line of this material for his travel guide. The old levity was gone: "The worst victory could not have changed us so radically as our staggering defeat, as this liquidation of good old Austria-Hungary plc. The firm has been wound up but the head office in Vienna is still running on idle."[22] Now Hirschfeld surveyed this head office in a completely new way. In the company of Viennese celebrities as well as everyday locals he explored the city, its restaurants, shops and theatres. Like many Viennese, Hirschfeld loved good restaurants and he urged his readers to take a wander past Hotel Sacher:

Sometimes Frau Anna Sacher stands outside the hotel with her world-famous bulldogs, making conversation with Austrian high aristocracy, which always gets very heated. Many a vitriolic attack and punch-up has taken place outside Hotel Sacher, but because these only ever involve the most feudal members of society, nobody gets seriously upset about it. We merely feel gratified that elegant society seeks out the most elegant places for their brawls.[23]

Hirschfeld realised that capable women like Sacher were what the country now needed. The female Schnitzler types – "upper-class doyennes of adultery and sweet girls from the lower class" – "have finally been laid to rest." The reason for this, according to Hirschfeld, were the dire economic circumstances.

The girls, in particular,

> are having a more difficult time than their literary prede-
> cessors who evidently had nothing else to do than to
> be happily or unhappily, sentimentally or frivolously in
> love. Anyone who gets up every day at six, tidies her
> room, makes breakfast for the family, then takes the tram
> for an hour to her workplace, her office, where for eight
> hours she has to sit, write, calculate, telephone, sort out
> tax and hospital deductions as an organised employee,
> such a working girl truly has no time for a tear in the
> corner of her eye [...] she is no longer naïve and clueless.
> On the contrary, she is very shrewd [...] all the sweetness
> has gone.[24]

Alice took a similar view and this new generation now opened
up an opportunity for her. "About 1923/24 [...] food was back,
plentiful as before the war," she wrote. "Many young women,
grown-up during the years of need [...] had never put to use
any of the good old famous recipes, had never tried their hands
on the famous Viennese varieties of food [...] My time had
come, though I was not quite aware of it!"[25]

Alice's career running a cookery school became possible
for three reasons: first, because this new generation of women
needed cookery lessons; second, because new apartments were
fitted with modern kitchens;[26] and third, because Viennese
society ladies had enough money once more to host large soirées
and needed to cater for them.[27]

Alice's sister Helene was one of these society ladies. She led a life that Alice only remembered from before the war. Helene was now married to the rich lawyer Dr Georg Eissler and they lived in a magnificent apartment in the first district. Although she had many talents, cooking was not one of them. And so Alice took over the kitchen for Helene's soirées. She did not find it degrading to cook for her sister's guests. On the contrary, she described how this job gradually instilled confidence in her. Particularly successful were her culinary creations for Helene's bridge parties. In the 1920s bridge became highly popular. All over Vienna, many a "bridge salon" was set up, a sort of mixture between club and casino.[28] Helene was one of the best players in Vienna and she organised her own bridge parties at home. The highlight was the food that Alice created for the evening. As bridge parties can go on for ages and nobody wants to put down their hand, it is not easy to satisfy hunger at the same time, and so Alice invented "bridge bites". In 2019 the Austrian newspaper *Die Presse* discovered and printed Alice's recipe (under the name Rudolf Rösch) in its lifestyle supplement:

The so-called bridge bites are varieties of open sand-wiches, fashionable of late. As their name suggests, they are bite-sized so that avid players can pop them in their mouths in one go without having to interrupt the game. To avoid the need for cutlery they are secured with toothpicks, allowing them to be picked up [. . .] The base of white or brown bread is usually shaped or cut very delicately. The toppings consist of a wide variety of savoury morsels. The bridge bites are served in paper cases, making them look like treats from the bakery. Once assembled most are quickly covered in cold liquid aspic.[29]

In the 1920s the bridge bites became very popular, but Alice believed her petits fours were in fact the key to her professional success:

> My sister's guests, all wealthy socialites, asked me to teach them – my art! [. . .] I could, in my moderate sized kitchen, not teach more than five or six at once. After a couple of months I had to do something about this [. . .] I had no business experience nor training; I had no money to invest. I simply went to a store down town where they sold gas and electric stoves for household use. I knew they had a test kitchen with plenty of room in the basement. The conversation between the owner of the shop and me was brief:
>   "Could I use your test kitchen twice a week for a few hours in the afternoon?"
>   "Yes, if you will pay the gas and electricity expense."
>   "Thank you, I will do that."
>   Thus, I was established. I put signs in the shop window:
>
> *"Lessons in Confectionery" by Alice Urbach*
> *Mondays and Fridays, 3 p.m. to 5 p.m.*[30]

On the first Monday, as Alice waited there with her maid Mitzi as assistant, only one woman turned up, the wife of a doctor:

This one lady as audience and the whole big room yawning empty! I was embarrassed and so flustered that I put the cake into the oven without adding the sugar called for in the recipe! Then [. . .] the same week the large room was full of ladies – old ones, young ones, cooks, girls in their teens, housewives – every chair, every standing place taken. I was just delighted! I had never dreamed that I could experience such a success![31]

Two things seem to have been responsible for the sudden popularity: word of mouth from Alice's many friends and her unusual method of recruiting pupils. "I always talk too much," she wrote apologetically, "but it was this irritating quality of mine that brought me success. I got half of my cookery school pupils by talking to every woman I met." Alice chatted to people everywhere – on platforms, in queues outside shops or in the hours spent waiting at some administrative office. And as Alice paused for breath she also listened attentively. She really was interested in what people thought and she was forever collecting good stories. With the test kitchen now up and running, every woman she met was a potential pupil for her cookery school; they just needed convincing. Alice became a strategic talker:

I would simply stand outside the most elegant delicatessens in Vienna, which displayed culinary masterpieces in their windows. Women of all ages stood admiring these glittering things. They didn't have the slightest idea how such miracles could be created. As soon as I realised that a woman really was interested I handed her my business card [...] And then she was bound to come to my cookery course. And she didn't come on her own, no, she brought her sisters, friends, mother, mother-in-law.

Quite apart from the fact that she never stopped talking, it must have also helped that Alice did not have the appearance of a strict teacher. She looked friendly, maternal and round. If you had asked a child what a cook looked like they would have drawn a picture of Alice. Finally she had found her role in life:

> Soon, two afternoons a week were insufficient for the demand. I had to have another place where I could work in the morning. The hardware store where I bought my pots had a storeroom behind the shop [. . .] Life was good. I was happy. I earned enough to provide my little boys with all the necessities! I don't think there was anything my little boys in those years missed, except the love of a father. I was very busy all day. I had, a long time ago, added lessons on hors d'oeuvres and cold dishes, on fancy canapés and sandwiches [. . .] Suddenly the authorities became aware, maybe notified by the licensed cookery schools who, of course, were envious.[32]

Alice had no licence to give courses, nor did the hardware shop have permission to hold them in its storeroom. She was summoned to the authorities. Fortunately, one of her pupils was the wife of the deputy mayor. He helped Alice obtain a trade licence and then, having found suitable premises, she was able to open her cookery school at 1 Goldeggasse. It was in a nice neighbourhood, close to the Belvedere Palace. After classes Alice's pupils could go for a walk in the park to work off the calories they had piled on. "I became so popular in this field," Alice wrote, "that it was considered a 'must' for any girl [. . .] to finish a course in my school or her education was not complete." Over the years Alice had all manner of pupils: "housewives of every age, girls in their teens, professional cooks, actresses, princesses, duchesses, with a few men sprinkled in for company!"[33]

Amongst the men there was even a prince from the house of Liechtenstein, "a tall, handsome fellow who, when he made a world cruise, wanted a little knowledge of cookery, in order, as he said, to be able to fix some food for himself and not be forced to eat French fried locusts while in South America." Many of her pupils had never cooked a meal for themselves before, including the American writer Princess Amélie Rives Troubetzkoy, Countess Aehrenthal, the former ballerina Grete Wiesenthal and the "beautiful daughter" of the British ambassador Walford Selby. Alice made all of them connoisseurs of the art of cooking.[34]

Helene helped Alice to recruit rich society ladies, but her half-sister Sidonie did all she could to support her too. They were close, despite the age difference of twenty-two years. Sidonie, whose name was shortened to Sida within the family, had red hair and a slight squint. Felix Mayer later wrote about his half-sister: "She had the kindest heart imaginable, always ready to sacrifice herself for others."[35] Sida had inherited a talent for writing from her father and was set on becoming a journalist. She chose a subject that was unlikely to bring her into competition with male journalists: housekeeping and fashion. To an extent Sidonie paved the way for Alice, as even before the First World War she was penning articles about housekeeping and giving talks on cooking.[36] In 1925 she and Alice wrote a book together: *Das Kochbuch für Feinschmecker* (The cookbook for gourmets). It was published by Moritz Perles, a Jewish house which would be Aryanised thirteen years later.[37]

Sidonie came up with countless ideas to help Alice offer ever-changing courses.[38] Once a week a famous cook would come along to present, as Alice put it, "the most astonishing dishes!" One of these chefs, who had cooked for the Habsburg family, showed the pupils the exquisite creations he had devised for the birthday parties of the imperial children. Alice also put on cookery exhibitions once or twice a year:

> The school made up its most lovely dishes, and all the pupils, former ones and those just attending were encouraged to bring forth a sample of what they had learned to produce [. . .] Hundreds of wonderful, appetizing edibles were presented to an admiring crowd or audience! I invited the editors and writers of all the fashionable magazines, periodicals and no musician, even a good one, could have waited more anxiously for the critics in the morning papers [...] The critics praised the exhibition extravagantly.[39]

By now Alice was giving talks throughout the city on subjects such as "Quick cooking for the working woman",[40] "The housewife and her attitude towards modern food" or "The girl at the stove".[41]

The newspapers reported on these talks and the *Neues Wiener Journal* printed a long article about Alice's courses under the headline "Is Cookery Modern?" The journalist was particularly impressed by the many foreigners at the cookery school, "whose foreign idioms enrich the cosmopolitan air of these courses". Alice could teach in Viennese English and Viennese French, and her audience listened with "keen interest to these polyglot and yet authentically Viennese courses, which under the tutelage of an educated lady, are destined to restore the reputation of Viennese cuisine."[42]

Because Alice was interested in international trends she was also the first person to offer a delivery service for ready-prepared meals in Vienna.[43] What we consider perfectly normal today was something new at the time, and highly praised by the press:

> Americanisation everywhere – now we in Vienna can also enjoy culinary delicacies delivered to our door in record time, hot and ready to eat. [Thanks to] Frau Alice Urbach, the famous teacher of modern cookery courses in Goldeggasse [. . .] The working woman who does not have time to cook herself, who cannot afford a domestic help and yet who wishes to spend the short time for dinner at the table with her family, the large army of employees with continuous working hours, the ailing person kept at home, all of these can get [. . .] delicious and nutritious home cooking![44]

At this time Alice was often away from home, giving talks, buying ingredients or delivering meals. Sidonie and a nanny helped to look after her sons. Whereas Karl was a good boy, there was always *zores* (trouble) with Otto at school. The older he got, the more he rebelled against the rest of the world. In 1928 he once again brought home a terrible end-of-year report from secondary school. Apart from PE (very good) and geography (good), his grade in all other subjects was merely "adequate". He was known as a troublemaker who rarely did his homework and was unwilling to submit to any authority. The antipathy he felt towards his teachers was mutual. Otto thought school wasn't important. His brain raced and he was full of ideas that shot randomly in all directions. He dreamed of inventing things and travelling the world. He had applied himself in geography as he was desperate to know where exactly the land borders ran so as to devise his escape plan. Occasionally he would skip school and take himself skiing. In summer he would go to one of the stations in Vienna to watch the trains depart. Westbahnhof, Südbahnhof, Ostbahnhof, Nordbahnhof and Franz-Josephs-Bahnhof – all of these became his stomping grounds. Apart from Südbahnhof they all lay in depressing parts of town, but for someone who had grown up in Ottakring poverty was nothing unusual. Otto blocked out the dreariness of the surroundings, dreaming instead that he was one of the travellers with the large trunks. He was especially fond of the colourful luggage stickers from big cities, shipping lines and elegant hotels. For a bit of pocket money he sometimes helped the porters load the suitcases and, if nobody was looking, he would peel off a few of the stickers for his collection.

Over the years he compiled a large assortment from all the capitals of Europe, although the most precious items in his collection came from America, Japan and China. Otto wanted to travel to these places one day, and when that day came he would put these stickers on a large, elegant trunk so that everyone would think he was a seasoned globetrotter.

Alice knew nothing of Otto's excursions, but she noticed him slipping away from her. She decided to involve him in her work, teaching him how to cook, and was delighted at how talented and creative he was. When he was sixteen he helped out with the courses too,[45] which brought them closer together. She was horrified, however, when Otto announced he was going to leave school. He wanted to design cars and had already secured an apprenticeship with Renault in Vienna. This was catastrophic as far as Alice was concerned. Successful Jewish men didn't become mechanics; they were doctors or lawyers. Otto ignored her objections. He finished his training and in 1932 he moved to England for eighteen months, working as an engineer for the United Mining Company in Wolverhampton. For him this was no more than an interim solution, as his real dream was to live far away from Europe. In 1934 he applied to emigrate to Palestine, but soon afterwards decided on America.[46]

Alice would have been in despair about Otto's chaotic life had Karl not been doing so well at school. He, at least, wanted to become a doctor, thereby salvaging the family's honour. Looking back, Alice wrote:

Nobody could have had better sons. My older one gave me trouble when he was about twelve [...] All the trouble he gave me when a boy, he made good a thousand times, when he was grown up and in the States. I should have really known, when he was a young boy, that he was someone special. But the times were so terrible [...] Bobby [Otto's nickname] was then in his first year – in a very modern school – and even there [was chastised] for bad behaviour. At home he never gave any trouble, perhaps the governess understood that he had to follow his own ideas. Then when he was a teenager no school wanted to keep him, because he never followed any rules! But Vienna was too small for him. He was a very wonderful and affectionate son, but wanted out. So I let him go when he was nearly twenty-two.[47]

In 1935 Otto went to Reed College in Portland, Oregon. Alice could not have known how important this decision would be for her life too.

4: SUCCESS AT LAST!

"No, no! The adventures first ...
explanations take such a dreadful time."
Lewis Carroll, *Alice's Adventures in Wonderland*

Reed College is situated in one of the most beautiful regions of America. The main building is in Tudor Gothic style, but the architecture is misleading. Reed is not one of the old American universities like Harvard or Princeton. In fact it was only opened in 1908, and since then has been anything but backward-looking. Along with Berkeley, Reed still has the reputation of being one of the most progressive educational institutions in the US. The college is also known for being the place where Apple founder Steve Jobs discovered his love of calligraphy in the 1970s, which later would have a key influence on the design of his firm.[1] Steve Jobs is certainly Reed's most famous student, but a few of his predecessors from the 1930s also deserve a closer look. They learned things at Reed which would lead them down unconventional paths in life.

From 1935 to 1936 Alice's son Otto, his friend Cordelia Dodson and an Italian aristocrat by the name of Emilio Pucci were three such students. As a trio they couldn't have been more different: Cordelia, the American from a smart family; Otto, the poor Austrian Jew; and Pucci, the Italian Fascist. Reed and the Second World War ensured that the three of them would never forget each other.

It was down to Dexter Keezer, the president of Reed College, that they met at all. Anyone taking a closer look at Keezer's life might wonder if it really was a coincidence that he allowed Otto to study there for free alongside a Fascist like Pucci. Keezer seems to have enjoyed social experiments. At any rate he believed that unorthodox methods were needed to get students to think. He himself had started to think during the First World War. Keezer came from a small town in Massachusetts where there was very little cultural stimulation. He might never have developed an interest in Europe and Europeans like Otto and Pucci had he not been sent to France as a soldier in 1917. His encounters with the French and British made him more worldly, dispelling his political naïveté. After his return he studied economics and later worked for Roosevelt's secretary to the treasury, Henry Morgenthau, on New Deal projects.[2] When Keezer became president of Reed College in 1934, he decided to give the sleepy ivory tower a thorough shake-up. In his opinion the students were too pampered and urgently needed to be stretched more.[3] This included sporting as well as intellectual challenges. Professors were shocked when Keezer announced that he wanted to bring the best baseball and American football players to Reed. His enthusiasm for sport also explains why he accepted penniless students like Otto and Pucci. Although neither could afford the high fees, they offered Keezer two things: they could tell their fellow students what was happening in Europe and set up a skiing team for Reed on the side.

The *Oregonian*, the biggest newspaper in Portland, reported in 1937 that Otto ended up at Reed College by pure chance: "Early in 1935 [Otto Urbach] heard of Reed through Dr Paul Dengler of the Austro-American Institute in Vienna. He wrote to President Dexter M. Keezer, asking if Reed could use a ski master."[4] Keezer said yes, and so Otto travelled to America in September 1935. As it turned out, Alice had to take in a Reed student in return, which she wasn't especially thrilled about: "The exchange student is already on his way," Otto wrote to Alice shortly after his arrival, "and I'm really sorry that you have to undertake this sacrifice for me. But I do believe that it's worth [the effort] because I really do have wonderful opportunities here. Everyone is incredibly friendly and helpful, and it won't be difficult to make Auntie happy."

Otto and Alice had agreed to use the codeword "Auntie" when talking about his residence permit. As an exchange student he had been given only a one-year visa, but he hoped to stay in America and send money back to Alice and Karl. Neither the Austrian nor the American authorities must get wind of this plan. As mother and son had little trust in the privacy of the postal system they would analyse the state of "Auntie's" health. Sometimes it was more hopeful, at other times less so.

There was something else Otto had to conceal – that he was earning money on the side. As a foreign student he didn't have a work permit, but still he got a job in the ski department of Meier and Frank (which is now part of Macy's):

I'm going to work four afternoons and all of Saturday and I'll be paid twelve dollars a week. The department store is absolutely terrific, it's brand new and done up in the most modern style. From the outside it looks like the national bank, but it's far taller. I work on the sixth floor. They've given me a small workshop, in the shop itself, where customers can see how to attach bindings and metal edges.[5]

Otto intended to save his money so he could hire a lawyer to help him out in "the matter of Auntie". His chances of earning enough were good, as his workshop soon had customers arriving in droves. Skiing was a new fashion in America and as a genuine Austrian Otto became the department store's main draw. Karl sent him original skiing posters from Vienna and all manner of Austrian knitted jumpers with which to decorate his workshop. Otto even built a roast chestnut stall and organised a Vienna week in the department store. His marketing ideas attracted the attention of the Jewish owners, Mr Frank and Mr Meier. Julius Meier (1874–1937) was a great philanthropist, and although not a member of any party he was elected Governor of Oregon in 1931. Otto could scarcely believe his luck when Mr Meier invited him to parties at the governor's residence. After all the misery of Vienna he was now surrounded by luxury. Even his college room seemed like paradise. He wrote to Alice:

The college is indescribably beautiful, in the middle of a garden, flowers everywhere, and the whole place has such a peaceful atmosphere [. . .] It's like being in another world. I have a small apartment with two other boys, both slightly younger. Three rooms, bathroom, a small fireplace [. . .] The food is excellent and plentiful [. . .] Almost all the students here have cars. The girls are all very pretty and smart, many of them have been to Europe. From my window I can see the cars arriving of those students who don't live in college. It looks a little bit like cars drawing up at the Opera House Ball.[6]

He seemed to be popular with the American girls too, as he revealed to Karl in a separate letter. Although he had broken up with a student called Jean he already had another girlfriend who drove a Packard. It was unclear which he found the more fascinating, the car or the woman.[7] Despite these distractions he did not neglect his studies. Overnight the school dropout had become a model student. To Alice he wrote:

I've passed all my quarterly exams with good marks. My psychology result was excellent, I got the eighth best mark in a class of sixty students. I'm not so good at political science, but above average . . . Some big news: next week I'm going to be on the wireless. [On the programme] "Neighbors of the Northwest". Each week they present an expert on a particular subject. Next week I'm the expert. The Americans really are quite naïve. Last week there was a minister on the programme and this week it's Mr Otto Urbach. It's a shame you can't listen in![8]

The newly found expert Otto explained skiing to the Americans. Very soon after his arrival he founded the Reed skiing team which would later participate in nationwide university competitions.[9] With a few helpers he also constructed an Austrian-style ski hut on nearby Mount Hood. The college magazine now regularly printed photographs of Otto's sporting innovations and published articles with headlines such as "Urbach to stage special flying mile event". Above the photograph of the dry ski-slope he had constructed himself, it read: "Why Wait for Winter? . . . Under the direction of Otto Urbach, Viennese ski expert studying at Reed, this wooden slide was put up last week, and two dry ski-courses, probably the first in America, are underway."[10]

With all these extra-curricular activities it is surprising Otto found the time to write essays. To make them more interesting he asked Karl to send political material from Vienna, particularly Fatherland Front publications,[11] and thus Reed students learned sooner than the rest of America that Austria was a clerical-Fascist state, led by Chancellor Kurt Schuschnigg since 1934. Otto was also able to explain why Austria had been dependent on Italy as its protector since 1933. His reports were of interest to the psychology students too. One young, attractive woman from Portland, who was particularly fascinated by what Otto had to say, was studying German, French and psychology. Her name was Cordelia Dodson.

Cordelia was a supremely confident woman all her life. She knew what to do in any situation (and how to get out of it unscathed). Her weakness for high heels, jewellery and make-up might have led some to regard her as superficial;[12] in truth she was exceptionally intelligent. Decades later Cordelia told a colleague that she was recruited by the American secret service while still a student at Reed.[13] Exactly when the recruitment took place has been impossible to ascertain. According to her CV, Cordelia began her studies in 1932, which were interrupted several times for semesters abroad in France and Austria. She graduated in June 1941.

Over the course of their lives both Cordelia and Otto became expert at keeping secrets, and this included their relationship. Whether they ever became lovers is unclear. But there are a few clues as to how important they were to each other. In her last interview Cordelia mentioned her friendship with Otto as key to the development of her interest in the National Socialist regime. Otto died before he was able to give eyewitness interviews, but his letters from the 1930s reveal his fascination for Cordelia. He makes frequent mention of her, and although what he says is relatively banal, the language is unusual for Otto. He was a man who dashed off letters quickly and preferred to be matter of fact. When writing about Cordelia, however, his tone changed quite noticeably. To Karl, for example, he said, "When you get this letter Cordelia Dodson might already be in Vienna [. . .] Tell her I think of her often."[14] By Otto's standards this was almost a declaration of love.

The psychology course at Reed would also have a long-lasting influence on the two students. Otto later employed his psychological skills to interrogate SS officers, and Cordelia used them on her former student friend, Emilio Pucci.

Whereas Cordelia and Otto would always work behind the scenes, Pucci played a very public role.[15] After the war he became a fashion designer, making clothes for celebrities including Jackie Kennedy and Marilyn Monroe. In 1962, Reed College invited him to give a talk about his life. He skilfully circumvented the controversial periods. Listeners only found out that he got a master's in sociology from Reed and a PhD from the University of Florence. Originally he had planned to enter the Italian diplomatic service, he told them, but instead joined the air force during the war. The rest of his talk was a lesson on how to dress correctly.[16] This seamless transition is testament to Pucci's elegance – he always was a superb slalom racer. In 1962 his American audience would doubtless have been horrified to learn that he'd been a highly decorated Fascist war hero and the lover of Mussolini's daughter, Edda Ciano. He had also omitted to say that he and another Reed student, Cordelia Dodson, had played the key roles in a spectacular secret service operation at the end of the war.

Pucci would become important for Cordelia during the war, but Otto and he had been rivals already during their student years. In 1936 Pucci took over the skiing team, taught Viennese waltzes to his female admirers,[17] and his final dissertation was a defence of Mussolini entitled "Fascism: An Explanation and a Justification". All of this understandably made Otto livid.

In a secret résumé of his life Pucci later explained that his enthusiasm for Italian Fascism had landed him in heated arguments with fellow students, beginning in 1935 when Italy invaded Ethiopia: "The Ethopian war had caused in America a wide-spread anti-Fascist feeling [. . .] Being away from my country I naturally reacted. I debated and discussed, trying to prove that Italy was justified in her action against Ethiopia. People listened to my remarks and answered in turn, leaving me often speechless, so great was my ignorance and so strong the logic of their arguments." For this reason in 1936 he changed to studying political science at Reed.[18]

Just as he had given Otto a place, Dexter Keezer accepted the Italian student into Reed, justifying his decision by saying that Pucci's "academic performance was first rate. And so was the zest and goodwill with which he tackled a variety of lowly chores on the campus [...] to acquire a bit of cash to supplement the bare subsistence being provided to him."[19]

Meanwhile, in Vienna, Alice was struggling with the Reed exchange student she had been sent. Ed Cerf, the son of a Reed professor,[20] turned out to be a spoiled egomaniac who would stay up all night drinking, and was forever borrowing money from Alice and Karl. When Ed invited his American student friend Bill to move in, Alice's patience came to an end. She asked Otto for advice and he replied immediately:

Write an airmail letter to his parents and tell them that you're not able to put Bill up too [. . .] You really don't need to be considerate and tactful. The Americans aren't. If I were in this position I'd be booted out. I find it most strange that he doesn't have a return ticket. Please don't be sentimental about this [. . .] don't think that if you send Bill away the same will happen to me [. . .] Please put your foot down [. . .] bear in mind that nobody in the USA wishes to give me something for nothing.[21]

At least everything else seemed to be going right for Alice in 1935. Karl had embarked on his first semester studying medicine at the University of Vienna and they moved into a spacious rented apartment at 7 Goldeggasse, a few doors away from the cookery school. As the unemployment rate in Ottakring had now reached 50 per cent and the social problems there were getting ever worse, the move came as a great relief.[22]

But the greatest excitement of autumn 1935 was the publication of Alice's second book. *So kocht man in Wien! (Cooking the Viennese Way!)* was 500 pages long and contained everything she had learned about cookery and housekeeping since the age of five.

Reconstructing the genesis of this book as precisely as possible is important because Alice's publishing house would later issue a version of events that bore little relation to the truth. Hermann Jungck, head of the publishing house since 1937, wrote his account of what happened in a 1974 jubilee publication. Why he discusses the Alice case in so much detail remains unclear. Perhaps he feared a legal dispute, or he was trying to justify his behaviour to himself. His story begins when his uncle, the founder of the publishing house Ernst Reinhardt, commissioned the book in 1934: "My uncle went to Vienna and visited his acquaintances there to find out who might be able to write such a cookbook. It turned out that all the women who ran cookery schools had already published a cookbook, except for Alice Urbach, who ran a smaller school, and had not written one yet."

The tale Jungck is telling here sounds like a Cinderella story: a publisher discovers an unknown woman who hasn't

Karl as a school leaver

yet put pen to paper. In reality Alice *had* published a success-ful cookbook with her sister Sidonie in 1925, and in cooking circles she was known as a real talent. Perhaps Jungck had no idea of this, but it is highly likely his uncle Ernst did know, for Moritz Perles, with whom Alice's first book appeared, represented several German publishing houses in Austria, including Ernst Reinhardt Verlag.[23] Jungck's shaky grasp of the facts here wouldn't be a problem had he not gone further and crossed a line in his story: "It was not long before Frau Urbach had compiled her cookbook — she once told me later that because she didn't have so many recipes of her own, she helped herself out by borrowing a number of recipes from other cookbooks but filing them under different names."[24]

It now becomes clear that Jungck is aiming to put in doubt the originality of Alice's book, and thereby cover up his own crime. In reality, Alice had assembled so much material that by 1938 she had already written two other cookbooks for Jungck: a vegetarian one entitled *Die fleischlose Kost* (Cooking without meat), and *Wiener Mehlspeisen* (Viennese desserts and pastries). Jungck does not refer to either in his jubilee publication; he had good reason not to. After the Anschluss of Austria he would publish all three books under the name of a different author. So it was in fact Jungck who had "borrowed recipes from other cookbooks", not Alice.[25]

In her memoir Alice tells a different story as to how the cookbook came about: "I got a letter from the publisher R. He wrote, 'I want a Viennese cookbook! Frau S. met you on a train to Gastein and she's a friend of mine. She is con-vinced that you ought to write such a book. Will you?'"[26]

Alice agreed and was pleased she could continue the family tradition:

> My father, one of my brothers, one of my sisters and several cousins, at least twenty members of our family, were either professional or occasional authors. Even one of my sons [Otto], working in a quite different field, wrote a film-script and sold it in Hollywood – to a firm. So, you see, I just followed the pattern! Of course, I never imagined that the book would turn out to be a bestseller.[27]

Jungck failed to mention in 1974 that *So kocht man in Wien!* became a bestseller; instead he described in great detail all the problems his publishing house had with it. In Austria the book appeared with the publishing arm of the Zentralgesellschaft für buchgewerbliche und graphische Betriebe (ZG),[28] who divided it into booklets to sell individually. This led to misunderstandings amongst buyers who for some reason thought the author was going on reading tours, offering cookery courses throughout Austria.[29] According to his own account, therefore, Herr Jungck had nothing but trouble with the book, because the sales representative made false promises and Reinhardt Verlag had to fend off these inquiries.

Jungck also neglects to mention the excellent critiques the book received. The first rave reviews appeared in December 1935, just in time for the Christmas market: "Alice Urbach, famous for her 'culinary' prowess, has now published a beautiful cookbook: *So kocht man in Wien!* The title says a lot, but doesn't tell you everything. For there is so much in these 500 pages and in such variety that it practically encompasses every aspect of culinary wisdom."[30] *Die Reichspost* came to the same conclusion:

So kocht man in Wien! This is the succinct and catchy title of an excellent new cookbook and housekeeping manual by Alice Urbach, famed for her traditional home cooking and owner of the renowned Viennese cookery school which also attracts many pupils from abroad [. . .] The thousands of recipes all bear the unmistakable hallmark of Viennese taste. Particularly thorough is the chapter on Viennese desserts and pastries, which of course have carried Vienna's reputation around the world: "stretched apple strudel", Carnival doughnuts, *Kaiserschmarrn* [shredded pancake] – we discover the best way of preparing all these delicacies so familiar to us, accompanied by realistic photographs showing the key stages of the processes. The experienced author dedicates a whole chapter to modern eating. We find sections on raw food, vegetarian cooking, various diets. Equally detailed and persuasive are the sections on infant nutrition [. . .] and weekend cooking. If, despite the variety of recipes, you are still unsure about what to cook the following day or for a special occasion, you only need to consult the appendix, where you will have no trouble finding the most exquisite but also economical recipes for every day of the year, for teas and coffee afternoons, for family occasions and dinners. In conclusion, there is no more apt way to

"Hard at work" –
illustrations from
So kocht man in Wien!

describe this inexpensive cookbook than by reiterating the words on the cover: 'Cooking the Viennese way!'[31]

The book contains many colour and black-and-white photographs, including several images of young cookery pupils stirring pots and pans. All you can see of Alice, however, is her hands – kneading dough or chopping ingredients. This omission was certainly not a reflection of Alice's wishes. She liked to be photographed and even though she didn't regard herself as especially pretty, there are countless photos of her posing proudly beside towering cakes. It would have been easy to photograph Alice's whole body at work in the kitchen, rather than just her hands. So why was her face not shown? One reason may have been that with her striking nose she simply looked too Jewish. The surname Urbach didn't sound Jewish (to this day there are Jewish and non-Jewish Urbachs) but her face would have told a different story. And in 1935 this was a story a German publishing house would not be keen to tell. Black cookery authors in the USA had a very similar experience at the time.[32] Their photographs were regarded as damaging to business, as were their "black-sounding" surnames, which were simply left out.

In 1935 Alice did not complain about a lack of photographs. She was too proud of her book and she celebrated its publication with all her Viennese friends.

She did not and could not know what the fate of her book would be.

5: SHANGHAI, OR THE AMERICAN SON

"be worried, letter follows."
Friedrich Torberg on the thrifty telegram style
of Jewish families[1]

"I can still smell the stench of burnt flesh, of blood and decay that lingers over Shanghai. The anti-aircraft defence is useless. They haven't been able to properly repel a single attack."[2]

It was Saturday, 14 August 1937. The first bombs fell on two hotels at 4.27 p.m.[3] Another wave hit the "Great World" entertainment complex. The number of dead and seriously wounded exceeded 2,000, all of them civilians. The day would enter history as "Bloody Saturday".

That evening Otto put on the uniform of the Shanghai Volunteer Corps (SVC), an international brigade of volunteers. A press photograph from 19 August 1937 shows him with other volunteers entrenched behind sandbags, rifle at the ready, close to the Bund, Shanghai's expensive promenade. The shops, restaurants and cinemas where he'd spent his free time for the past year had been destroyed.

But what was Otto doing in Shanghai in 1937? And why did Alice have to worry that he might never emerge from the city alive? She was no longer used to worrying about her elder son. When Otto moved to America his life finally seemed to be on the right track, and during his first college vacation in 1936 he wrote reassuring letters to Alice. He had a summer job running a YMCA camp at the idyllic Spirit Lake in Washington state: "I'm here at a camp about 100 km from the nearest human settlement. A wonderful lake, huge forests and sunshine [. . .] I'm supervising 45 boys, all between 12 and 16 years of age. We've got a cook, doctor, washerwoman, motorboats and electric light."[4]

Otto got on well with the boys, but from the start he locked horns with the cook. Alice had taught her son many culinary tricks; he knew how to make a lot out of a few cheap ingredients, and so his tolerance of poor food was very low. When the YMCA cook once again managed to burn lunch he sacked her.[5]

There was one problem Otto couldn't solve in this summer idyll. The "matter of Auntie" had proved much more complicated than expected. Otto urgently needed an extension for his residence permit, without which he would not be able to continue his studies or take a job in America. Until then it had been possible to travel to Canada or Mexico and return to America after a few weeks with a new visa, but the US government had unexpectedly put a stop to this practice. In June 1936 Otto wrote to Alice, "Unfortunately I don't have good news this time. I went to Canada and was thrown out, after which I went to Mexico, where the same happened. I've discovered that the new rules state you can only immigrate if you have relatives."[6] And a few weeks later: "Now I have to master the art of patience. Cursing or getting angry doesn't get you anywhere, and in this respect it's a valuable experience. I'm happy to be here, that's to say away from Austria, and yet I don't know what the future holds for me, although nothing should make me want to swap here for Europe [. . .] I'm glad, that apart from you, I feel no ties to Vienna and Austria."[7]

In search of a country where he could stay provisionally, Otto recalled his old collection of stickers pilfered as a child from Viennese train stations. A favourite had been one from China, and it was this country that offered the way out of his predicament. Applying for a residence permit for Shanghai was relatively uncomplicated, but financing the passage might be a problem. Otto wrote to Alice, "Tomorrow I'm meeting the boss of a shipping line between here and Shanghai. I've been promised a job on a boat. I'm not sure yet, but I think it's as a winch operator. The ship is mainly carrying planks as its cargo, so if it sinks at least I'll have something to hold on to."[8]

Otto banked on spending several months in China. He found it difficult to say goodbye to Reed College, especially when he learned that Pucci would now be running the skiing team for the 1936–37 season. He could only hope the Italian wouldn't also try to seduce Cordelia with his skiing flair.

Otto's official title on the ship was "second deck engineer". For a deck engineer he had impressive letters of introduction, including from Reed president Keezer and the Governor of Oregon, Julius L. Meier.[9] For Otto this did not appear out of the ordinary; in his world there were some days when you were turned away at the Mexican border and others when the Governor of Oregon invited you to his house. He had learned to get along in both worlds. On board ship he was as interested in the crew as he was in the officers. To Alice he wrote:

> Life on a freight steamer is quite different from how you'd imagine. It's more like a well-organised factory and without any of the romance normally attributed to the sea. The captain has very little to say and the seaman's union or trade union, who have a representative on the ship, determine who has to do what.[10]

And in a letter to his brother he wrote, "I eat at the officer's table, which is most agreeable. I have my own cabin with ice box and fan [. . .] The captain on board is a German, but he's not a 卍. He's been in the US for a long time."[11]

By the time the ship made a stopover in Japan, Otto had learned a little Chinese and Pidgin English, "which is the main language in Shanghai. The Chinese mess boys fall about laughing at my pronunciation."[12] He could only hope that it would suffice for the time being.

Shanghai in the 1930s was a magnet for those wanting – or needing – to begin a new life. In 1936 one immigrant described it thus:

> They come to China and want to get rich, they think that when they've got their dollars they'll go home again and

build themselves a nice house. That's what the Germans want, the English, everyone [. . .] They settle in Shanghai, they build skyscrapers and plant flowers, but it's all temporary because they're determined to return to Europe. Sometimes they can't cope with the loneliness anymore and they really do go home. But then they miss China. They miss the sun, they miss the servants, they miss the big country. They've lost the ground from under their feet and they no longer belong anywhere.[13]

In other parts of China the political situation was far less stable. Warlords tyrannised the population. Although General Chiang Kai-shek and his Kuomintang fought the warlords, they were battling the Chinese communists at the same time. These internal power struggles weakened the country, a situation exploited by Japan. In 1931, five years before Otto arrived in Shanghai, the Japanese found a pretext for occupying Manchuria. Although the League of Nations condemned this blatant infringement of Chinese sovereignty, it failed to deter Japan. It simply left the League of Nations in February 1933 and pursued plans for expansion in China – in a more subtle way. At the same time the Soviet Union, the USA and European powers began – also covertly – to amplify their involvement in the region. This was the dangerous situation Otto became caught up in months after his arrival in China in September 1936.

It all began relatively harmlessly, with Otto moving into the YMCA in Bubbling Well Road. "Forty dollars per month with full board, including swimming pool and library," he reassured Alice. From here he could explore the city:

Shanghai is a big muddle, filthy but also impressive. Lots of unemployed Russian refugees, much poverty amongst the Chinese next to the luxury of the rich English and Americans. Huge contrasts. Skyscrapers and mud huts stand side by side. A colourful mixture of rickshaws and Rolls Royces. Every nation you could imagine. Like Babel in its dimensions and confusion. I've had a lot of invitations but met relatively few nice people. I spend a lot of time with the secretary of the American chamber of commerce. A former Reed College student.[14]

It is understandable that Otto didn't tell his mother about the high rates of criminality and the opium dens,[15] nor that the port of Shanghai was a lure for prostitutes. Sixteen-year-old Chinese girls wearing lots of rouge and provocative clothing would routinely wander the streets. The endless beauty salons earned well from them, but also from the middle-class Chinese. Western clothes and make-up were regarded as very progressive. At weddings Chinese brides liked to be photographed in white. Since 1923 an American radio station had operated in Shanghai, broadcasting its own programme of entertainment for the city and featuring commercials for Western products. The city centre, with its tirelessly flashing neon advertisements, reminded Otto of Times Square in New York, but although the American influence was strong, the British still played the dominant role. After the Opium Wars of the mid-nineteenth century they had been awarded the island of Hong Kong and trading rights in the port cities of Canton and Shanghai. With their villas modelled on English country houses they shaped the suburbs of Shanghai, turning them into a garden idyll that was supposed to be reminiscent of the home counties. For the Chinese upper and middle classes an English schooling was equated with high social status and they would send their children to local English-speaking schools where they performed Shakespeare plays. Those who fancied rather cruder entertainment went to the English greyhound races, for which a stadium had been built specially in Shanghai. Here you could place large bets and lose a fortune.

In his letters Otto told Alice nothing of the manic passion for gambling that pervaded every class of Shanghai society (perhaps he knew that his father had been a gambler and he didn't want to worry Alice, but it may be that she had hidden this shame from her sons). Only once did Otto mention in passing that he'd bought a ticket for the Irish lottery. In truth, however, almost everyone around him gambled – Europeans, Americans and locals. Shanghai was home to endless gambling dens where addicts would lose themselves for days. Chinese fortune tellers earned handsomely from this addiction. They sat at small tables by the side of the road and told their customers which lucky numbers they should put their money on. It was a world of confusion, and in his letters Otto spoke highly of the new Shanghai novel by Joe Lederer, *Blatt im Wind* (A leaf in the wind), which best described what he was experiencing.[16] Lederer was an Austrian Jew and had worked as a journalist in Germany and in 1934 she emigrated to China. She secured a job as a nanny, but before she could settle she caught tuberculosis and had to return to Europe. Her protagonist describes the beauty and ugliness of Shanghai: "In summer, when you sit in your garden in Shanghai the cicadas shriek and the sky is blue [. . .] White herons in the blue sky. And cholera. And the lotus flower. And the typhoon. And the Dragon Boat Festival. And the stench of the canals."[17]

But for Lederer's characters the agonising loneliness is worse than any stench. It was a loneliness that Otto was familiar with too. In spite of the huge distance separating them, Alice could sense this. She reminded him several times to look up his second cousin, Dr Robert Pollitzer. Pollitzer belonged to a group of Western doctors working in Shanghai who later ensured that thousands of Chinese patients would survive the epidemics of the war.[18] For Otto too the Pollitzers and their children were a lifesaver of sorts. They offered him a sense of family before the chaos erupted.

To earn money Otto had taken a poorly paid job at the American Ford factory. He wrote to Karl: "I suppose you could call me a dogsbody. I oversee the unloading and loading of all automobiles [. . .] When there's work to be done in the factory I help out on the assembly line. I make a lot of technical drawings and check automobiles [. . .] About 200 automobiles pass through our hands every month."[19]

To prevent his mind from becoming deadened he tried to learn languages: "I'm taking Chinese and Russian lessons and I'm also attempting to make myself understood in about five other languages. Filipinos, Japanese, Russians and Mongolians all work in the Ford factory."[20]

Although the factory appeared very international, at lunch the Europeans would sit at their own table and eat their Chinese food with a fork and spoon. Otto soon tired of this; he was eager to meet Chinese people. Some invited him back to their homes and he gave return invitations which occasionally became quite pricey: "I try to save wherever I can, but as I have to spend quite a lot to save face I don't get anywhere."[21] The invitations were worth it, however, for his understanding of the language improved: "I can already make myself understood to some extent in Chinese although I still make plenty of mistakes and can read hardly anything yet."[22]

There are two sources for Otto's time in China. The first are his letters to Alice and Karl, in which he occasionally remarks that he hasn't written for a while because he's been travelling around the country. Sometimes he mentions places he plans to visit. He writes tersely: "In the next few days I'm going to Tientsin. Will probably spend a week or two up there."[23] Or: "There's a possibility I might go to northern China for a few weeks, where we have a big delivery for the Chinese government."[24] So far, so vague.

The second source is provided by a route map Otto drew himself, as well as black-and-white photographs taken with a Leica. On the map he marked his stopovers and the various modes of transport: to Nanking, Peking and Lanzhou with the Chinese airline Eurasia Aviation, then by car to Yungtang and Xining, and back to Kaifeng by plane.

At first glance there is nothing striking about the photos. They show landscapes, Buddhist monks and aeroplanes. His route, however, was highly sensitive. Several of the places he passed through were in Japanese-occupied Manchuria and other Chinese regions where Japan was trying to build up political influence.[25] What exactly was Otto doing in these dangerous regions?

There are two possible answers to this. The innocent answer is that Otto worked for Ford, and Ford was keen to do business with the Japanese, even in those areas which until recently had still been Chinese. Like other big firms, Ford – free from any moral encumbrance – sold to both sides. If war broke out the company would be able to earn handsomely. So Otto's travels may have been for purely commercial reasons.

The second theory is more complicated. Knowledge about Japanese activity in China had become politically important. The USSR and USA were – unofficially – cooperating to obstruct Japanese expansion in China.[26] Did Otto take other photographs on his unusual trip through Manchuria and Inner Mongolia which he didn't stick in his album? Were these "other" photos for his new friend at the American consulate in Shanghai, or for his employer Ford? They would have been of interest to both. Ford needed good situation reports; the firm had to protect its investments in China *and* Japan. American governmental circles also needed information from the occupied areas. In an affidavit Otto later admitted to having done some intelligence work on the side: "In Shanghai I volunteered for the US Marines as an intelligence agent."[27] Understandably he mentions nothing of the sort in his letters to Alice and Karl. All he writes about Japan in early 1937 is: "I got an invitation to a Japanese skiing competition, but couldn't accept it of course. Japan is very keen on skiing, and the sport seems to be becoming of nationwide interest. There's a possibility that the 1940 Winter Olympics will be held in Japan."[28]

After his travels through Manchuria, Otto knew very well that the Japanese wanted more than skiing. He also suspected that further Japanese attacks on Chinese territory were imminent.[29] As he waited for Japan's next step, a personal crisis occurred somewhere totally different – Vienna. The Austrian economy had deteriorated since his departure, and the cookery school was no longer thriving. But in September 1936 Otto had assumed that everything at home was proceeding more or less as normal. To Alice he wrote: "You must be working on reopening the cookery school [after the summer break] . . . I hope that there's at least something in it for you. As soon as I get a job I'll send money."[30]

Alice's letters to Otto have not survived, but his replies are in the family's possession. Over the next few weeks one question kept cropping up: Otto wanted to know from Alice how she was managing with her "struggles". Alice was facing increasing financial difficulties, even though her cookbook was a commercial success. She had received only a one-off payment in 1935 and enjoyed no share of the receipts.[31] Just one year after publication she was already seriously short of money.[32]

Along with financial worries there were political concerns, since the situation in Austria had deteriorated. In July 1936, Chancellor Schuschnigg signed an agreement with Hitler that, on the face of it, seemed to bolster Austria's sovereignty. Hitler asserted that he had no intention of meddling in Austria's internal affairs and was not planning an annexation. In return Schuschnigg issued an amnesty to Austrian Nazis. At the same time, however, Mussolini had increasingly distanced himself from Austria in favour of Hitler.[33] Until then Italy had provided the Austrians with a certain degree of protection from their powerful neighbour to the north. "Our political situation seems to be getting ever darker," Sigmund Freud wrote to a colleague in March 1937. "There is probably no holding up the Nazi invasion [...] Unfortunately the only protector we have had hitherto, Mussolini, seems now to be giving Germany a free hand."[34]

Both politically and financially, therefore, Alice's future looked perilous. She had to change her life before it was too late. Britain seemed to offer a way out; an elegant hotel in Brighton was looking for a star chef and Alice already envisaged this role for herself. She decided to emigrate.

In faraway China, these plans took Otto by surprise. His mother loved Vienna – why did she now want to abandon her homeland and all her friends? He knew that he had little chance of dissuading her from taking this step. Once his mother had made a decision she would carry it through. So he tried to support Alice remotely: "I'm sure life won't be too difficult for you in England. You probably won't like it to begin with, even though Brighton is supposed to be beautiful."[35] Otto had plenty of experience of immigration. He knew only too well how hard the first few months could be.

At the end of 1936 Alice closed her cookery school and gave notice on the apartment in Goldeggasse. Nineteen-year-old Karl had to move in with his student friend Willy. In February 1937, five days after her fifty-first birthday, Alice registered her departure from Vienna and travelled to London.[36]

Surviving letters from her sons reveal she must have had problems with her residence permit in the UK. On the other side of the world in China, Otto felt helpless. He wrote to Karl:

8th March 1937

Dear Karli!

I got your letter and an unhappy one from Mother. I'm feeling very gloomy, but there's nothing I can do. I did let Mother know, however, that in an emergency I can wire her some money, because I can borrow some here [. . .] I'm pleased you're keeping your head above water, but I'm less worried about you than about Mother. If you're having problems with money write to me. If necessary I could send you $15 per month.[37]

In March 1937, after only a month in England, Alice had to return to Vienna. It was a terrible setback for her.[38]

Otto guessed that the political situation in Austria was not going to improve. He wanted to return to America as soon as possible, so he could earn money to pass on to Alice and Karl. And he seemed to be in luck:

Shanghai, 14th May 1937

Dear Karli!

Some great news: I've obtained an entry visa for America. You can imagine how delighted I am. I was in Nanchang for a fortnight and when I came back the visa was there. Now it's going to be another couple of months until I get the quota number from the American consulate in Vienna [. . .][39]

Otto was hoping, therefore, that he would only spend another couple of months in China. But just then the situation became dangerous.

In May 1937 the weather gradually turned hotter in Shanghai. The first pith helmets appeared in the streets, and Otto too bought "one of these ridiculous things" to protect himself from the sun. It would come in very handy on his many trips. With war on the horizon, his employer was delivering lorries non-stop. Otto was working continuously and in July 1937 he found himself with his new pith helmet in the wrong place at the wrong time: in Beijing. Whether the Japanese or Chinese were responsible for the exchange of fire at Marco Polo Bridge is still a matter of dispute. The bridge was only fifteen kilometres from the city centre and this military incident on 7 July 1937 heralded the start of the Second Sino-Japanese War. Some historians also regard the date as the beginning of the Second World War. For Otto, at least, it marked the start of "his" very long war, even though he could not know it at the time. To Alice he wrote:

Dear Mother

Please excuse my long silence, which was not entirely of my own making. As I'm sure you've read in the newspapers, there have been serious clashes between the Chinese and Japanese in northern China. It's been in the air for a long time now, and the Ford Motor Co. has known for a while that it would blow up at some point. For the past two months both armies have been buying as many lorries as they can get hold of. About three weeks ago I accompanied a transport of 50 lorries to Peking [Beijing], where the Chinese were meant to receive them. I arrived safely and was supposed to take the train back to Shanghai a couple or so days later. You can imagine how surprised

I was when I woke up in the middle of the night to the sound of heavy artillery. There was no chance of my leaving, and the following day I went with all the other foreigners to the American consulate hospital, where we were accommodated. We reckoned that the whole thing would blow over in a few days, but we were mistaken. On the fourth day I received a telegram from Shanghai informing me that the transport division of the Chinese army needed more help with the lorries. Very reluctantly I left the consulate hospital, where the food and drink were excellent, and went in search of the company, which had headed to the west somewhere. After a few hours of looking I found them near Fengtai, about 10 km from Peking [Beijing]. The lorries were in such a terrible state as they'd tried to drive them without oil. We set up a makeshift workshop in a water buffalo shed and began reconditioning the engines. It was all going smoothly until the Japs got wind of it and started firing at our idyll. All the Chinese drivers vanished, and I left with a Russian and a Ford tractor, driving straight across the paddy fields. I had problems getting back into the city, but I finally made it to the hospital and its dependable rice dishes. Two days ago I came back via Tientsin to Shanghai, where they were already quite worried.[40]

Otto did not mention why there was every cause for concern. Beijing and Tientsin were now in Japanese hands. There was no reason to expect that the Japanese would simply halt their advance. The words with which Otto signed off his letter sounded highly optimistic, therefore: "One more month and then Shanghai will be behind me, which I'm desperately pleased about." It would turn out to be a long month. What happened soon after his return to Shanghai was so appalling that even Otto could no longer downplay it as an anecdote.

By now the heat made it unbearable to stay indoors. The poorer people put their folding beds onto the pavements at night, and anybody with electricity kept their fans going permanently. Otto slept badly and during the day he dragged himself exhausted to work like the other residents of Shanghai. Everyone was craving cool air. Some restaurants installed ice blocks, and people could even dance around them in dance halls – if they still had the energy to do so.

The oppressive weather also led to overreactions. Just as in the Marco Polo Bridge episode there are at least two versions of the following account: a Chinese and a Japanese one. Afterwards it was impossible to establish exactly who provoked whom.[41] On 9 August a Japanese lieutenant was stopped by a Chinese guard as he tried to enter the airport at Hongqiao, leading to an altercation. According to the Chinese report, the Japanese soldier shot the Chinese guard dead, upon which he was killed by some other Chinese guards. According to the Japanese version, the lieutenant was shot by the Chinese guard for no reason whatsoever; it was clearly a cold-blooded murder. Obviously there had to be an immediate response to such a "provocation", and this "spontaneous reaction" was well prepared. The Japanese sent their battleship *Izumo* to Shanghai and anchored it in the Whangpoo (now Huangpu) River.

Although it had started raining in Shanghai, the residents'

relief and joy was limited. The rain turned into a violent storm that destroyed telegraph poles and hampered communication. For the Japanese this was an advantage. On 12 August they began shelling Shanghai from the *Izumo*. The Japanese artillery's target was the northern district of Shanghai where the inhabitants were almost exclusively Chinese. It was clear that the Japanese wanted to avoid hitting the Shanghai International Settlement which was home to 48,000 foreigners of all nationalities. Had they been harmed, international public opinion would have been far more outraged. While the residents of the northern district tried to flee in panic to the International Settlement, the question arose as to how the Chinese leadership would respond to this act of war. And more importantly: Who would help them against the Japanese?

The wife of the Chinese commander-in-chief, Chiang Kai-shek, came from the wealthiest family in Shanghai. Madame Chiang Kai-shek was a Christian and had been educated in America. She was incredibly well connected and in this crisis she automatically turned to the Americans. One of her American military advisors suggested bombing the Japanese warship from the air. As the *Izumo* was anchored close to the International Settlement, however, this would entail a certain risk. Shanghai was the fifth-largest and most densely populated city in the world. What would happen if the Chinese pilots, inexperienced as they were and hampered by poor weather, missed their target? Notwithstanding these reservations, Madame Chiang Kai-shek gave the order to bomb the *Izumo*. On 14 August the Chinese aircraft took to the skies.

It was a Saturday, a working day in China. Otto was busy

by the river. As he cursed the bad weather, he had no idea that 14 August would go down in history as Bloody Saturday for quite different reasons. He wrote to Alice:

The Japanese provoked a conflict with the Chinese in Shanghai to give them a reason to sail a huge fleet of battleships up the Whangpoo River. They lined up along the riverbank and started shooting wildly at the city [...] That afternoon I was down by the river loading lorries onto a ship when all of a sudden the Japanese ships started firing their anti-aircraft guns like crazy [...] We left half of the cargo in the dock and sent the ship off straightaway. I was about to return to the factory in our motorboat when I saw that the Chinese had now completely blocked the river above the Settlement with a variety of boats and junks laden with sand. The factory was totally shut off from the outside world. I went to the office and filed a report (telephones had stopped working by now).[42]

The first aerial bomb, weighing 900 kg, landed directly on the International Settlement at 4.27 p.m.[43] It struck the Palace Hotel, while another bomb hit Nanking Road and parts of the Cathay Hotel. To begin with the situation was confusing. Those under attack assumed that these were Japanese bombs. Shanghai had been the target of Japanese air attacks back in 1932 and history appeared to be repeating itself. People were well aware of the devastating effects of aerial bombardment. A few months earlier, in April 1937, the Spanish town of Guernica had been flattened by the German Condor Legion. In Guernica around

1,000 civilians had been killed in the attacks; in Shanghai the death toll passed 2,000. In his letters Otto mentioned the figure of 3,000 deaths.[44] Even today the precise figure is hard to verify.

Slowly the news trickled out as to who had dropped these bombs. Not the Japanese, but the Chinese had bombarded their own city by accident. The chaos of these days was so overwhelming that Otto could send only a few scrawled lines:

> I just want to tell you quickly that I'm fine. An aerial attack is not one of life's pleasures but you get used to everything. I'm wearing an English uniform, driving for the SVC [Shanghai Volunteer Corps], which has been organised by the English army and works well. The situation here is a complete muddle and we can only wait. Don't worry about me, because as soon as boats start leaving I'll be on my way to the US. So don't worry if you don't hear from me for a while.[45]

In another letter he explained to Alice and Karl, "The SVC is an international volunteer organisation, supported by the English, and it has about 600 members who are well trained. In an emergency, of course, any man who can hold a rifle can join, but that doesn't mean he can shoot it . . ."

Otto underestimated the number of volunteers – there were 1,500. For some reason Scottish and Jewish SVC members were together in one group, Russians in another, and Americans, Portuguese and Filipinos in another. Most of them had never been in uniform before and suddenly found themselves torn from their everyday lives. A Russian who was seventeen at the

Otto's letter to Karl, on the writing paper of the Shanghai Volunteers, 23 August 1937

time later recalled sitting in the cinema watching the film *Hollywood Cowboy*. In the middle of the showing a message flashed up onto the screen: All men who are registered SVC members must report for duty immediately. When he and several volunteers got up to leave they were applauded by the entire cinema.[46]

SVC volunteers had to put on a brave face to avoid causing even greater panic in the population. Not all had such acting talent. An American journalist watched a group of SVC men who had to clear dead bodies away from the streets. When they saw body parts scattered everywhere some threw up. Later they went to a bar and tried to cope with what they had experienced with the help of black humour and plenty of alcohol.[47] When one of them found a finger on the floor he asked the group, "Anyone lost this?"

Otto's way of dealing with the situation was to photograph everything with his Leica. When later he put the pictures into an album he tried to keep his laconic distance. Beneath the picture of a road with wrecks of cars at all angles he noted: "Nanking Road. Shanghai's 5th Avenue. Doesn't look so good after an aerial attack." Another bombed-out building was captioned: "Sun department store (closed for the time being)." And beneath the photograph of an Indian hanging dead over a balcony: "19th August. This Sikh gave me two parking tickets. He was killed by shrapnel."

His album also shows, however, how furious he was. On one page he stuck the now-famous "apology telegram" from Madame Chiang: "None deplore more than we terribly tragic accidental dropping of bombs." Beneath this Otto placed a photograph of piles of corpses and wrote: "A Chinese 500-pound bomb fell on this crossroads. 'By accident', according to Madame Chiang Kai-shek. I took this photo on 22nd August, two minutes before I was injured by shrapnel that had ricocheted off a wall. AP [Associated Press] paid 15 dollars for it."

Other pictures had shorter captions. One shows shopfronts that must once have been elegant. Bodies lie on the street in front of them. Otto comments on the image with a single sentence: "Ah-Ling was killed here." But he doesn't explain who Ah-Ling was. Did she work in one of the shops, was she a member of the Chinese family that often invited Otto to dinner, or was she a girlfriend? Another of his photographs shows several dead whose bodies had been piled on top of each other. Below Otto has simply written: "Mass slaughter in Avenue Edward VII."[48]

Otto knew, of course, that he could not impart the details of this slaughter to Alice, so he played down the situation in his letters to her:

In the days leading up to the intervention of English and American troops it was the task of the SVC to protect the Settlement from incursion by the Japanese or Chinese [. . .] I first drove a private car for some bigwig and then did all manner of things [. . .] from working in the field mess to transporting pigs. The most dangerous job was evacuating 5,000 inmates from a prison that lay in the centre of the combat zone. There were dead and injured, and I was lucky not to get hurt.

What he described so tersely here would later bring him a medal. Not, curiously, for the evacuation of prisoners from Ward Road Jail, but for his feat of having transported pigs through the combat zone. The Chinese valued pigs as an especially important foodstuff; they seemed to have been less concerned about the survival of the prisoners. Otto did not regard his behaviour as particularly courageous. To Alice and Karl he wrote: "I've always considered myself to be quite brave. That's totally wrong, for I was pretty scared the whole time. Thank God everyone else felt the same way, because it didn't matter." The SVC volunteers were frightened by the aerial bombs in particular. Otto's letter went on: "Shanghai is the first city in the world to endure modern air attacks. You can imagine what European capitals would look like if enemy aircraft dropped a few well-aimed TNT bombs."[49]

Clearly Otto had forgotten what had happened in Guernica a few months earlier; the civil war raging in Spain was far removed from his own life. Stuck in Shanghai, he believed that this level of destruction was unprecedented, and that he was experiencing the warfare of the future. To show the devastation these bombs could cause he wanted to ensure his photographs were published, and indeed they would later be printed in several newspapers. But none of his pictures triggered such an emotional response as the one taken by the Chinese cameraman Wong Hai-Sheng. It changed the attitude of the Western world towards China overnight, and even today still evokes horror. The photograph shows a Chinese baby sitting upright on the platform of South station in Shanghai. His body is covered in burns and his mouth is wide open, emitting an

Edvard Munch-like scream. This image of the solitary, badly injured child in the middle of the bombed-out station had such force that it unleashed a wave of sympathy in the USA for China and was chosen as 1937 Photograph of the Year. The Japanese, by contrast, felt vilified as "baby killers" and doubted the authenticity of the photo. They accused Wong of intentionally dramatising the image, claiming that he himself had put the child in the middle of the chaos and touched up the smoke. The anger at the photographer was so great that later the Japanese even put a bounty on his head. Wong had taken several photographs of the incident, however, and even filmed part of it. His pictures show that the father was looking after several children and in the end took the wounded baby to safety. Later it is seen lying on a stretcher. Irrespective of whether the smoke was artificial or not, there can be no doubt that this child was seriously injured.

For Otto too it was absolutely clear that a terrible crime had been committed that day. He was on SVC duty at the station and his report of the incident was published under the headline "South Station Bombing at Shanghai Described". Now he let go; even today his report – not unlike the photograph – comes across like a cry of rage:

> The bombing of the South station in Shanghai tops all atrocities ever committed in modern warfare. On the 28th of August, the Shanghai municipal administration notified the Japanese high command [. . .] that from then every day at three o'clock trains of refugees would be dispatched into the outlying smaller cities [. . .] where comparative safety was to be had [. . .] There would not

be any movement of Chinese troops on the railroad lines used for the purposes of evacuation at the specified hour. The Japanese consul [. . .] promised to refrain from any shelling and bombing of the vicinity of the South station. The Chinese also agreed to refrain from any military movements during the time of the daily three o'clock evacuations. Six thousand women and children assembled at South station ready to embark on trains going into the interior when a squadron of twelve bombers and pursuit ships roared over the station [. . .] A shocked city of Shanghai watched one plane after another drop missile after missile [. . .] The pursuit planes power-dived low and riddled the milling persons who were still alive with machine-gun fire.

Chinese anti-aircraft batteries in the vicinity were not prepared [. . .] as they had agreed to evacuate in order to permit the undisturbed departure of the trains. I don't want to over-sentimentalize. But there is only one term for such an outrageous atrocity – murder.[50]

By now everyone was worried about Otto. Although we no longer have Alice's letters, Karl's and Cordelia's remain. Cordelia was travelling through France at the time and had been regularly receiving correspondence from Otto. When the letters stopped abruptly, she wrote to Karl, whom she had met on her Europe trip: "We were terrified as we scoured the papers for news from Shanghai. I hope Otto gets out of this chaos and doesn't get it into his head that he has to win the war for China."[51]

Otto had given up on this ambition. All he wanted now was

to escape the madness. An American newspaper later published an article on how he succeeded: "The *President McKinley* lay off the Whangpoo, eight miles at sea, and the only way [Otto Urbach] could embark was by riding on a Japanese tender [. . .] Japanese officials forced him to leave most of his goods, and in particular a Leica camera [. . .] Before surrendering the camera, however, he rescued his films which graphically depicted the war horrors of Shanghai."[52]

As soon as he was on board ship he wrote long letters to Alice: "Right now I'm trying to forget it all as quickly as I can. I'm really recovering [. . .] and eating so much that the steward says the ship isn't earning a penny from me."[53]

He did not mention that during the combat in Shanghai he had lost a lot of weight. Cordelia, who was still in Europe, wrote to Karl:

I received a letter from my mother and she said that Otto had arrived [in Portland] and had already had dinner with my family. It seems he is safely out of that Chinese mess and very happy to be back in the USA. Mother says he is very thin because he had to work very hard getting the women and children out of the city. My father thinks there may be an opportunity for him in the new big hotel that has just been built on Mount Hood. I hope that he does get a job there because he certainly deserves some peace after what he has been through.[54]

Cordelia's next letter shows that Otto had been in a much worse state of health than originally thought: "My mother wrote me that Otto had had an attack of appendicitis and had to be taken to hospital. The poor kid certainly does have the worst luck, but if he stays in Portland and works it won't be so bad. Also it is a good thing he had the attack in Portland and not in China in the midst of that horrible mess."[55]

Otto spent his twenty-fourth birthday in Portland Hospital, where he fretted over how he was going to find the 100 dollars to pay for his appendectomy. What unsettled him even more, however, was the worry about his Shanghai friends, especially the Pollitzers and their children. After the bombing of the station Otto was convinced that the Japanese would commit further crimes against the population. For this reason, he gave a number of interviews in which he painted the situation in the bleakest terms possible. One newspaper took the story of his escape as a starting point and entitled its article: "Twice Refugee, Austrian Ski Expert Returns to US".[56]

In all the articles Otto was at pains to warn about Japan. Under the headline "Japan Fooling World" he explained that Shanghai was just a sideshow, and that the Japanese military would overrun the whole of north-east China within the next three months.[57] Although he overestimated the advance of the Japanese army, he was right about their brutal methods. A few months after the interview, in December 1937, the Japanese captured Nanking. According to estimates they killed more than 200,000 civilians and carried out mass rapes over a period of six weeks.[58]

Otto had escaped the war at the right time. But he could not afford to study any longer; he had to earn money as quickly as possible. Although he got a job as a designer for the ski manufacturer C. A. Lund in Minnesota and could finally send money to Alice, China continued to trouble him for a long while. He wanted to document what had happened – for Austrian readers too. In a letter to Karl he wrote: "Enclosed you will find a manuscript I wrote in a hurry. I don't know if it's good enough to be published. Maybe you can get in touch with Victor Pollitzer as he has good contacts in journalism. If you can make it happen keep the money."[59]

Shortly before Christmas 1937 Otto received some post from Shanghai. It had been redirected, first via the Ford Motor Company in Michigan, and then for some reason forwarded to Hong Kong, finally ending up at Otto's workplace in Minnesota. In the package was a Shanghai Volunteer Corps medal for unusual bravery.[60]

There is a photograph of Otto holding up the medal. Shortly afterwards he lost it in one of his many moves. He no longer needed it as a souvenir because he had finally found a way to digest what he'd been through. He started learning Japanese in accordance with Sun Tzu's saying: "If you know the enemy and yourself, you need not fear the result of a hundred battles."

6: THE YOUNG LADY'S VISIT

*"The conundrum facing the Viennese:
you can't cope with living in Vienna anymore,
but nor can you cope with anywhere else."*
Helmut Qualtinger

Alice returned to Vienna in March 1937. In her memoir she does not say exactly what happened in England; she did not want to be pitied. But there was no sugar-coating her situation. She no longer had an apartment or cookery school in the city and had to start again from scratch. Karl was now living with his German student friend Willy Schultes in a small apartment on Wiedner Gürtel, and Alice didn't want to be a burden on him or her sisters.[1] First she moved in with her best friend Paula Sieber. The two women had known each other since the 1920s and were almost the same age. Paula's marriage had been as disastrous as Alice's. Right after the birth of their son, her husband had cheated on her. But she reacted far more decisively than Alice. Paula got a divorce and brought up her child on her own. A big cinema fan, she had the idea of turning her passion into a career. Together with her sister Selma, she opened the Palastkino (Palace Cinema) in Josef-städterstrasse in 1914.[2] The name hinted at splendour, and the interior, with its luxurious red-velvet seats and golden flourishes, was indeed reminiscent of a plush opera auditorium. As in the opera house, the Palastkino had an atmospheric live orchestral accompaniment to the silent films.[3] Paula loved dramatic films, just as at times her private life took dramatic turns. At the beginning of the 1920s she married her second husband, the lawyer Dr Hermann Sieber, with whom she had another son, Peter.[4] But this marriage too was short-lived, as Sieber died in a car crash in 1926. Like Alice, Paula had to bring up two sons alone.

The two women had much in common, therefore: they had to feed their children and survive as businesswomen in economically testing times. Like Alice with her delivery service, Paula also had a keen instinct for new trends. She tried to react as flexibly as possible to her audience's wishes, and when talking films came to Viennese cinemas in 1929 she rapidly converted her establishment with the necessary technology (though the cinema musicians proved less enthusiastic and demonstrated in Vienna against their dismissal).

Paula and Alice endeavoured to help each other, especially when one of them was in particular financial straits. In 1937 Paula was clearly the more successful businesswoman, and so Alice moved in with her and her sixteen-year-old son Peter. The Siebers lived at 3 Schreyvogelgasse, an elegant building in the Viennese neo-Renaissance style. The apartment was also appealing to Alice because it was round the corner from her favourite café, the Landtmann.

No sooner was Alice back in Vienna than she and Karl received urgent letters from Otto in China. His student friend Cordelia Dodson was planning to come to Vienna, and he begged them to find the best but also cheapest guesthouse for her as quickly as possible. Otto was desperate for Cordelia's first visit to Vienna to be a success, and so he persuaded Karl to assume the role of tour guide. "Please don't forget to be very polite. Her family was incredibly nice to me and invited me over often."[5]

Karl felt insulted by his elder brother's exhortations. Otto seemed to have no idea how much he had grown up; he was now a nineteen-year-old medical student, and he no longer blushed whenever he found a girl interesting. Admittedly, he was no connoisseur of Viennese nightlife and he still didn't dare to dance, but this would soon change, with the help of his friend Willy. They had got to know each other in the last year of school. Physically Willy was the opposite of Karl, a hulk of a man and a heart-throb. He himself was not Jewish, but he hated the Nazis. Karl knew that together they would make Cordelia's stay a triumph.

For Karl and Cordelia, the eleven months from April 1937 to March 1938 would prove decisive. Karl kept a diary of this time (in student English, to practise) and Cordelia's letters from the period have survived too. The occasional comment suggests that the world around them was becoming more menacing, but at their first encounter nothing of this was evident. Cordelia wrote to Karl:

> You probably won't have much trouble recognizing me, American tourist will probably be written all over me. Anyway, I am dark haired and eyed, rather tall, I will wear a rust-colored suit with tan fur collar [...] I will be travelling third class, having spent too much money in Italy.[6]

The description was spot-on, but as Karl waited on the platform for the Venice train that April evening he was seized by a troubling thought:

> Ten more minutes. Suddenly a horrible thought comes in my mind. What shall I do if that girl is bad looking? [...] It would be terrible to lead one of those horrible skinny-looking girls all around Vienna for fourteen days. But no, that is impossible. After all, my brother always had good taste when it comes to girls. I have hardly finished worrying when the heavy train rolls in hissing and puffing. The second car bears the unmistakable sign: Venice–Trieste–Klagenfurt–Semmering–Vienna. People emerge with happy faces [...] I run along the long row of cars [...] Suddenly I hear my name. I look up to the car window [...] Oh, boy, she is certainly above all expectations [...] She really is stunning. Dark full hair, dark, vivid eyes, very characteristic and interesting features, and beautiful and slender hands. Even the red fingernails fit her well as much as I dislike painted fingernails.[7]

Seeing the amount of luggage Cordelia had brought with her, Karl fetched one of the station porters, an institution in Vienna.

In his alternative 1927 tourist guide, Hirschfeld explained that as soon as you get off the train, you should look for men in blue-and-white coats, then shout "Porter!" as loudly and energetically as possible. The next challenge, he went on, is to understand their dialect. Then you have to go to the motor taxis, more stylish than the old horse-drawn fiacres, according to Hirschfeld: "[The fiacres are] in the process of becoming extinct and make surprising demands if you disturb them as they die out."

Karl could not afford a fiacre or a motor taxi and so plumped for the tram. Cordelia was enthused by everything. In 2003 she would write, "During that short visit I was enamoured, loved Vienna and loved the two young students, Karl and Willy, who introduced me to [the real Vienna]."[8]

Karl and Willy were eager to invite their guest to dinner in their apartment already on the second evening, but as they weren't sure how an American woman would react to such a swift invitation (Willy had suffered bad experiences in this area), and as they were ashamed of their run-down accommodation, they discussed it at length. In the end they took the plunge and tidied up. When Cordelia came for dinner, Karl cooked his special dish – Wiener Schnitzel – and Willy decorated the table with Austrian and American flags. Cordelia arrived with her American records. "They sound fantastic," Karl wrote. "It feels as if Fred Astaire and the Broadway Melody of 1936 have moved in with us. Now we're 42nd and Broadway Street!"

But Karl had one exam still to take before the end of the semester, and he was dreading it. In the Austrian corporate state[9] universities were expected not only to undertake research and teaching, but also contribute to the students' civic education. Every student had to attend compulsory ideological lectures and sit an exam on the "theoretical and historical foundations of the Austrian state". Karl had not even glanced at the 120 pages of educational material, and he only had twenty-four hours until his oral examination. He had the idea that Alice could keep Cordelia company during this time. But he was worried that the two would not get on, as they came from completely different worlds: Cordelia was a young American girl, whereas his mother had "all the charms and faults of the Viennese post-war generation."[10] On the positive side, both were broad-minded and were used to people from other countries.

It was worth a try. He had the two ladies meet in Café Sacher, and Alice began by telling Cordelia precisely what she thought of Americans (not a lot). Sixty-six years later Cordelia wrote about this meeting:

> During that first, short visit to Vienna, I met Alice Urbach, learned of her cooking fame. She also indicated fairly clearly that Americans were not her favourite nationality. I think she had an unhappy experience with [. . .] Ed Cerf, who was the exchange student for Otto in Reed. I gathered that Ed was a spoiled and mischievous teenager.[11]

Cordelia was amused by Alice's directness. Over the next few years, she would succeed spectacularly in giving her a better image of Americans.

As a Jewish mother Alice expected that Karl would return from his exam in triumph. "You've never failed an exam yet,

Karl!" she said as he was leaving Café Sacher. In Cordelia's presence he found these words terribly embarrassing, but Alice would be proved right. Karl passed the exam because he'd learned by heart the necessary patriotic phrases about Austria's glorious history. From now on he could devote all his time to Cordelia. During the day he showed her the sights of Vienna, and in the evening they toured the bars with Willy. Their first stop was the new Vienna skyscraper in Herrengasse with its elegant dance hall in a glass tower.[12] Karl would never have gone there on his own, but together with Cordelia and Willy it seemed perfectly natural. He tried a cocktail for the first time and was surprised by how expensive such a small drink could be. But the investment was worth it:

Cordelia awaits us in a very nice black dress [. . .] She certainly is an elegant person. Otto has no bad taste at all. Well, I am glad of her being here and his being in Shanghai [. . .] One man at the next table starts to talk to me in English. I must smile. He asks if we are English. "No, I reply," hesitating a little. "We are American." That is rather bad I think but then it is so much simpler than going into a long explanation. And it really is a swell sensation to take a little glory of being American onto oneself. One can see how the faces of my neighbors become pleasant with admiration. But that doesn't last long. One of them has been in New York once. His English is worse than mine but he starts to ask a few questions which I can escape only by telling him that I have never been in New York.[13]

At the time Karl was unsure why he'd been feeling so happy since Cordelia's arrival. As she was four years older, he concluded that there was no way he could be in love with her; you didn't fall in love with older women. All the same, everything about Cordelia seemed exciting and he proudly introduced her to his friends. He described one of these encounters in great detail:

The evening before some friends of mine had invited Cordelia and me for dinner. Cordelia discusses the people she had met there.

"What were these two German refugees we met there, Karl?"

"What do you mean?"

"Oh, I wondered if they were Jewish."

"Yes, I believe so. Why?"

"No particular reason. I just wondered."

I wonder suddenly if Cordelia knows that I am Jewish.

"Do you know that I'm Jewish too?"

It is painful but I look at Cordelia straight in the eyes.

"No, Karl, I didn't know it."

"Does it make any difference to you?"

"But Karl, you should know me better by now. You are almost insulting."

"Thanks."

She answers only with a sympathetic understanding look.

"Do you think the Nazis will come to Austria?"

"Maybe."

"Well, what are your plans in that case?"

"Oh, it is not that serious. I hope that I'll finish my studies before they come and then I want to go away anyway."

"Where do you want to go?"

"I would like to go where my brother is, of course."

"China?"

"Oh, no. I hope he will be back in the United States by that time."

"I wonder if you would be very happy in America, Karl."

"Why?"

"Oh, I don't know. It's a different life there. First, realistic, not very romantic."

"That's just what I want. I would be very happy, I think. But then, that's all dreaming. I don't know where I'll end up."[14]

What is surprising about this exchange is that Otto had evidently kept an important detail about his family from his American friend. Although he'd spent months discussing Fascism with the other students at Reed and had written essays about the Fatherland Front, he'd never revealed how, as a Jew, he was directly affected by all of this. Apart from the university president Keezer and the – Jewish – governor of Oregon, nobody appeared to know. Karl was much more open about his background, however, and even went with Cordelia to the city where the Mayers hailed from. One beautiful spring day they took the boat from Vienna down the Danube towards Bratislava. When they crossed the Czechoslovak border Karl was momentarily surprised to see the houses by the river flying the red flag of the Social Democratic Party. He hadn't seen these for several years in Vienna, and for Karl it felt "wonderful" to be in a country where political parties existed, and proper May Day celebrations.[15]

The May Day celebrations had been abolished by the Austrian corporate state in 1933, and replaced by marches displaying loyalty to the government. This was another reason why Karl dreamed of being able to live somewhere else one day. That weekend with Cordelia in Bratislava was like being in a different world. Karl knew Czechoslovakia well; he had often spent the summer holidays with elder cousin Poldi (Leopold) and his children in Janovice (German: Janowitz).[16] During the First World War Poldi had been taken prisoner by the Russians, and ever since had been plagued by the worry that his entire family might go hungry. He often sent money to Karl in Vienna and urged him to learn Czech. Poldi was a Czech patriot who refused to speak German and, keen not to disappoint his cousin, Karl did in fact try to improve his knowledge of the language. His Czech was good enough for Bratislava, at any rate. Cordelia was extremely impressed and Karl dreamed of accompanying her on the rest of her European trip, translating everything she wanted to know. He didn't say a word of this to her, of course, and as his Easter vacation was now over they returned to Vienna.

On the day of her departure, he gave her his parting gift: a cigarette case with sixteen Chesterfields and four Camels. It had taken him some time to get hold of these as American cigarettes were scarce in Vienna. Cordelia had an appropriate gift for Karl too: one of her American records. She promised to come back, but Karl wrote gloomily: "Someday I want to leave on this train for America myself. It's hard to see people off all the time and always stay behind."[17]

While Karl was trying to convince himself that he hadn't fallen in love, once again Alice was having to grapple with far more prosaic problems. She could not stay with Paula Sieber for ever, and in April 1937 she found a solution. A Jewish doctor running a sanatorium in Hietzing was looking for a dietary cook for his patients. Alice moved into the nice building at 111 Speisinger Strasse, where she was able to live and work for almost a year until the owner fled in 1938.[18] Although it was only a part-time job, she enjoyed it. She could build on her theories about healthy eating, and she planned to reopen the cookery school and delivery service. In the *Neue Freie Presse* she announced for autumn 1937: "Frau Alice Urbach's modern cookery courses will now take place at 57 Untere Viaduktstrasse, 3rd district. Course begins 1st October, menus for home, the very best cuisine."[19]

Alice knew she would urgently need this extra income to be able to support herself and Karl. Although she never went on holiday herself, in summer 1937 her savings were not even enough to finance a trip for Karl. She suspected that her "not-in-love" son was very keen on joining Cordelia in France. But Alice also hoped that his life would improve as soon as he'd finished his studies. To speed up the process Karl decided in summer 1937 to get the obligatory university camp over and done with. Under the Austrofascist regime, every male student had to stay at one of these camps for "physical and mental military training". The idea behind it was to offer an ideological alternative to National Socialism and educate the students as "new Austrians".[20] Karl thought he was Austrian enough already, but he wanted to tick off the camp as soon as he could:

All my friends tell me I am stupid to take it the summer before the anatomy exam. I think it is quite a lucky idea to get away from the books and still do something required by law [. . .] When we arrive at our destination I am pleasantly surprised. Our camp is situated in an old monastery [. . .] directly on a rather large lake[21] [. . .] In the afternoon a colonel and a lieutenant of the regular army who are in charge of the camp make a few speeches about discipline [. . .] The training itself is not very strenuous though it is rather boring [. . .] Gas drills are rather uncomfortable as every move brings forth streams of perspiration and one thinks of being choked till one gets used to it a little better. One morning I sit for the first time behind a heavy machine gun. I am terrified and there is so much noise before I pull the trigger that I forget all about aiming. We never think that any of us will actually need this someday. It seems all play and sport.[22]

Karl made the best of his time at the camp. He loved the lake and the mountains, and he went swimming and rowing with his campmates. One of them had brought an accordion and they would sing together in the evenings when not on night watch. It was an idyllic summer, until one night the camp leader came into the dormitory and barked:

"Everybody on the court in ten minutes in full uniform!"[23] We can't understand it at all. I leave my pajamas on underneath the uniform in the hope to be in bed again soon [. . .] Suddenly the lieutenant appears and addresses us in a very tense voice. "I had to dismiss one of your comrades a few minutes ago. It was reported today that he greeted a German motorcyclist with the Hitler salute. I warned you in my first address that I shall allow no politics here. I will have to report the case to the authorities. You may go back to your beds. Good night." This incident feels like a bomb. We all knew that there are some Nazis among us. But we [. . .] didn't spend a lot of thought on it. But this brings the matter into the foreground again. I don't feel so happy anymore.[24]

The only person who could cheer him up was Cordelia:

One day during the last week of my stay I receive a letter. It is blue and so I know it is from Cordelia. It is dinnertime and all the boys at the big table make some funny remarks about the letter. I feel annoyed, blush a little, and stick it in my pocket without opening it. Of course, I wait until dinner is over and soon I sneak away and sit down in a hidden corner among some trees to be alone with the letter. It is from Paris. Cordelia writes about the exposition, the expensive stores, the cafes, and some American girls she has met. I realize very suddenly that I haven't seen any well-dressed women for quite a long time and am amazed by how completely one can change in a few weeks. The letter gives me the same feeling as a message from civilization to a member of a North Pole expedition.[25]

Cordelia was especially interested in the World Exposition. Some pavilions were not yet finished, but the Soviet Union's and Germany's were already up:

> The German and Russian ones are enormous and a funny thing they are opposite each other. Not so funny but rather dangerous looking. There are two huge statues on the top of the Russian building, a man and a woman marching and waving a hammer and sickle [. . .] These two figures are facing the huge eagle of the Third Reich which is on the top of the German pavilion.[26]

The creators of both pavilions were later awarded gold medals: Boris Iofan for the Soviet one, and Albert Speer for his martial design of the German pavilion. Karl was not convinced that he necessarily wanted to see these buildings, but as a reply to Cordelia's letter he sent a photo of himself with a gas mask, which she remarked on: "You certainly are beautiful in a gas mask."[27]

Karl's studies resumed in autumn 1937, and occasionally he helped Alice with her delivery service. Life was monotonous. And then finally an interesting letter arrived from Portland. Otto wrote:

> I don't know if you are already aware that all the Dodson children will be in Vienna this winter. Cordelia's sister

wants to go to Vienna to study music. Cordelia and her brother Daniel will also do some study in Vienna in the winter. I know you'll be pleased because, like me, you're really keen on Americans. Please ask Mother how expensive top-rate singing lessons are, and what the fees are at the Konzerthaus academy. Send this information directly to Mr W.B. Dodson, Portland Chamber of Commerce, Portland, Oregon AIRMAIL. I'm enclosing two dollars to cover the cost [. . .] I'd be really grateful if you could do something for the Dodsons in Vienna. I'm thinking more about the social side. I haven't had a letter from Mother in a while, even though I've sent two or three, plus a telegram. What's going on? I'm sure Mother could at least write me a few lines, even if she does have a lot to do. The aunts have been silent too and I feel as if I'm being boycotted. It makes me livid and takes away my desire to write if I never get a reply back.[28]

Otto could not have imagined the effect this news had on Karl. Cordelia was coming with her siblings and would be spending an entire winter in Vienna. The year 1938 was going to be a fantastic one.

Sixty-six years later Cordelia wrote of this time: "That winter of 1937–38 was the end, I know, of our romantic student dream of a life." What happened soon afterwards opened her eyes "to the reality of the world, not beautiful but there it was."[29]

7: THE HUNT

"We wrote books
We made people better
We stayed true to the flag
And still we were driven out,
Robbed, tortured and ridiculed."
Ernst Lothar, December 1938

New York, 1962. The form for the Austrian assistance fund lay on the dining table in Alice's small New York apartment. It had been there for a number of days – untouched and looking reproachful. The longer Alice neglected it, the greater the reproach. She had read it through, of course, several times. She was unable to answer two simple questions and she could not understand how she had forgotten these important details? It was not like her, she had always had a phenomenal memory. She could recite pages of verse and recall every telephone number, but now a crucial piece of her memory was missing. More precisely, an entire six months. Whenever she thought of the period between March and October 1938, her brain

124

immediately became foggy. The spring and summer of 1938 seemed to have been deleted. Alice guessed, of course, why the memories had gone, but she was not able to admit it.

She put a sheet of paper in the typewriter and read the questions once again:

Question 7: Full address on 13/3/1938.

Where was she living shortly after the German invasion? At 111 Speisinger Strasse or back with Paula Sieber? Alice simply typed the address of Paula's apartment: 3 Schreyvogelgasse, 1st district. She put a question mark after it.

Then to question 8, which was more difficult to answer: Last address in Austria before emigration or deportation.

Once more nothing but fog. She had spent some time at a guesthouse, but had she gone to ground again at Paula's in October 1938? She could not remember. So first she typed, "the same", then crossed it out and wrote by hand the address of her sister Helene: "last days: 10 Ebendorferstrasse, 1st district", with another question mark afterwards.[1]

She found it hard to write Helene's last address. Helene had been the cleverest of the siblings, a lawyer who believed in justice and the law, and who refused to understand what it meant to live in a country where the rule of law was absent.

Alice could not have known that her torment with the questionnaire was completely unnecessary. Each move had been registered by the city of Vienna and even today, for a small fee, you can view Alice's addresses at the registry office. She had in fact spent her last five days before her flight at Helene's. "24–28 October 1938: 10/12 Ebendorferstrasse, 1st district. Changed address: England"[2], the document says curtly.

The failure of Alice's memory at this point was an amnesia that kept her alive. What happened back then has been recounted so often, but Alice was never able to formulate it in words herself. It did not fit with her refusal to be a victim. Her unofficial memoir simply states: "I should write more about the months in Vienna, during the Hitler time. I cannot – it is a horrifying remembrance. To go in the street never knowing whether you might be arrested for no reason at all [. . .] And I went early, those who stayed behind, had much more to suffer, were deported, tortured and killed."[3]

In March 1938 Austria was "attached" to the German Reich, but the end of Austrian sovereignty had begun a few weeks earlier. On 12 February 1938 Chancellor Kurt Schuschnigg signed the Berchtesgaden Agreement and took the National Socialist Arthur Seyss-Inquart into his cabinet as minister of the interior. It was the start of a gradual bankruptcy. Otto watched the events unfold from America and wrote to Karl on 10 February:

> I'm very concerned by the recent political developments in Austria. I hope that the American newspapers are exaggerating and that it's not as they describe. In any case you must brace yourself for the possibility that you might have to finish your studies elsewhere. You can count on my helping you as much as I can. Prague or Switzerland would be obvious options. Financially I wouldn't be able to cover all your outgoings, but I'll do whatever I can if necessary.[4]

Otto believed that it was just a matter of time before a Nazi-friendly regime came to power in Austria, and he knew what that would mean for his family. But he also anticipated how difficult it would be to bring Alice and Karl to America.

While Otto was making plans, Karl appeared not to have understood the gravity of the situation. In December 1937 he and Willy had organised a large welcome party for the Dodsons and he had been in high spirits ever since. Elizabeth (Lisbeth) Dodson was even more beautiful than her sister Cordelia and only one year older than Karl, an age difference that seemed perfectly acceptable, and so he resolved that Cordelia would be his soulmate and Lisbeth his new crush. Twenty-year-old Daniel Dodson brought some variety to Karl's life too. He was also good looking and took intensive "German instruction" with a number of Viennese girls even though his American girlfriend, Lucia, had followed him to Austria.[5]

The gaiety in Vienna began to trouble Otto. To Karl he wrote, "Please don't start frittering the time away and don't fall in love with one of the American girls either unless you can marry them. Otherwise there will be headaches when they leave . . ."[6] Otto had lived long enough in the US to know what American girls expected from a relationship, and apart from anything Karl should sit his exam as soon as possible, rather than wasting his time on private matters. By February 1938 the political situation was far too grave for flirtations.

On 24 February 1938 Chancellor Kurt Schuschnigg gave a speech that combined courage, despair and false hope. He

Cordelia and Lisbeth, *c.*1939

concluded with the words: "Thus far and no further! . . . Unto death! Red-white-red! Austria!"[7]

As Cordelia noted later, these words became a slogan over the coming days. With Karl and other like-minded people the Dodsons walked through Vienna chanting, "Unto death! Red-white-red!"[8] Alice would not have been with them, but for the first time she too was on the side of the Austrian chancellor. She had to hope that he would offer a show of strength against Hitler.

On 9 March Schuschnigg unexpectedly announced a plebiscite on Austria's sovereignty, to be held on 13 March. Hitler and Hermann Göring managed to get the plebiscite cancelled on 10 March, however, and simultaneously accelerated their plans for annexation. The people of Vienna realised that the situation had escalated to a dangerous level. Nonetheless the Dodsons went to the State Opera on Friday 11 March to see Tchaikovsky's *Eugene Onegin*, as planned. Karl and Willy stayed at home listening to the radio, and at 7.47 p.m. heard Schuschnigg's resignation speech, which was a mere three minutes long. When death was outside the door the Austrian chancellor had decided to let him in. He would give way to Nazi force and transfer power to Seyss-Inquart. His speech ended with the words, "And so, at this hour, I say farewell to the Austrian people with a heartfelt wish: God protect Austria!"[9]

Karl was twenty, but that night he felt like a hundred-year-old. In the streets Austrian Nazis were already chanting, "One people, one Reich, one Führer! Sieg Heil, Sieg Heil, Sieg Heil." Their wishes were fulfilled the following day. On 12 March 1938 the German army marched into Austria and Heinrich Himmler flew to Vienna to begin his "cleansing" of political opponents and Jews. During this time Cordelia tried to capture the mood in Vienna through photographs. A few weeks later she wrote to Karl, "I finally remember that on the night of the coup the Englishman (Rofe) went around with my camera taking snaps everywhere. The stupid chap said that he was an expert and then he just took my camera away. I'm really angry when I think about it now . . ."[10]

None of these photographs have survived, but enough images and film clips exist that show what happened over the following days. On Monday 14 March Hitler entered Vienna to the sound of the church bells ringing. A euphoric Viennese woman described the day with these words:

> You really cannot imagine the jubilation unless you saw it with your own eyes! Whenever the convoy of motor-cycles, tanks and motorcars came to a standstill, girls would rush at the soldiers to the resounding cheers of thousands and smother them with kisses!! Because we couldn't find any space this time, not even on the roof of a motorcar, we dashed to Mariahilfer Strasse where the endless procession was making its way in [. . .] We immediately found a space on the street in the front row. The passage between the lines of people was so narrow that it took much skill for the military vehicles to get through. There we were, all six of us, shouting our heads off, waving our flags, shaking the soldiers' hands and asking them questions.[11]

In their letters Alice and Karl do not mention the term anti-Semitism until March 1938. This doesn't mean, of course, that they did not experience it, but it was something they had got used to, a whistling in the background like tinnitus. Sometimes the noise was more painful, sometimes less so. The ideas of Vienna's leading anti-Semite, Karl Lueger, lived on. Alice's father Sigmund had been spared the sight of Lueger's supporters becoming Hitlerites in the 1920s. Mayer had always regarded his former party colleague as an opportunist rather than a true anti-Semite. But he could not have said this about the National Socialists. They hated the Jews out of sheer principle – those who had come to the capital from the east because they were poor, and the established Jews in Vienna because they were rich. It was a diffuse mixture of disgust and social envy. All Jews, rich and poor, seemed to have become more visible through the misery of the post-war years. The surnames of Viennese lawyers and doctors now sounded suspiciously Jewish, while every hawker with sidelocks appeared to be doing murky business. It was quite a while since Alice had been one of the rich Jews, but neither did she belong to the poor ones from the east. She was somewhere in the middle. Had she been asked who or what she was, after some astonishment she would have probably replied: I am Viennese. Her father had exhorted her to keep her faith, and beyond that to assimilate. Alice's sons were circumcised and they occasionally went to synagogue on religious holidays, but that was all. Alice had no time for a deeper analysis of her Jewish identity; she had to work.

Of course she knew only too well what was going on around her. As a cinema fan she had watched the 1924 silent film *Die*

Stadt ohne Juden (The City without Jews), in which Hans Moser plays a crazed anti-Semite.[12] The film is based on the novel of the same name by the Jewish journalist Hugo Bettauer, and deals with the same issues as the life's work of Alice's father – the question of whether the Jews belong in Vienna. A chancellor by the name of Schwertfeger hounds all the Jews from the city, and soon afterwards cultural and commercial life collapses. The coffee houses decline into beer halls, the theatres show nothing but farces, everyone wears loden coats and nobody gives good tips anymore. The film ends on an optimistic note, however. The anti-Semite played by Hans Moser is admitted to a sanatorium and the Jews are called back to Vienna. In reality the Jews waited in vain for such a recall, and the author Hugo Bettauer was himself granted little mercy. Only a few weeks after the film's premiere he was shot dead by a Nazi.

The events of 12 March 1938 surpassed anything the Viennese Jews had experienced before. The Austrian director Ernst Haeussermann came to the conclusion: "The difference between Germany and Austria as regards anti-Semitism was that the Germans were anti-Semites because they were Nazis, but the Austrians were Nazis because they were anti-Semites."[13]

This was surely correct, but there was another specific reason for the intensity of the orgies of hatred that erupted now. During the period when they were outlawed, the Austrian National Socialists serving prison terms were made to efface their own Nazi slogans in cleaning troops. These "humiliations" had brutalised them still further. Now they intended to get even with their old "enemies". They used all the methods that had been tried and tested in Germany and added a few sadistic details of their own. Numerous photographs show how citizens dressed in hats and coats were forced by bellowing Nazis and onlookers to kneel on the ground and clean the pavement. These so-called "scrubbing groups" became a new popular sport. Nowhere is this better explained than in the 1961 play *Der Herr Karl*.[14] Herr Karl, a fictitious average Viennese, wallows in memories of the Anschluss:

I remember all of us were standing there on the Ring, at Heldenplatz. It was like at the wine tavern, like a huge wine tavern, but there was a sense of ritual, rapture [. . .] The police stood there with their swastika armbands, looking smart [. . .] We felt a certain greatness [. . .] There was a Jew from the block of apartments, Tennenbaum. Otherwise a nice chap. They'd written things against the Nazis on the pavement [. . .] and Tennenbaum had to clean it off. Not on his own, the other Jews too [. . .] I brought him along. The caretaker laughed, he never missed out on any fun [. . .] He came back after the war, Tennenbaum. I met him in the street and said, "Good day to you, Herr Tennenbaum," and he didn't look at me. He's angry now, I think. And yet, someone had to clean it off. The caretaker wasn't a Nazi either [. . .] Everything they say about it these days is wrong. It was wonderful, lovely [. . .] I wouldn't want to give up the memories. But I didn't get anything out of it. Other people really lined their pockets. Fortunes were made back then, shops Aryanised, houses, businesses, cinemas. All I did was drag a Jew along, I was a victim. The others got rich. I was an idealist.[15]

Otto was well aware of Viennese anti-Semitism (and people like Herr Karl), but in far-off America he could only guess at what was happening in Vienna now. His letters to Alice and Karl were already out of date when he took them to the post office.

13th March 1938

Dear Karli,

I'm very concerned by the situation in Austria and I hope there's no unrest. Personally I don't care what happens in Austria, but for you it's terrible. Please do what I said in my last letter [find a university place in Prague]. If I or you had money you would be here in a matter of weeks, but we have to look at things realistically. With two or three thousand dollars you could come over, but where are you going to get that? For my part I will do whatever I can [. . .] If you were here I could possibly find a place for you in a college, but that too takes time to organise. Please be careful and send me newspapers so I can find out what's actually happening. Meanwhile, chin up![16]

Alice must have sent Otto a gloomy letter that very same day. She told him she had not only lost her job at the Hietzing sanatorium, but her little dog Fido too. Even by Otto's standards, his reply was remarkably nonchalant:

28th March 1938

Dear Mother

I didn't get your letter from 13th [March] until much later [. . .] I'm very sorry that the little dog has died. Fido was a nice dog and I'm sure it will be very hard to get used to living without him. It's very sad you've lost your job, seeing how happy you were there. But what can one do? I'm excited to hear whether Karli will go to Prague. I'm prepared to help him out financially as best I can. If you urgently need money I can send you some too. Although I'm pretty broke myself I can rustle some up [. . .] Otherwise I can only hope that nothing unpleasant happens to any of you in Vienna.

Yours affectionately, Otto[17]

Otto knew that all letters from abroad were opened, and so of course he was not going to risk writing what he really thought about the "unpleasant" things that might happen to Alice and Karl in Vienna. As neither appeared to understand how danger- ous it was to speak their mind in letters, Otto spelled it out on 10 April, writing in English in the margin: "LETTERS ARE READ! USE DISCRETION IN ANSWERING."[18]

Friedrich Torberg wrote about how emigrants began to invent a secret language. A threatening word like Gestapo became "teacher", and concentration camp was replaced by "concert hall". This gave rise to bizarre sentences such as "Poor Uncle Sigi has been at the concert hall for a fortnight" or "Yesterday the teacher ordered us to come to the Hotel Metropole". (What that meant was patently clear, as the Gestapo made Vienna's Hotel Metropole its HQ in 1938.)[19] Torberg tried to encapsulate the despair of this period in a joke, telling the story of two Viennese friends who corresponded with each other in 1938. One had already made it abroad; the other was stuck in Vienna and pretended to be an enthusiastic Nazi: "A wonderful era has dawned. In the city centre a few more Jewish shops have just been Aryanised. We took the owners to the Prater to make them do gymnastics. It was a marvellous sight and far too little for these leeches. Hopefully I'll be able to give you more good news soon. Heil Hitler! Yours, Sami Grünzweig."[20]

The reality was not much different from the satire, as the problems of communication suffered by Alice's brother Felix would show.[21]

As well as mourning the loss of her dog and her job in March 1938, Alice was most upset when Karl was thrown out of university. The hope that he might manage to finish his studies before the arrival of the National Socialists was definitively buried. Karl was so angry and despondent that he wanted to leave the city at once. Cordelia wrote sixty-six years later, "Karl again came to our rescue. He arranged for the whole show to go to Lech am Arlberg and stay with a local family, Wolf. I doubt we realized what a magnificent place Lech was and what a magnificent solution it was."[22]

But bad luck seemed to have followed them to Lech. The Dodsons and Karl were enthusiastic skiers and they ignored the villagers' warnings. Just a few days after their arrival Karl, Daniel's girlfriend Lucia and Lisbeth Dodson were caught in an avalanche. Cordelia was at the edge of the piste when it happened: "My memory is primarily the horror of seeing the three [of them] show only a ski tip and then another snow block and then an arm or ski pole."[23]

Compared to the political avalanche that had swept through the country, the mass of snow in Lech was a trifle. But Karl was well aware that he could not hide with the Dodsons in the mountains for ever. He had to return to Vienna to accelerate his and Alice's emigration. The Dodsons had seen enough of the braying Nazis in Vienna and chose instead to move on to St Georgen in the Attergau. From there Cordelia wrote to Karl in April 1938: "I am terribly sorry and upset about the difficulties you are having. Isn't there any way for you to get away? It is so peaceful and lovely here that one almost forgets things."[24]

Karl's replies have not survived because Cordelia destroyed his letters as a precaution. Like Otto she urged him to be more circumspect in his choice of words: "Karli, it might be better not to write too much against our Friend – I don't think letters are opened between here [St Georgen] and [Vienna], but for your safety be a little more cautious."[25]

"To emigrate" is a verb that implies a certain proactiveness: it is your decision to leave. In 1938, however, nobody left the country of their own free will; they *were* emigrated. The composer Georg Kreisler insisted on describing emigration as an act that had been imposed on him – in 1938 he had "been fled".[26] Nobody would do this voluntarily, but even so it has often been asked why "the Jews" did not leave earlier. In reply one could cite the playwright Johann Nestroy – "Everyone is a good prophet in retrospect" – or ask a question in return: "Where should they have gone when nobody wanted them?" Even those who did find another country faced an additional problem: who was going to finance their flight? With newly devised restrictions and taxes the emigrants were systematically plundered. There was now a "Jewish capital levy", a "Reich flight tax" and a "compulsory levy to the Jewish community".

Despite this, no stone was left unturned. The hunt for official stamps began immediately after Anschluss. Nothing was now more important than the scramble for the right stamps on the right documents. For America you needed an affidavit; that is to say, an American guarantor had to be found who would pledge to the US authorities in writing that they would support the emigrant financially. Over the coming years Otto would provide a number of affidavits for family members, but as he didn't earn much and was yet to obtain US citizenship these declarations didn't carry much weight. You needed to be able to show more than an affidavit from Otto Urbach.

Every potential emigrant now frantically tried to think of relatives or friends abroad. The briefest encounters were dug out of people's memories. Who did you know in New York or Texas? In desperation Alice's cousin Lily Bader recalled two American women she had met on holiday in Norway. Although they had only spoken on two or three occasions, she wrote them a letter anyway. To her surprise Lily actually did get an affidavit from both women and thus her departure came one step closer. People without acquaintances abroad had to be inventive. One particularly creative refugee got hold of an American telephone directory and wrote to everyone with the same surname as him. Although he was not related to any of these people, one of them ended up acting as his guarantor. But even if you had all the necessary papers, you had to reckon with the arbitrariness of the authorities. Lily Bader's thirteen-year-old daughter Dorit described the hounding of her parents:

On the day after the Nazis marched into Austria the world descended into darkness [...] The grown-ups in my life suddenly looked ashen-faced, spoke in whispers and were dealing with things we didn't understand[27] [...] On one occasion we children had to accompany our parents to an official place. I recall a dark building with crumbling plasterwork. Several floors were connected by spiral stairs. A family stood on each step. As soon as one lot of applicants left the office, the families would climb a step. Those coming down looked either delighted and relieved or down in the dumps. We spent hours going up the steps, one by one, in this dark building. Nobody spoke. An icy, unnerving silence had settled on the stairs [...] When we finally reached the [desk] I saw terror in my parents' eyes. As they were strong people who didn't usually show their worries to their children, I'd never seen them like this before. It made me scared.[28]

Alice knew how difficult it was to get a work permit for Britain. Now everything seemed to be repeating itself, but she could not afford another failure. She was once again living with Paula and Peter Sieber in Schreyvogelgasse, but the Aryanisation of Paula's apartment was hanging over them menacingly. Since it was in the elegant 1st district, it was to be expected that a "deserving" Nazi would covet the apartment (between March 1938 and May 1939 around 44,000 apartments in Vienna were

Aryanised). Alice was also worried about her sisters. Sidonie's husband, Julius Rosenberg, was seriously ill, and Jews were no longer treated by "Aryan" doctors. Although Sidonie did all she could to keep Julius alive, he died five months after the Anschluss, on 10 August 1938.[29] Sidonie and Karoline were now widows and no longer had a connection to Vienna; they wanted to leave. But as both were over seventy, it seemed almost impossible to find a country that would accept them. Of the Mayer siblings only Alice, her brother Felix and her youngest sister Helene Eissler were still able to work. All three now tried to get out of Hitler's "Ostmark".[30] Otto still thought that Czechoslovakia would be the best refuge:

24th April 1938

Dear Mother

I'm always pleased to hear from you, even if all the letters I get from you have been opened. As far as Karli is concerned there's nothing that can be done for the moment. I personally think it's best if he does his PhD in Europe as it would be almost impossible to get him into university here. He would have to spend at least two years at a college, and that's almost unaffordable. But when he's got his doctorate it will be much easier for him to come, and he would only have to take a state exam [. . .] If it's at all possible Karli should finish his studies in Prague. It's easier for me to help you out financially in Europe than here because the dollar is worth more over there.[31]

But Otto soon realised that Czechoslovakia would be Hitler's next target. After the annexation of Austria, in April 1938 the National Socialist regime began a propaganda war against the Prague government. As Goebbels noted in his diary, Hitler had already announced to his inner circle on 20 March 1938 his intention to "crush" the neighbouring country.[32] In Germany the following rhyme was doing the rounds: "In April Hitler does as he will, in May Czechia is his prey." Now Otto thought that Karl ought to come to America straightaway:

8th May [1938]

Dear Karli

I'll send you an affidavit in a month or two. It obviously depends on whether the consul in Vienna finds it convincing enough. Personally I don't think my affidavit is good enough on its own, as I don't have sufficient cash [. . .] I can find you [. . .] a job. But don't mention this when you go to the consulate, just emphasise that you want to finish your studies here [. . .] I'll get you [. . .] approval from some college [. . .] Do you think you're on good enough terms with the Dodsons to ask them for an affidavit? [. . .] A few more points to take on board. Don't mention at the consulate that you're looking for work (contract labor exclusion clause) or that someone's financing your emigration. It must look as if you have enough money yourself to pay for the crossing and keep your head above water for a while. If it works out I'll open a bank account in your name here and you'll have to lie that you've been sending money over here for a while now. *This is important* [...] In any event you must be patient and wait, because it's bad if you've been rejected. In the worst case you can try again in Prague. But there you'd have to hide the fact that you were already turned down in Vienna [...]

Yours affectionately, Otto[33]

This letter contravened Otto's own precautions. He was so exhausted that he had forgotten to censor his words.

Highly awkward though it was, Karl now had to ask the Dodsons for an affidavit. His chance came when Daniel Dodson returned from his skiing holiday and moved in with Karl and Willy. Otto, too, had made some progress:

5th June 1938,
Alpena Hotel, Michigan

Dear Karli

I've received your last letter in which you say that Daniel [Dodson] is staying with you. In the meantime I've arranged for my firm to give me an employment statement that you are to show together with the affidavits. It will be a few more days before I can send the affidavit, but I'll hurry the process as best I can. I beg you to do without maudlin sentiment [...] It's completely unnecessary to gush with gratitude in your letters. Of course you're happy to leave Austria and of course I'm doing all I can to make this happen [...] Please give everyone my warmest greetings, Otto[34]

On 16 June 1938 Otto finally found a notary to certify his affidavit. It stated that he was working as a designer and technical advisor for the C.A. Lund Company, earning 240 dollars per month and had no financial commitments apart from paying off his car. It was his wish to enable his brother Karl to come to America so he could finish his studies in medicine. Otto stated in the affidavit that he would assume full financial and moral responsibility for his brother until he had completed his doctorate.[35]

Mr and Mrs Dodson did not fail Karl either.[36] Cordelia wrote to him – in German – from St Georgen: "Is it true, Karli, that you might be able to come to America in the fall? That would be so lovely. My mother writes to say they're making every effort to get you away."[37]

But the obstacles for all refugees, Karl and Alice included, remained enormous. At the Évian Conference in July 1938 practically all participating countries refused to take in Jewish refugees from Germany and Austria. Franklin D. Roosevelt did not appear in person even though he had instigated the conference himself. The Zionist leader Chaim Weizmann came to the conclusion: ". . . the world is divided into places where [the Jews] cannot live and places where they cannot enter."[38]

The biggest winners from Évian were the National Socialists. In an internal Nazi memo, "Reports from the Reich", it stated with satisfaction:

At the Évian Conference [. . .] the whole world was shown
that the Jewish problem is not merely an issue provoked
by Germany, but that it is a problem of current global

political importance. In spite of the Évian countries' unanimous rejection of the way the Jewish question is being dealt with in Germany, no state apart from America has declared itself prepared to accept any number of Jews unconditionally. It was notable that the Australian representative even talked of the danger to the country's own race posed by Jewish immigration.[39]

Although the US delegation did not voice such anti-Semitic comments, ultimately the Americans committed themselves to nothing. On the contrary, immigration was made more difficult after the conference. With this in mind, Otto advised Alice to set her sights on a European country.[40]

Although Alice was working on her emigration to the UK, she was depressed at the prospect of being separated from Karl as well as Otto. Karl wrote to his brother:

Got your letter [of 23 July] yesterday [. . .] Obviously I'm upset about Mother. She placed all her hopes on being able to go to the USA and fairly soon. I hope it will somehow work out later. I mean, Mother doesn't have to work as a domestic employee. But you're right, I have to come over first and then we'll find a way. Mother knows this too. I hope she'll find a job in England in the meantime. If that doesn't happen, it will be a real tragedy because when you write that you can support Mother more easily in Europe than in America, that may be true, but it's also deceptive. For we cannot go to Hungary, Switzerland, Czechoslovakia, Italy, the Balkan countries, the Netherlands, Belgium or France. Nor further north to the Nordic countries. So you see there is practically no country in Europe that will let us in. We cannot stay here either, because sooner or later we'll be expelled, and second – I'm not being soppy now – it's unbearable mentally. Wait until I can tell you. Mother is also trying to arrange her emigration and hopefully she'll find something halfway suitable in England [. . .] Still no sign of Mr Dodson or the affidavit. So I braced myself and after mulling it over for quite some time I wrote to him personally yesterday. I started by thanking him most politely for everything he'd taken the trouble to do for me, and then I asked him to send the affidavit via Washington, if he hadn't already sent it, because it will be checked there and otherwise will be sent back from Vienna to Washington for checking [. . .] As you can imagine, I was as polite as possible. I now hope that I'll get an answer from Mr Dodson by the end of this month [. . .] When you come to New York, please if at all possible look up Arthur Horowitz. His address is 190 Miller Avenue, Brooklyn, NY. He's a friend and studied with me. If for some reason it doesn't work with the Dodsons, though I can't imagine that happening, I need to find someone else.[41]

Cordelia seemed to assume that the affidavit was a mere formality. On 8 August 1938 she wrote – in German – to Karl from her travels: "We're going to Salzburg this week to see a festival production – Salzburg is horrible this year. Nothing but Reich Germans, ugly people. All the atmosphere has vanished.

The expectation is that 'they' will do away with Salzburg and concentrate everything in Bayreuth."[42]

Whether the Bayreuth Festival would replace the Salzburg one appeared a trivial concern compared to the reality of Karl's situation. The Dodson affidavit still hadn't arrived and he was getting increasingly nervous by the day. Otto had to reassure him:

> Please don't be impatient, Karli. I promise I'll get you over here and you know I've done everything I can. Don't despair and look forward to your future in the US. The main thing is that you can speak good English. Promise me that even if you don't have any opportunity to speak it, you'll at least read a little English every day. That's the crucial thing.[43]

While Karl could think of nothing but affidavits, Otto tried to distract him with the dream of owning a ski hotel together: "This is my new plan . . . Alongside my job with the C.A. Lund factory I'd like to build a small ski hotel [in Laconia]. I know it sounds like a pipe dream but it would not be so difficult if you and I worked together. Laconia is in a beautiful location, by a lake, and in winter it's a skiing area a little like Semmering."[44]

As Otto and Karl envisioned their future in America, Alice's chances of emigrating were improving, at least. She made contact with her twenty-year-older cousin Rose in England, whose mother Regine had, together with her brothers Sigmund and Albert Mayer, helped the family business make its international breakthrough in the nineteenth century. Rose had been trained as a classical pianist in Vienna and would have happily stayed in Austria, but in 1901 she had moved with her husband Adolf Landstein to London. There they anglicised their surname to Landstone and set up an umbrella firm that didn't do particularly well, in spite of the British weather. Perhaps it was also down to the fact that Rose was primarily interested in music and continued to live with one ear in Vienna. She considered England to be a musical desert, where one could only survive with deliveries of Austrian records. The arrival of the Nazis cut short her escape into music. Although Rose was already seventy in 1933, she decided to survive Hitler and make this a possibility for her friends in Germany and Austria too. Thanks to Rose's tireless efforts many, if not all, did survive, including twelve of the Mayer, Landstein and Squarenina families.[45] Rose's son Charles Landstone, who later became a well-known dramatist and theatre producer, described in his memoir how his mother begged countless business friends to draft fictitious work contracts and was permanently going to the authorities to submit visa applications.[46] The British officials found it hard to fob off an elderly lady who would go as far as camping outside offices to reach her goal. Charles Landstone later gave his autobiography the apt title *I Gate-Crashed*.[47] It was a trick he had learned from his mother.

Thanks to Rose's determination, Alice had renewed hope for emigration to Britain. In September Otto wrote excitedly to Karl: "It's really encouraging that Mother has a chance to go to England, because even if she doesn't have a job there I can send money to make it bearable for her at least. The pound is very low."[48]

After the Nazi Party Rally at Nuremberg in September 1938, it became critical for Alice and Karl to redouble their efforts to leave. In his closing speech on 12 September, Hitler issued new threats to Czechoslovakia. War seemed imminent. Prime Minister Neville Chamberlain travelled to Germany for final negotiations and Karl must have feared that the borders would close at any moment. He sent a desperate telegram to Otto, who replied: "After receiving your cable I've pulled out all the stops. I hope to be able to send all the necessary papers to Vienna in a few days' time. In the meantime please don't lose heart and be patient. I'm sure we'll see each other again soon."[49]

On 30 September Chamberlain's policy of appeasement towards Hitler proved successful. The Munich Agreement prevented war for the time being, at the cost of Czechoslovak sovereignty. The Dodsons learned about this in France, on their way to the port. Because of the threat of war, their father had ordered them to return to America immediately. On board they received a telegram from Karl and Willy that read: "Hurrah for peace!"[50] At that moment Karl was not thinking of his cousin Poldi, the Czechoslovak patriot, whose world collapsed on 30 September,[51] rather he was simply relieved that war had been averted at the last minute. As ever, Cordelia's reaction to events was the most prudent. After the ship arrived in New York she wrote:

Yes, hurrah for peace, but you have to get out before another such crisis arises. Do you understand? Karli — my father has written to Washington about the affidavit. I think you'll find something out very soon. But for goodness' sake don't give up hope – your last letter scared me, darling. You wrote as though you were not expecting to see us again. Please, please, Karli, keep your chin up and your courage. We are all expecting to see you here in USA soon and also [to hear] that Willy is in England. Don't disappoint us.

Lisbeth added some words of her own, urging Karl to take one last good look around before leaving, as he would never see the same Europe again.[52]

After going from pillar to post, Alice finally managed to emigrate at the end of October. She had to leave Karl, her siblings and Paula Sieber behind in Vienna, but she was certain that Karl at least would be setting off for America soon. Otto thought so too in November 1938: "I'm delighted that Mother is in England and I'm sure it won't be long until we . . . see each other in the USA."[53]

Otto's letter didn't reach Karl; Willy received it. He was in turmoil. Karli had not been seen since 10 November.

8: BOOK THIEVES

"A bird of prey
sinks its claws deep inside me,
stealing what I hadn't yet thought of."
Karl Kraus

In 1913 Egon Erwin Kisch published the report *Magdalenenheim*, in which he described his visit to a Prague institution for "fallen girls". The woman running the place shows the famous journalist around the building, explaining to him at length how much she despises her charges. When Kisch enters one of the workrooms he is recognised by the girls and given an enthusiastic welcome: "Egon's here! [. . .] Give me a cigarette, we don't get any here [. . .] Send my regards to the boys in Bar Brasilia." At this point the visit comes to an abrupt end.

More than two decades later, now in exile, Kisch discovered that a certain Hanns ut Hamm had plagiarised his account. Hanns ut Hamm was the pseudonym of Hans Reimer Steffen, who wrote in northern German dialect and was an ardent Nazi.

He had simply transposed Kisch's reportage from Prague to Hamburg. Now the girls spoke Low German and greeted their "Hans" rather than "Egon". For this report Steffen won 1,000 Reichsmarks in a short-story competition organised by the city of Hamburg.

Maybe he ought to have made more changes, for when those who eulogised his writing found out that they had honoured a "Jewish composition", Hamm/Steffen got into trouble. It soon blew over, however, and during the war he was again permitted to publish such witty gems as *Hier lacht die Front* (Jokes from the front). For potential Nazi plagiarists, however, the affair was instructive. Narrative texts, it seemed, were not ideal. For despite all the burned books, too many people remembered the original stories. It was far better to steal non-fiction works.[1]

The Aryanisation of books is a subject that has not been investigated until now. There is not even an agreed term for the process. "Aryanised books" has hitherto been used to describe another Nazi crime – the plundering of Jewish libraries.[2] But nobody has yet systematically explored the far more serious intellectual theft of the work of Jewish authors and publishers. There are no statistics relating to the approximate number of those affected. The subject simply doesn't appear in research.

Paradoxically, the book burning of 1933 is one of the reasons for this. The campaign seemed to have solved the problem, as books by unwelcome authors were simply destroyed. The new rules of the Reich chamber of culture had been in force since November 1933, and in May 1935 they were tightened even further.[3] It was forbidden to publish "damaging and undesirable literature", i.e. books which ran "counter to the cultural and political goals of the National Socialist Reich."[4] With that the matter seemed to be settled. But these rules were kept very vague and behind the scenes a struggle raged over who would determine National Socialist book policy. At least seven institutions considered themselves responsible.[5] This chaos of jurisdiction was an opportunity for publishers as well as a problem. With good relations and the right contacts they were able to successfully manoeuvre their way through the system for a long time. In the 1970s Alice's publisher Hermann Jungck recalled that:

> until the end of the war there [was] no pre-censorship of publishing houses' output. The Nazis had intended to do this and [. . .] had set up an office to which all manuscripts were to be submitted prior to publication. What happened, however, was that this office suffocated under a mountain of submissions [. . .] The office was then disbanded and it was decreed that every publisher was personally responsible for what they published. In other words, they could (albeit under their own responsibility) continue to determine their output independently until the time during the war when they had to submit a form in writing to the propaganda ministry.[6]

This leeway puts the role of publishers in a new light. Did they submissively hurry to censor themselves after 1933 to comply with the new regime? For why should publishing houses differ from other businesses, which also came to a rapid accommodation with the new power structure? As a publisher, you didn't have to believe in Hitler to have a financial interest in being able to continue operating under the new regime.[7] Volker Dahm says of the Börsenverein (German book trade association): "[it] displayed such political zealousness that the National Socialists could expect automatic compliance."[8] Already in 1933 the association had "unnecessarily – promised unreservedly to implement the Reich government decrees relating to the 'Jewish question'".[9]

In an essay on the publishing landscape during the Third Reich, the publisher Klaus G. Saur emphasises how negatively the repressive measures of the Nazi regime affected countless German publishing houses and how powerful the Party's own house, Franz Eher Verlag, became.[10] But that was only one side of the story. Although after 1933, as Saur highlights, "around 800 publishers and booksellers" emigrated,[11] this also meant that undesirable competitors vanished from the scene. The departure of these competitors left a vacuum that the "Aryan" presses rapidly and willingly filled. From a commercial viewpoint it was an ideal situation.

A lucrative solution was also found to the problem of Jewish non-fiction books: "Non-fiction books and novels based on real events were amongst the most successful genres in the Third Reich."[12] It was therefore more profitable to find ways to continue publishing them, and one such way was to steal them. This was a logical step, for in a country where Jews had gradually lost their legal protection since 1933, their intellectual property – just like their material assets – was at the mercy of others. It meant that every "Aryan" author and publisher could now help themselves to this intellectual property without having to fear the consequences.

Which was exactly what happened to Alice's book. In 1938 it acquired a new author.

To date, few publishing houses have opened their archives. Requests for access are frequently met with the answer that the archive holdings were destroyed in the Second World War. The CEO of a children's publisher put it thus, "Most publishing houses bade farewell to National Socialism in the form of a major fire."[13] When a request was made to consult the Ernst Reinhardt Verlag archive to find out what happened in Alice's case, the assistant to the managing board sent an e-mail in 2018 regretting that "there was no longer" an archive on Alice Urbach. During the war, she continued, the publishing house had left Germany and continued its operations in Switzerland for a number of years, before later returning. But owing to the "turmoil" there were "very few documents left [. . .] much had gone missing."[14]

To put this into context, it should be pointed out that in 1974 and 1999 Ernst Reinhardt Verlag published two jubilee volumes based on archival material from before and during the war. Their response was thus less than convincing and, indeed, documents *were* found when Alice's case became public in 2020.

Not all publishers have had such difficulty uncovering the whereabouts of their archive holdings. The historian Angelika Königseder has researched the academic publishing house De Gruyter. She shows how from 1933 De Gruyter began by trying to pay off Jewish authors.[15] Such an offer was made, for example, to the linguist Hans Sperber. Like Alice, Sperber came from Vienna and they were almost the same age. As a Jew, he had his licence to teach at the University of Cologne revoked in

1933 and soon afterwards his publisher developed serious reservations about keeping him on as an author. Sperber had already published one book with De Gruyter and assumed the "overall management" of *Trübners German Dictionary*. For this monumental project he had specifically turned down a research trip to America. In the middle of the preliminary work for the dictionary in 1933, he received a letter from his editor: "Regretfully I have to request that you step back from overseeing the publication of the dictionary, at least in an official capacity."

In compensation Sperber was offered 500 Reichsmarks as well as the opportunity to continue to write articles for the dictionary – anonymously.[16] Sperber was deeply insulted, a grievance he would never recover from, not even in exile. The publishing house, on the other hand, was able to use Sperber's preliminary work for the project and adapt the rest of the dictionary to Nazi ideological lines.

Sperber's treatment was comparatively fair. Other Jewish writers were fobbed off with hopeful words for the future: "Wait until the political situation has calmed down."

Inside the publishing house, however, the tone was clear. An internal document said the following:

1. When reprinting check if author is Aryan (according to the Nuremberg Laws).
2. For books written by non-Aryan authors check whether reprint can be authored by an Aryan.
3. Publicity for books by domestic Jews to be omitted from prospectuses etc.[17]

Point 2 is of particular interest. How could "non-Aryan" books be transformed into "Aryan" ones? A method was developed for this, which Alice's publishing house employed as well.

Ernst Reinhardt Verlag is proud of its long publishing history. In 1899, the Swiss Ernst Reinhardt moved to Munich to open a bookshop. He befriended the writer Ricarda Huch and established a small publishing house. For the time the subjects of his books were remarkably progressive, including sexuality, psychiatry and healthy eating. Many of his authors were socialists or Jews, the most famous being the psychotherapist Alfred Adler, who had converted to Christianity. Another, the left-wing commentator Elga Kern, had to emigrate before her book, *Führende Frauen Europas* (*Europe's Leading Women*), was banned.[18] Although Ernst Reinhardt was a board member of the Börsenverein,[19] privately he was critical of the National Socialists. In 1937, however, the publishing house's orientation changed. Reinhardt died unexpectedly and his Swiss nephew Hermann Jungck took over.

A photographic portrait from the post-war era shows Jungck as a serious-looking man with an angular face and black horn-rimmed spectacles.[20] His ancestors were Swiss pastors, and visually at least Jungck too conforms to the stereotype of a harsh preacher – severity appears deeply etched in his face. Jungck was born in 1904 in the Alsatian town of Weissenburg. His birthplace made him learn to adapt: the town became German in 1871, French again after the First World War, German once more in the Second World War, and finally French (Wissembourg) after 1945. The Jungck family escaped from this political fluctuation, settling in Switzerland, where Hermann became a member of the Swiss Wandervogel movement.[21] Until he finished school in 1923 his education proceeded serenely, but then came a disruption. In his memoir Jungck only mentions this as an aside: "As my father (who ran a stationery shop) lost his fortune in the inflation, my uncle Ernst Reinhardt suggested I become a bookseller and his successor, as he was unmarried and had no children."[22]

His father's bankruptcy must have been humiliating for Hermann, as he was no longer able to study and had to earn money instead. But he soon realised the great opportunity his uncle's offer presented him with. Ernst Reinhardt was a generous man who invested a large amount in educating his nephew over the next few years, enabling Hermann to undertake traineeships in Paris and New York, and then have a permanent job in the publishing house. In the 1930s Jungck studied law for a few semesters, but abandoned his degree when Reinhardt died in 1937. From now on Jungck ran the company with a firm hand, though the situation he had inherited seemed less than ideal. Over the decades his uncle had successfully published works by many Jewish authors, and now they had become a burden. Jungck soon discovered that other academic publishers faced similar problems, publishing series and non-fiction titles by Jewish writers and editors. This "Jewish excess" was no doubt down to the fact that publications and educational certificates were always valued very highly in Jewish families. The playwright David Mamet describes it thus: "For 2,000 years we braced ourselves to have someone to knock at our door and say: 'Gotcha!' And so we wondered: what can't they take away from us? The answer's quite simple: education."[23]

Education seemed theft-proof. Alice's father had always reminded his children that the Mayers had escaped the ghetto through education and hard work. The book he had written on the subject reinforced his viewpoint. For the "People of the Book", to have an author in the family meant enormous social prestige, and it was firmly believed that a book would last for ever. Because Alice had failed to gain any educational qualifications, she felt particularly proud to have published two books. Even though her father was no longer alive to see these works appear in print, she felt that she hadn't completely fallen short of his high expectations. But, as many Jewish authors now discovered, even authorship could be stolen.

Right after Hitler's takeover of power, the Jewish lawyer Max Friedlaender chanced upon a new legal publication in a book-shop. It had the "gripping" title *Kommentar zur Rechtsanwaltsordnung* (*Commentary on the Code of Conduct for Lawyers*). When Friedlaender began to read the book, it seemed remarkably familiar. The introduction claimed that the Jews had dragged the status of German lawyers down to its lowest "moral level" and that the Nazis would now change this for all time. Surprisingly, however, they had stolen the work of one of these "immoral" Jews for this new book.

> After [...] half an hour I found more than twenty instances of clear plagiarism. These were not word-for-word tran-scripts of entire sentences, they were excerpts from our book, using slightly different words, but reproducing the exact lines of thought, indeed the logical reasoning and

arrangement of entire passages. Or questions that otherwise had been addressed very differently, or not at all, contained our findings without explanation, as if they were obviously the right ones. This really was a new form of combating Jewish thought and Jewish literature. They presented both as inferior, but then copied our work without giving any credit, and touted it as Aryan innovation.[24]

The plagiarist, a man by the name of Erwin Noack, worked originally as a lawyer in Halle. Since 1931 he had been an ardent National Socialist and was given a chair soon after the takeover of power. Later he rose to become the vice-president of the Reich chamber of lawyers and proclaimed the "De-Jewification of the German legal profession".[25] He himself profited greatly from this "De-Jewification". His colleague, the president of the People's Court, Roland Freisler, heaped praise on Noack's work, coming to the conclusion that the "German legal profession [had] to face up to the shameful fact that [until then] their code of conduct had been annotated by Jews." Thanks to Erwin Noack, a "German commentary" had finally appeared.[26]

Surprisingly Friedlaender did not lose his sense of humour. Looking back on it he wrote: "In university circles they soon knew what to think of the book; many people were calling it the 'little Friedlaender'."[27]

Another plagiarist was the businessman Ludwig Reiners. In 1944 he published *Deutsche Stilkunst. Ein Lehrbuch deutscher Prosa* (German style. A textbook of German prose), based in large part on the work of the Jewish author Eduard Engel.[28]

As with Friedlaender, sentences were simply rewritten and examples lifted in full. Reiner had the advantage that the plagiarised author Engel could no longer object, as he had died in 1938. The book became a commercial success that continued into post-war Germany. In 1956 *Der Spiegel* even devoted a lead article to the plagiarist Ludwig Reiners, in which his work was roundly celebrated.

One of the most spectacular cases of Aryanised specialist literature, however, relates to *Knaurs Gesundheitslexicon* (Knaur's medical encyclopaedia). This practical reference book first appeared in 1930 and became an instant bestseller. Its creator, the Jewish doctor Josef Löbel, was stripped of the editorship when the war broke out. Deleting his name required a large dose of chutzpah because Löbel was famous in his time. As a doctor, writer and journalist he was known as a master of imparting knowledge with humour. He published his brilliant, witty articles in newspapers in Berlin, Vienna and Prague, and wrote a number of best-selling books on popular medicine, which were translated into sixteen languages. Löbel was also keen to educate the public. He advocated the early recognition of cancers and encouraged people to take vitamins. Löbel was so well known that he even appears as a character in Joseph Roth's novel *Radetzky March*, as the wise philanthropist Dr Skowronnek from Franzensbad. In fact Löbel used to work there every summer as a spa doctor.

As the medical historian Peter Voswinckel discovered, a certain Peter Hiron took over *Knaurs Gesundheitslexikon* in 1940. Hiron was the pseudonym of the Nazi Dr Herbert Volkmann, who immediately set about Aryanising the encyclopaedia. He added entries such as "hereditary health", "race" and "poison gas intoxication", and deleting others like "homosexuality", "prison psychosis" (which the Nazis had now made a commonplace affliction) and, to be on the safe side, "megalomania".[29]

Hiron/Volkmann had an outstanding record in the Aryanisation of specialist literature. Just prior to appropriating Löbel's encylopaedia, he had already "replaced" another Jewish writer, Dr Walter Guttmann. This too was an astonishing achievement, for Guttmann's textbooks were standard works and, like Löbel's publications, existed in a number of languages. One of Guttmann's most important books was *Medizinische Terminologie* (Medical terminology), which he had continued to improve since its initial publication in 1902. In a foreword he describes it as his life's work. Guttmann's life's work was taken from him when it was in its twenty-ninth edition. No mention was made of the expropriation. The book sold handsomely, whereas the penniless Walter Guttmann committed suicide in 1941.[30]

This act of desperation links him to Josef Löbel. Both were robbed by the same man, and both committed suicide. Löbel took his own life in Prague, after the Nazis had deported his wife.

The practice of Aryanising books was carried out not only by large publishers, but also by smaller presses such as Ernst Reinhardt Verlag. Two of its authors were affected: Alice and a man by the name of Dr Paul Wessel.

Paul Wessel's story begins at the University of Munich, where he ran a so-called "crammer", a private refresher course for students. Wessel specialised in the natural sciences, teaching medical students what they needed to know to pass their exams in physics, chemistry, biology and zoology. For this he developed lecture notes that were divided into four parts: "outline, brief review of material, exam questions and answers".

At the beginning of the 1930s Paul Wessel decided to turn his notes into books. Hermann Jungck's uncle, the founder of the publishing house, was still alive at the time. On 4 April 1933 he signed an initial publishing contract for a "physics refresher course for students of medicine". The contract anticipated that other titles would be forthcoming, and over the next few years a series of nine volumes appeared entitled *Reinhardts naturwissenschaftliche Kompendium* (Reinhardt's scientific compendium). Paul Wessel created the outline of the series and wrote several of the books himself. For the other volumes he enlisted his crammer colleagues. His employee Dr Max Ott wrote the volume on organic and inorganic chemistry, and Dr Felix Pagast the one on zoology. Both adopted Wessel's outlines and edited their manuscripts with him.

Just like Alice, Paul Wessel was discovered by the old publisher Ernst Reinhardt. And like Urbach, the name Wessel didn't sound Jewish. After all, everyone knew of Horst Wessel, the "martyr" of the National Socialist movement. Dr Paul Wessel, however, was not in the least related to Horst Wessel and, more seriously, was a half-Jew according to the Nuremberg Race Laws.

In his jubilee history Jungck describes in detail his first meeting in 1937 with Wessel, who turned up at the publishing house in SS cavalry uniform: "As he later told me, he had borrowed it to impress me and imply his Aryan descent." Wessel told Jungck he was planning a trip to China and so wanted to appoint a good acquaintance of his, Frau Dr Viola Riederer von Paar, in his place for "all rights and obligations relating to the publishing contract". On 7 May 1937, therefore, a three-way contract was signed between Paar, Wessel and Jungck. From now on Riederer von Paar became acting editor of the series.[31] Now her name – instead of Wessel's – was on all the individual titles, and Paul Wessel was erased as the editor of his own series. Only on his physics book did his name still appear, alongside Riederer von Paar's as editor.

Jungck's story about their meeting in 1937 is reminiscent of bad burlesque. Did Paul Wessel really appear in SS uniform? And why would he make such far-reaching concessions to the publishing house because of a visit to China? Was the three-way contract really his idea?

Viola Riederer von Paar studied medicine in Munich from 1930 to 1935, and so could very well have been a student in Wessel's crammer. Nonetheless in 1937 she published a book with Reinhardt Verlag on Nazi genetics.[32] This was exactly the sort of "science" that would have seen Wessel – a half-Jew – carted off to a concentration camp. Would he, therefore, hand over his publishing rights to a woman who specialised in racial theory? Maybe Paul Wessel suffered from a serious form of Jewish self-hatred and the two were good friends, as Jungck claimed. It is more likely, however, that Jungck proposed this solution so that the entire series would acquire beyond all doubt an "Aryan" editor. It was probably also his intention to make Riederer von Paar the new academic star of his publishing house. She now had her own series, which meant extra publicity for her book on genetics. In his version of the story Jungck also neglects to mention that Riederer von Paar was a good friend of *his*. She came from an old family of the Lower Bavarian nobility and in 1943 ensured that Jungck's books were taken to safety from bombing. Jungck personally transported countless crates to the Riederer von Paar family castle. According to Jungck, these included "valuable books that would likely be sellable later".[33] Among them must have been Alice's and Wessel's works, for Jungck was able to bring them back on the market immediately after the war.

After his conversation with Jungck, Paul Wessel fled Germany for Switzerland. In Jungck's version of the story this move comes as a complete surprise – he had, after all, been thinking of a trip to China. Jungck concluded that the situation had become "too hot" for Wessel. His choice of words has connotations of the criminal underworld, and indeed Jungck goes on to describe Wessel as a kind of crook. Although he emphasises several times how unimportant Wessel's contribution was to the series, he seems to have needed a final volume from his author. In 1938 Jungck even took a special trip to Zurich for this purpose. Once there he discovered that Wessel was burnt out after his flight from Germany. Jungck noted with disgust that Wessel had tried to fob him off with a substandard text: "He showed me a manuscript, but when I leafed through it I realised that large chunks had been pasted together from his book on physics." It is hard to verify the truth of this claim. According to Jungck's version he then rejected the manuscript.

We can only guess at the desperate state Paul Wessel must

have been in when Jungck met him in 1938. He was not granted another residence permit in Switzerland and so had to flee to Britain. Just like Alice he lived there in poverty, without ever earning anything from his works.

During the war, however, his physics book as well as the entire series enjoyed excellent sales. In his 1974 publication Jungck described this success with great pride. As there was a greater need for doctors during the war, "all volumes saw an increase in sales and kept being reprinted."[34] (Wessel's physics book was a success in Spain too, although Jungck does not mention that it was translated into Spanish in 1942.)

It is interesting to note that Jungck's version of the Wessel story is not mentioned again in a later history of the publishing house. The author of the 1999 jubilee publication is Hermann Jungck's son Christoph, who writes:

A project instigated by [Ernst Reinhardt] proved to be groundbreaking: the publication of scientific compendiums based on notes for exam preparation. The most successful was a concise physics textbook [. . .] It soon achieved high sales figures and, as it was regarded important to the war effort, we were able to keep printing it until late in the war.[35]

Paul Wessel is not mentioned here by name, but the book still pokes fun at him: "Shortly after the publishing house was taken over, the author of the aforementioned physics compendium appeared in SS uniform. Later it turned out that he, who was half-Jewish, had merely borrowed it to make an impression [. . .]

There were no further consequences to this episode; the author concerned was able to abscond to England in time."[36]

In this version, Paul Wessel's story has a happy ending; he is able to "abscond". And there is no mention of the three-way contract or Frau Dr Riederer von Paar acting as a front woman. Only her book on genetics had to be explained in 1999, when Christoph Jungck showed himself to be understanding of his father's motive for publishing such a book: "We have the right, indeed the duty, to read the works of the time with the knowledge we have today. It becomes problematic if our judgement too quickly becomes moral condemnation."[37] And so the 1999 history did not condemn crude racial theories either.

The genetics expert Viola Riederer von Paar had several honours conferred on her after the war. The Catholic Church bestowed on her the Papal order "Pro Ecclesia et Pontifice", and in 1971 the Deutsche Caritasverband gave her the "Goldene Ehrennadel" (golden badge of honour). By contrast Paul Wessel had a very different fate.

The "front man" method worked very well in 1937 and Jungck soon had opportunity to use it again. The events of March 1938 were a blessing, for now business was more straightforward: "When the Anschluss of Austria took place, shipping to Austria became of course a much simpler process, as everything could take place directly from Munich."[38] Only Alice Urbach remained a problem. Until that time she had been a foreigner, but now all Austrians became German citizens and were thus subject to the Nuremberg Laws. Jungck decided that Alice could no longer be the author of her own book. In 1974 he wrote tersely: "After the Anschluss of Austria I was obliged to find a new author for the cookbook because Alice Urbach was a Jew and otherwise the cookbook could no longer have been sold."[39]

Alice had heard of stories about front men from her father. In the Pressburg ghetto Jews were not permitted to own property. They could try to buy, however, using a front man. But there was a risk here too: you could never be certain that the front man would stick to the contract.

When, in 1938, front men had a renaissance in the Third Reich, Jews experienced an eerie déjà-vu. From one day to the next Alice was no longer the author of her own book. In the 1970s she wrote: "The book was less than three years old when Hitler's legislation forbade any Jewish author to have a book on the market! Thus, the publisher gave this book, my book *copied word for word with just another's name* . . ."[40]

Only in 2020 did new sources allow us to recreate what happened at the time. In September 1938, as Alice was trying to organise her flight to Britain, she received a letter from Munich. She had been sent a "clarification". From this it emerged that Alice had in the meantime written two further cookbooks for the publisher that hadn't yet been released. One was on vegetarian cuisine and the other on Viennese pastries and desserts. In the "clarification" Alice was now asked to hand over: "The copyright and all publishing rights." She was also asked to give up all her rights to *So kocht man in Wien!*[41] She signed the document.

Contracts signed after the implementation of the 1935 Nuremberg Laws and which led to a loss of assets are no longer legally recognised and fall under the law of compensation for those persecuted during the National Socialist regime. By this time, it was commonplace for Jews to have to surrender their assets under pressure, and for far less than their real value. The Austrian house Perles, for example, which had published Alice's first cookbook, was targeted by "Aryanisers" immediately following the Anschluss, on 22 March 1938. Richard Hollinek forced the Perles family to hand over one of their most important periodicals, the *Wiener Medizinische Wochenschrift* (*Viennese Medical Weekly*). Paul Perles, who survived the Holocaust, recalled how he and his family were "presented with a piece of paper to sign which transferred ownership of the *Wiener Medizinische Wochenschrift* to Hollinek in return for the cancellation of all outstanding printing bills. We were told that if the owners (my father and uncle) didn't sign, the [Nazi] party would discontinue the paper at once and it would be published by Hollinek the following week with a differently coloured cover. Personally, I had to agree, without remuneration, to spend several weeks showing Hollinek how to run the paper. When I asked what would happen if I refused, Hollinek said there would be ways of convincing [me]."[42]

The function that Frau Dr Riederer von Paar had assumed in the Paul Wessel case was now assigned by Jungck to another person, surprisingly a man. Jungck wrote in 1974: "I found [a new author] in Rudolf Rösch, who not only revised the cookbook, but also brought some of Frau Urbach's extremely rich dishes up to date (in line with the findings of modern nutrition), so that it was in fact his own work, albeit based on Frau Urbach's cookbook."[43]

There were indeed some rewordings, deletions and additions. The Austrian historian and cookbook expert Walter Schübler has compared both books with forensic precision and comes to the following conclusion:

> Rösch did some rearranging, reordered some of the recipes that were lifted word for word, made minor amendments to chapter headings – the attempt at camouflage is palpable – rewrote the various introductions, deleted a few short sections such as "cooking for the weekend" or "provisions for touring and journeys", but besides the 200 illustrations he reproduced entire chapters running to dozens of pages verbatim or with only minimal changes.[44]

The first deletion was of Alice's "preface" from 1935, in which she underlined the international character of Viennese cuisine. It read:

> Viennese cuisine justifiably enjoys an international reputation. It is exceptionally varied, being able to draw on a rich seam provided by the colourful mix of peoples that made up the former Austro-Hungarian monarchy [. . .] The strudel and goulash, for example, are both Hungarian inventions, dumplings are of Bohemian origin and various tasty little morsels are taken from French cuisine.[45]

Terms such as "colourful mix of peoples" and "international reputation" were less popular with the Nazis. The "preface" was entirely replaced by a "foreword". In it, Rudolf Rösch praised himself with the surprising observation: "It takes an incredible amount of detailed work to design and put together a cookbook like this."

He then thanked two colleagues – Maria Gerhardt and Elfriede Goll – for their "industrious efforts" with this detailed work. Perhaps their mention was a way of explaining why only women's hands were to be seen in the book's photographs – Alice's hands. Rösch's foreword concluded with the words: "Now this book will find its way into every German Gau [district] [. . .] as testament to the fact that in the second largest city in the Reich we are masters [of the culinary arts] too."[46]

Jungck's claim that Alice's book needed "bringing up to date", therefore, referred to the Nazification of the text. And indeed, the comment about "every German Gau", or the observation that Vienna was now the "second largest" city in the Reich, could not have been more up to date. Recipes with Jewish names, such as "Rothschild sponge", "Rothschild omelette" or "Jaffa torte" were removed, and foreign names of recipes Germanised: "Beef fillet Parmentier" was given a native appellation, while "Beef Wellington" became "Beef in blankets".

Jungck's assertion that Frau Urbach's "rich dishes" needed bringing up to date (in line with the findings of modern nutrition) was untrue – after all, the book had only appeared three years earlier, and in addition to typical rich Viennese desserts it also contained hints on healthy eating. Alice had not spent years giving talks on vegetarian food and balanced diets for nothing. What the publisher did delete, however, were the passages that had quite clearly been written by a woman, largely in the second half of the book where Alice made very personal suggestions for running a household. Her advice sounded far too empathetic for a male author's voice. Gone, for example, was this short passage in Alice's sub-chapter "How the housewife should treat her maid": "When dealing with her maid, every housewife should always bear in mind that she is in a privileged position compared to the girl: she has a fixed, secure home, whereas at the housewife's request the girl may have to leave this home from one day to the next, sometimes without knowing where she will find work or somewhere else to live."[47]

No doubt these observations did not sound sufficiently masculine (and at the beginning of the war would no longer have been applicable to the treatment of a Polish forced worker). Alice's ideas that touched on emancipation disappeared too, including this sentence: "Not all women are fully aware how much [the housewife] contributes to the economy, for nine-tenths of all money spent in the country is spent by women; most money passes through their hands. For this reason, she must be trained for her difficult and responsible job."[48]

Rösch deleted these remarks, only citing Alice again when it came to thrift: "First comes what is necessary, then what is useful, and only then what is pleasurable and what is gratuitous."

Apart from these changes, the Rösch book was very similar to Alice's original. Her book was now the work of a man. But who was he?

In all the editions that appeared between 1939 and the end of the National Socialist regime, Rudolf Rösch was presented as an "established master chef in Vienna and employee of the

Reich food agency". (After the war the second part was understandably deleted.) But research in the German Federal Archives did not turn up a Rudolf Rösch attached to the Reich food agency. Nor was there a Rudolf Rösch in the Reich chamber of literature.[49]

Rudolf Rösch is not an uncommon name. In Germany and the new "Ostmark" there were many Rudolf Röschs who were members of the Nazi Party, whose professions are noted on their membership cards. These include clerks, labourers, drivers, a locksmith and even a major general. Only one Rudolf Rösch of the right age had an Austrian background, a Salzburg business graduate who served in the Wehrmacht from 1939 to 1945.[50] It is rather unlikely that he would have worked as a chef on the side during this period. Was Rudolf Rösch a pseudonym, therefore, or maybe even a phantom invented by Jungck? The current CEO of Ernst Reinhardt Verlag stated in 2020 that there are no documents in the archive relating to Rudolf Rösch. She does believe, however, that he was a real person and not an invention of the publisher.[51]

If Rösch didn't work for the Reich food agency and wasn't a "Viennese master chef", it is most likely that he was a resident of Munich. In 1932, 1933 and 1935, a man of that name appeared in three programmes on Munich radio. According to the radio magazine, he talked about plum dumpling recipes and grape diets.[52] It is perfectly possible, therefore, that in 1938 Jungck decided to make this Rösch an author, employing the same method as other publishing houses. Just like Volkmann/Hiron, Rösch became a best-selling author overnight.

9: ARRIVAL AT THE CASTLE

"The horror of that moment," the King went on, "I shall never, never forget!"
"You will, though," the Queen said, "if you don't make a memorandum of it."
Lewis Carroll, *Through the Looking-Glass*

In the Bloomsbury district of London, near the British Museum, is Woburn House. At the end of the 1930s this imposing building was the first port of call for Jewish emigrants.[1] To prepare refugees for their visit, the British government made an information film about Woburn House, some disjointed scenes of which have survived.[2] In one we see an Austrian émigré couple entering the building. They are both about forty and well dressed. The man is wearing a pristine warm coat; the woman has a large white bow on her dark dress. In the next scene, which the director repeats several times, the couple are sitting opposite a British employee at Woburn House. He speaks good German and the following dialogue ensues:

Employee: "You were in Switzerland?"

Man: "Yes, I was in Switzerland."

Employee: "Did you enter without a visa?"

Man: "Yes, I had to leave Vienna within 48 hours, in which time I wasn't able to get myself a visa. So I had to escape through Vorarlberg [. . .] through the forest and mountains with my wife."

Employee: "How did you manage to enter the country?"

Man: "I had to flee illegally [. . .] over the mountains, which I knew very well as a tourist. That way I hoped to avoid any border guards."

The director now cuts and repeats the scene. In the next version the nameless emigrant explains in greater detail why he had to flee. He had been imprisoned for five weeks and upon release he signed a declaration stating he would leave the country immediately. He embarked on his flight over the mountains with his wife at five o'clock in the morning, in the hope of avoiding border guards so early in the day. While the man talks his wife sits silently beside him. At the beginning of the film she looks composed, but in the course of the interview her body gradually slumps, as if she's so ashamed she wants to disappear. And that is exactly what happens in the next shot. The camera is now focused only on her husband, who is visibly uncomfortable about having to tell the story of his flight again, but who endeavours to keep calm until the director is finally happy with what he has filmed.

Alice went through a similar procedure at Woburn House. Like the Austrian woman in the film sequence, she also wore dainty bows with her outfits. Apart from this feminine detail, however, Alice was not a girly, timid type. Outwardly, at least, she played the strong woman who could not be fazed by anything. She too would have found the situation in Woburn House humiliating, but by now she had a fair amount of practice in skilfully covering up her humiliations. She knew only too well that there was no return ticket; Britain was the only country that would take her in.

As she liked to talk, we can assume that she chattered relentlessly to the Woburn House employee. We can also assume that the man, exhausted by her torrent of relevant and irrelevant information, waved Alice through as quickly as possible. Maybe he took the time to give her an information brochure which listed all the important rules for refugees. The brochure had the long-winded title, "While You Are in England. Helpful Information and Guidance for Every Refugee". It had been produced by Jewish organisations in agreement with the British government, and the title hinted hopefully that this was an interim solution, and that the refugees would not stay long in Great Britain. But while there they should stick to certain rules. Alice understood what was expected of her. Thanks to her impeccable memory she had soon learned the brochure by heart, and over the next few years she would follow the rules to the letter – not always to the pleasure of her charges.

The brochure was divided into two. On the left-hand side was the English text, on the right a German translation. Alice ignored the right-hand side and studied the first few paragraphs which were designed to prevent the refugees from being afraid of the police. This was crucial, as many refugees had been in situations where their local policeman, who they may have known for years, looked on impassively as Jewish citizens were mistreated, their homes and businesses plundered. Police uniforms were now equated with arrest, violence and prison. Refugee children in particular later described how surprised they were when British police gave them a friendly smile. This was the first key message of the information booklet: "The police are your friends and are ready to help you wherever you are." In return a certain amount of monitoring had to be accepted. When moving, each refugee had to register their change of address within forty-eight hours.

The Jewish community also urged all refugees to adhere to the following guidelines:

1. Spend your spare time immediately in learning the English language and its correct pronunciation.
2. Refrain from speaking German in the streets and in public conveyances and in public places such as restaurants. Talk halting English rather than fluent German – and *do not talk in a loud voice*.
3. Do not criticise any Government regulations, nor the way things are done over here. Do not speak of "how much better this or that is done in Germany". It may be true in some matters, but it weighs as nothing against the sympathy and freedom and liberty of England which are now given to you. Do not forget that point.
4. Do not join any Political organisation, or take part in any political activities.
5. Do not make yourself conspicuous by speaking loudly,

nor by your manner or dress. The Englishman greatly
dislikes ostentation, loudness of dress or manner, or
unconventionality of dress or manner.[3]

Alice resolved to speak softly and she checked her clothing
again for colourful items. She did not find anything out of
the ordinary; she hadn't been able to afford to buy beautiful
items to wear for several years. So there was no danger of her
standing out.

Another point was more important. According to Home
Office regulations, Alice could stay in Britain only while she
could prove she had work in service. She was not permitted
to do a different job.

On her first visit in 1937 Alice had noticed that there was a
shortage of servants in Britain. Very few English girls wanted
to work as maids: "The girls much rather worked in factories
and had their evenings for themselves [. . .] Though they earned
less because they had to provide food, their clothing, their
living in general, they still preferred their freedom!"[4]

Thanks to the work permit for servants (the "domestic
permit"), refugees now filled this gap in the British labour
market, but this did not always function smoothly, as Alice
described:

Thousands of former well-to-do men and women of the
best society did not see any other means of escape [. . .]
than domestic situations. It was hard for women who
never in their lives had to make their own beds, or wash a
cup – to turn suddenly into maids and scrub bathroom

floors! Worse for men with white collar jobs – to turn suddenly into valets and butlers. These were men such as lawyers and bank managers who used to be waited on hand and foot themselves. I know also that it must have been very trying for the British housewives to have such an untrained staff on hand. It was, of course, easier for girls of a simpler upbringing, who had worked all their grown-up lives, even if they were dressmakers, milliners and so on. However, they were not allowed to follow their line. Whatever they were, they had to be domestics![5]

It was obvious that Alice would work as a cook. One could find out about available jobs at Woburn House, and she immediately secured a position. The offer sounded promising. She would be working at Harlaxton Manor.

Harlaxton Manor is a large estate in Lincolnshire. Since the 1970s this palatial property has been used as the setting for many a costume drama. Victorian carriages ride up the long drive to the main entrance and ladies in hooped skirts float through the endless succession of rooms. There is something eccentric about the theatricality of the building, and so it comes as no surprise that it served as the location for such films as *The Haunting* and *The Ruling Class*, which feature characters who succumb slowly to madness. When Alice took a position on this country estate in the winter of 1938–39, she rapidly came to the conclusion that its owner could not be of sound mind.

To prepare herself for the job, Alice first wanted to learn all she could about British food. Having read Shakespeare and

Byron at school, Alice was convinced she was fluent in English and thus prepared for any eventuality. But doubts crept in after her first trip to buy groceries. She was keen to try "marmalade", only to discover that the English word means a bitter preserve of citrus fruits, whereas in German it is a general word for jam. Her English teacher had clearly failed here. Many other English words seemed to make no sense either. A "biscuit" was nothing like the German "Biskuitkuchen", which is a sponge cake. A Viennese "Biskuit", on the other hand, is more like a scone, while the word "cake" in English could be either a "Kuchen" or a "Torte" in German. The English "tart", however, is not a "Torte" but an "Obsttörtchen" (and it was a long time before Alice realised that the same word could be used to refer to a prostitute). Hardly anybody in Britain seemed to have heard of petits fours, and those who had thought they were too complicated and time-consuming to make. Alice was particularly shocked that British children were allowed to eat ice cream whenever they liked. In Vienna, ice cream was thought to be loaded with calories, which children should be given only on birthdays and after a successful trip to the dentist. For a pastry chef like Alice, the jellies so popular in Britain were a culinary crime.

Friedrich Torberg describes British cuisine in the 1930s as "known to be inedible".[6] For Viennese like Alice and Torberg, used to Austro-Hungarian–Czech–Jewish fare, Britain was on the bottom rung of the European culinary hierarchy. If, as an Austrian, you had the misfortune to have to eat here, there was only one way to survive: you had to find a kosher restaurant. Only there could you find meat dishes and pastries with any flavour, and so it is unsurprising that the ravenous diners who frequented these restaurants were not only Jews.

Although Alice was aware that she had ended up in a culinary wilderness, she had to keep her opinion to herself to avoid risking losing her "domestic permit". Nobody would be willing to hire a cook who mocked the eating habits of a country which had saved them from the Nazis.

Alice endeavoured, therefore, to avoid letting her dissatisfaction show. Like the wonderland of the fictional heroine after whom she had been named, her world too had been turned upside down since the Anschluss. At her cookery school she had been the one hiring staff, and a whole chapter of her book *So kocht man in Wien!* had focused on how to treat maids kindly. Now Alice herself was in the reverse position and, as she was soon to find out, her experiences would not be pleasant. This was chiefly due to her first employer and the owner of Harlaxton Manor, Violet Van der Elst.

These days barely anybody in Britain remembers Mrs Van der Elst, but in the late 1930s she was a colourful figure who was a regular feature of the country's gossip columns. "Violet", as she was called by her admirers, came from a modest background and worked her way up the social ladder with great energy. She was born in 1882, the daughter of a washerwoman, and started work herself as a scullery maid. Pretty and intelligent, she was able to make the leap from servant to dancer,[7] appearing in some rather dubious establishments, where she met her first husband Henry Nathan. Nathan was a Jewish engineer fifteen years older than Violet. As a career in a nightclub did not appear to have much of a future, she accepted his proposal of marriage. It offered her material security and the opportunity to climb socially into the middle class.

Although it was Henry Nathan who provided the initial capital, ultimately it was Violet who turned it into a fortune. Ever since her days as a scullery maid she had been working with soap, and this gave her the idea of developing her own products. She invented a shaving cream and, later, several face creams for women. Soon after Henry Nathan died in 1927, Violet married her manager and secret lover, the Belgian John Van der Elst. Together they expanded the business, developing an extremely successful skin lotion called Doge. Everything appeared to be going well until John also died in 1934, after which Violet fell into a deep depression. From that day on she became unbearable.

When Alice arrived at Grantham station in November 1938, she knew nothing about her employer Mrs Van der Elst or her success in the cosmetics industry. After fleeing Vienna Alice couldn't afford expensive skin creams, and besides, she had more to worry about than facial care. First she had to register at the local police station and provide her new address: Alice Urbach, Cook for Mrs Violet Van der Elst, Grantham Castle.

Grantham Castle was a fantasy name for Harlaxton Manor dreamed up by Violet Van der Elst. In 1937 Harlaxton had been advertised for sale in *Country Life*, and as soon as Violet saw the photographs she wanted to add it to her collection of opulent properties. The manor house was set in a vast, magnificent estate boasting several lakes and ponds. It was a sort of retro product built by the architect in Elizabethan style in the 1830s.

It has been claimed that Mrs Van der Elst's offer trumped those made by other interested parties such as the Duke of Windsor and Henry Ford's son, but that seems rather improbable.[8] Such individuals would not have been interested in a house without electricity or running water, but Violet was not put off by such details. Within a year she had electric lights installed as well as eight bathrooms. Eschewing understatement, she decreed that henceforth Harlaxton was a castle and gave it its new name, after the nearest town.[9]

At first Violet did not have enough furniture to make the place habitable, and so she embarked on a grand shopping tour. She began, as ever, at the very top, her first port of call being Buckingham Palace. Through an antiques dealer she was able to acquire Gobelins that Queen Alexandra had once been given by her brother-in-law, Tsar Nicholas II of Russia. They depicted the changing seasons and Mrs Van der Elst developed such a passion for tapestries that over the years she purchased more than one hundred Gobelins (with a combined value of £30,000, a vast amount of money at the time). As she also had a weakness for the Middle Ages, the corridors of Grantham Castle were decorated with suits of armour and mediaeval weaponry.

One of her most spectacular acquisitions was the 150-bulb chandelier for the marble hall. It had been manufactured in Czechoslovakia and originally destined for the Royal Bank of Madrid. When the Civil War broke out in 1936, however, delivery of the item was impossible. Mrs Van der Elst was now able to purchase it at a knockdown price and she was fond of telling all her visitors that she owned the largest chandelier in the world. On a mantelpiece beneath it she placed the urn containing the remains of her second husband. One of the maids' most important tasks was to dust the urn every day and decorate it with fresh flowers.

This sumptuously furnished castle was thus to be Alice's new home. At Grantham police station she spelled her name several times. This was another typical experience of the emigrant: "'How do you spell it?' was the inevitable, humiliating question we hated with a passion."[10] Over the years Alice would turn spelling her name into quite a routine, always with a thick Viennese accent, of course.

As Alice was about to leave the police station she was spoken to in German by a man who had also been in the queue. His name was Arthur Pan, like Alice a product of the defunct Habsburg Monarchy. Originally from Hungary, Pan was a painter whose wartime portraits of Winston Churchill are still well known. Back in 1938, however, several years before these commissions, he only had one client: Mrs Van der Elst. Pan told Alice all about his acquaintance with this woman, who had commissioned him to paint a representative portrait. Mrs Van der Elst had proved to be an extremely difficult model during their sessions, insisting on being painted wearing only black, on a chair that the doges of Venice had sat on before pronouncing the death sentence. Regarding herself as a highly talented painter too, she wanted to have a say in all the artistic details. Although she was satisfied with the end product, more problems emerged when it came to the fee. Violet Van der Elst was notorious for her tardiness in paying for services rendered – and often for not paying at all, for which she was sued several times. In one instance she refused to pay a portrait artist because

Violet Van der Elst in front of her portrait by Arthur Pan,
having just paid the artist

she did not look sufficiently attractive in the painting. In court, her long letter of complaint was read out: "I have too much hair [in the picture] and bottom part of my face too weak. I have a square chin [. . .] I have beautiful hands and these hands are too bony."[11]

In Arthur Pan's portrait Mrs Van der Elst looked younger and slimmer than in real life, so he didn't have to worry about any angry letters. He eventually got his money too (albeit only after some protracted wrangling) and told Alice that he had been invited to spend Christmas at Grantham. His excitement at the prospect was limited, but he promised to visit Alice in the kitchen.

After they parted company, Alice had to make her way to Grantham Castle. Weighed down by a heavy suitcase, it was hard to reach the house on foot, and just for once the chauffeur came to pick her up. It was an interesting car ride. In Alice's recollection the car took fifteen minutes just to negotiate the castle's long drive (here she must be exaggerating somewhat as the drive is about one mile long, which means the car would have been going at a snail's pace). As the chauffeur wasn't usually allowed to ferry staff, all the servants had bicycles. Alice could not ride a bike, however, and so during her entire time at Grantham she did not leave the estate even once.

Although she had grown up in the Habsburg Monarchy and knew Schönbrunn Palace well, Alice was impressed by the size of Grantham Castle. It had its own orangery full of exotic plants and peach trees that blossomed even in winter. In total, the house boasted more than one hundred rooms, although nobody seems to have counted exactly. No sooner had Alice arrived than she realised that there were too few staff employed at Grantham to care for this abundance of rooms. Most were never cleaned, and the servants seemed to be in a permanent feud with the eccentric mistress of the castle.

The prevailing atmosphere at Grantham Castle had little in common with the fictitious Granthams of *Downton Abbey*. The television Granthams are a nice family who touchingly attend to the cares of their servants. Violet Van der Elst was quite the opposite, deeply suspicious of her staff. She wasn't only in court because of outstanding payments; she often appeared as the plaintiff too, accusing servants of stealing clothes, jewellery, cheques, rugs and furs. One of her methods of testing servants was to place banknotes beneath the rugs (probably to find out whether they cleaned under them too) and wait for the response. One maid was so incensed by this that she nailed a banknote to the floor. She was especially furious with Mrs Van der Elst because she was repeatedly woken by her at three in the morning to change the bedclothes.

The staff also had to put up with Mrs Van der Elst hurling objects about during emotional outbursts. For this reason, she could not expect much sympathy. When she fell down the stairs one evening the butler hissed, "I hope she's broken her neck." Even her young secretary Ray, with whom she had an on-off relationship, later admitted that Mrs Van der Elst demanded absolute subordination and treated her staff like "slaves" (he himself had to put up with several jealousy dramas).

Because the staff saw Mrs Van der Elst as the common enemy, there was great solidarity between them. Alice never mentioned having any problems with her colleagues, and yet such harmony was not obvious. A growing number of British servants at the time reacted against new arrivals such as Alice. Between 1933 and 1939, 20,000 Jewish women fled to Britain. All of them had to look for positions in domestic service as a condition of their immigration, generating a competition that threatened the livelihoods of British staff. Some reacted by joining far-right movements. The number of servants who supported the British Union of Fascists increased dramatically at the end of the 1930s.[12]

Anti-Semitism was absent at Grantham Castle, which may in part have been down to the fact that two important men close to Mrs Van der Elst – her secretary and lover Ray, as well as her chauffeur – were Jewish.[13] Finally, Alice appeared to be safe, far from the horrors of Austria. But she knew that she had not escaped Vienna altogether; Karl was still waiting for his affidavit, and while her son was stuck in Austria, Alice could not be free.

She knew that every letter was opened and she didn't want to put him in danger by asking direct questions. Alice would have understood whatever Karl had written to her, but his letters ceased to arrive in November. Alice suspected that something terrible must have happened.

On 9 November 1938 Karl celebrated his twenty-first birthday with a few friends. He had held the party at home because Jews were now forbidden from visiting restaurants and coffee houses. Since Karl was kicked out of university, he had seen only a few of his student friends. Willy continued to stand by him, however, and the two of them still shared a small apartment. They could not know that as they were celebrating Karl's birthday, synagogues were being set alight and Jewish shops plundered throughout Germany. A few hours after the party was over, at 4 a.m. on 10 November, all Viennese SS and SA formations were ordered to get to work too and arrest as many Jews as possible. Although the Austrians started later, they launched into the pogrom with even greater gusto. Karl had no idea what awaited him when he left the house on 10 November to obtain one final document for his emigration:

As there are always people standing in front of the office, I have to get up early to be ready by noon. The alarm clock rings at 6. I am tired and don't want to get up. However, I must go down town so I jump out of bed and get started. At a news stand I see a headline in big letters: "Herr von [sic] Rath dies. Jews will pay for it." I feel rather shocked, but feel that there isn't much more they can do to us after all they have already done. I also feel secure with my summons to the American consulate and my boat ticket. I arrive at the Jewish emigration office at 8 am to file my papers. How strange, I think, that no people are waiting today. I immediately realize that something is wrong. I turn around and start to leave as quickly as possible. A man dressed in civilian clothes approaches and asks what I want. I reply that I want to get my papers in order. "Well," he says, "just walk in and get what you want." It is too late to get away. Many people are standing around who look like Gestapos [. . .] So I go to the door and open it, and there, lined on each side of the stairs, are a row of beefy looking big storm troopers in full equipment, steel helmets and field uniforms. The first one grabs me by my coat and shouts, "So we got you." No sooner do I turn around than he socks me with his fists, then the others start in. One slap after another, kicks in my face and boots in my back. But I don't feel anything, it's too big a shock. They throw me up and down the stairs, it seems great fun for them.[14]

When the SA troopers had tired of beating Karl, they shoved him into a little room. He saw twenty men, women and children, some of whom were crying. An SA man was sitting at a desk, taking telephone calls. He greeted each caller with the same message, delivered with sarcastic politeness: "I'm sorry, our phone doesn't work today. I can't get you a connection to the office you want, but you had better come down and investigate for yourself. Or if you will give me your address I will send someone to help you later on."[15]

The man's accent sounded so Prussian that Karl was sure no Viennese Jew would fall for it. Anybody with their head screwed on would avoid the emigration office now. But for him it was too late:

We stand there waiting and waiting. Later a Gestapo official asks all the women and boys under sixteen to come with him. They may go home. One man tells the official that he has heart trouble and asks if he may go, too. "Shut up," is the answer. "We know your dirty tricks. We will cure you." He signals a storm trooper, "Take this dirty pig in an upper room and cure his heart trouble."

We are loaded into several trucks which were waiting

outside. In the rear sits a storm trooper with his pistol ready. "Now you keep quiet and don't move," he commands. "If you make any trouble I'll shoot, but it doesn't matter, because we're going to shoot you anyhow." One elderly man loses his nerve and starts to cry and shout. He already has one son in Dachau, and he has just returned from a Nazi prison himself. Later I am to see this man in the concentration camp. He will have gone mad. The truck hauls us to a well-known prison. It was a Viennese school before the Anschluss, but Hitler needs more prisons and barracks than schools. We stay there five days.[16]

Karl could not have known that his uncle Felix Mayer was in a similar situation at the same time. The two of them were among the 6,500 men (and 200 women) who were arrested during the November pogrom in Vienna. Felix was arrested on 10 November in his apartment at 39 Döblinger Hauptstrasse and the place was looted.[17] Like Karl, for days he was then transported from one makeshift prison to another. First to the riding school in Porzellangasse, then to a school in Kenyongasse, followed by another school at 14 Karajangasse (the future Austrian chancellor Bruno Kreisky had been detained here back in April 1938).[18] Most prisoners went from Karajangasse to Dachau, but Felix was fortunate. He was transferred to a building in Elisabethpromenade, where he was released on 28 November 1938, probably thanks to falsified papers and a bribe. Franziska Tausig, a distant relative, later wrote about this practice: "Some 'offices' [for forged papers] were set up in Vienna. Relatives of those imprisoned whispered the addresses to each other." For a lot of money Franziska bought false affidavits there to prove that her husband was able to emigrate.[19] Felix's wife must have arranged something similar for him. He never told anyone in the family what happened to him on his tour of prisons. The only clue is in an application he made to the Austrian assistance fund in 1956, in which he stated: "In prison (Kenyongasse) I was the victim of severe physical abuse and suffered nervous disorders (hallucinations) as a result."[20]

Karl's prison story turned out differently:

During the first two days one truck after another arrive. People stagger in with torn clothes and bleeding faces. There isn't even room to sit on the floor. Occasionally the Gestapo holds inspections in the middle of the night. Sunday morning a man suddenly loses his mind and jumps out of the window. The commander of the whole prison comes into our rooms afterwards and says that because of this atrocity we must stand up for two hours. I had thought it would be impossible to stand for two hours without moving, but we did, and it is good training for what is to come. One fellow has heart convulsions and falls on the floor. Nobody can help him, nobody dares move. After that the commander tells us that if anyone jumps out of the window he will shoot ten of us, and we believe him.[21]

Because the November pogrom had been especially brutal in Vienna, Willy feared that something must have happened to Karl. When he did not return home, Willy attempted to inform

Alice's siblings and all the Urbachs.[22] But it was a while before he tracked them down. Some time later Otto wrote from America to his "Aryan" aunt Marie Urbach:[23]

I got a letter today from Karli's friend Willy [. . .] in which he told me that Karli disappeared without trace on the tenth of this month. Apparently it has something to do with a debt that Mother left behind in Vienna. The whole matter is very unclear and although I intend to take immediate steps I cannot do much without knowing precisely what happened [. . .] I'm terribly worried about what has happened to Karli, and I cannot imagine any reason why it has come to this. Apparently Karli already has a ticket to America, and although I don't know if he had his American visa, I am fairly certain that the American consulate gave him the visa. I will get in touch with a lawyer today to see if he can do anything. His name is Dr Hardt and I believe he has good connections.[24]

By the time Otto wrote this letter, Karl had already been transferred:

Monday morning a storm trooper comes in and announces that we have stolen some blankets and everyone will have to pay for them. We haven't seen a single blanket during the whole time, but everyone has to pay a mark. Later, another fellow comes in and announces that some plates have been stolen. Everyone has to pay again. If one doesn't have the money, someone has to

Nov 27. 1938.

Liebe Tante Marie:

        Ich erhielt heute einen Brief von Karlis Freund Willy mit dem er
zusammen wohnte, in dem er mir mit teilt das Karli am 10 dieses Monates
spurlos verschwand. Es soll angeblich im Zusammenhang mit irgend einer
Schuld sein die Mutter in Wien hinterlassen hat. Die ganze Sache ist sehr
unklar und obzwar ich sofortige Schritte unternehmen will kann ich nicht
viel tun ohne genau zu wissen was geschehen ist.Ich waere Dir vom Herzen
dankbar , falls Du mir per Flugpost all Details mitteilen wuerdest. Karlis Fr
Freund Willy hat sich angeblich mit irgendwelchen Verwandten in Verbindung
gesetzt. Ich weis nicht mit wem, aber ich bin ziemlich sicher das er Robert
von diesen Vorfall informiert hat.Ich schreibe Robert ebah auch einen
Brief um ihn zu bitten mir mit Auskunft zu bitten.

        Ich bin schreklich besorgt, was mit Karli los ist und ich kann mir
absolut keinen Grund vorstellen , der zu so etwas fuehren koennte.

        Karli hat angeblich schon sene Fahrkarte nach Amerika und obzwar
ich nicht weiss ob er sein amerikanisches Visum hatte glaube ich zimlich
bestimmt das das Amerikanische Consulat ihm das Visum erteilt hat.

        Ich setze mich heute mit einem Wiener Rechtsanwalt in Verbindung
um zu sehen ob er etwas tun kann.Sein Name ist Dr. Hardt und ich glaube
das er ueber gute Verbindungen verfuegt.

        Geld kann ich im telegrafischen Wege umgehend anweisen falls es
notwendig ist.Ich moechte aber das Geld nur an jemanden wirklich vertra-
uenswuerdigen schicken.Bitte teile mir mit wenn etwas gebraucht wird.
Wenn du mir ein Cable sendest brauchst du nur den Betrag zu telegrafieren
und ich weis dann schon was gemeint ist.Ich gebe dir weiter unten meine
Adresse unter der ich fortwaehrend erreicht werden kann. Ich hoffe das Du

diese schweren zeiten so gut wie moeglich ueberstehst.Ich kann mir vorstellen
wie euch allen zu mute sein muss.
        Dir im voraus dankend verbleibe ich Dein Neffe

                                        Otto

Otto B. Urbach , 2306 Hampden Ave St. Paul, Minn.Diese Adresse ist fuer
                        U.S.A.   Briefe.

Urbach,Northland Ski Co , St. Paul,Minn.   Diese Adresse fuer Cablegramm

Otto's letter to his "Aryan" aunt Marie Urbach, 27 November 1938

pay for him. Shortly after this they load us like cattle into trucks again [. . .] I hope they will give us a trial [. . .] Well. I got my trial. First in a little room a physician in storm trooper's uniform asks me just one question:

"Healthy?"

"Yes," I say. Another S.S. man kicks me into the next room. A high Gestapo official sits behind a huge desk like God himself. He asks what steps I have taken to leave Germany so far. When I hear this question, I feel absolutely sure that I will be free within the next ten minutes. I show him the summons to the United States consulate, my passport and my boat tickets and say that I'll be leaving Germany on December 20.

"That's fine,' he says. "You have lots of time."

He then marks a big red "D" on my paper. "D," he says to the waiting S.S. man. Again a kick, and I am in the corridor, forced to stand with my face to the wall as usual.

"Don't move, don't talk."

[. . .]

Then a voice behind me says [. . .] "So you dirty dogs want to kill us Germans? But wait, you'll see. Do you know where you're going?"

"No," I say.

"Well, my friend – Dachau."

I couldn't believe it. I wouldn't believe it. It was so impossible. Dachau! This word meant murder, slaughter, hell. I believed it in the evening when my train left the West railroad station.[25]

For Alice it was traumatic that she was unable to help Karl. After having read about "Reichskristallnacht" in the English newspapers, she managed to get in touch with her half-sister Karoline in Vienna. "Karla" told her that there had been a huge number of arrests, amongst them Karl and Felix. Karoline thought that like many others Karl might have been taken to Dachau by now (and everybody knew what Dachau meant. A whispered Viennese joke from the time went: "Silence is golden, talking is Dachau"[26]).

This was the most devastating news in a life that was not lacking in crises. Alice had experienced the brutality of the first wave of arrests in March/April 1938 and so could all too well imagine what had happened now.[27] But there was nothing she could do. She was in an English castle, totally cut off from her family. Apart from Rose Landstone she knew nobody in Britain who could help her; she had not even had the opportunity to talk to her new employer or at the very least impress her with her culinary skills. From the other servants she had heard that Violet Van der Elst was overweight and was adhering to a strict diet of toast and apples. Although Violet spent hours on an exercise bike, she never slimmed down. It was assumed, therefore, that she binged at night, secretly plundering the pantries.

Officially Alice's job was to bake for the house guests and plan the Christmas menu. A large party was expected to descend on Grantham Castle for the holidays. Violet Van der Elst surrounded herself with impoverished aristocrats who were known far and wide as scroungers and accompanied their rich benefactor on casino trips to France. Mrs Van der Elst also socialised with local politicians who were meant to help her secure a parliamentary seat. She planned to stand for the Labour Party and lobbied for the abolition of the death penalty in Britain.[28] As with the sale of her cosmetic products, she used the most current marketing strategies for her campaign. Whenever someone was sentenced to death, she would open a petition and collect a large amount of signatures. On the day of the execution she would arrive in her Rolls Royce at the prison where it was being carried out and deliver a speech against the death penalty by megaphone. While she was speaking a specially chartered plane would fly over the prison, trailing a black banner. This was no more than a brief distraction from events on the ground, however, for invariably there was a tussle between Mrs Van der Elst's supporters and the police. Order would only be restored when the death of the condemned prisoner was announced and the protesters sang "Abide with me". Afterwards Violet was usually arrested for disturbing the peace and would spend a few nights in police custody.

For all her eccentricities, Mrs Van der Elst had impressive social commitment. Her methods were in the long tradition of the suffragettes, and it was in part thanks to her persistence that the death penalty was finally abolished in Britain in 1964.

In 1938, however, most of the servants, Alice included, thought that Mrs Van der Elst's crusade against the death penalty was one big egotistical spectacle, in which she merely posed as the great campaigner. In the eyes of the servants Violet simply could not be a good person, and Alice accepted the opinion of the long-suffering staff without giving it much thought. She was also misinformed about Mrs Van der Elst's business

Violet confronts
the police

success, believing that Violet's Jewish husband had been solely responsible for building up the cosmetics empire and that she was now just "blowing" the money.

This misinformation was not a good basis for their first encounter. When Violet Van der Elst, after some hesitation, received her new cook, the two took an immediate dislike to each other. This was nothing unusual as far as Mrs Van der Elst was concerned. She had an innate distrust of other women, even treating the wives of her guests with frostiness. She believed that only men were worthy of addressing her.

By contrast, since her disastrous marriage to Max, Alice had avoided men and preferred the company of women. For this reason, Alice had no doubt imagined that she would get on with Mrs Van der Elst; they were roughly the same age, after all. But the social divide was too large. Whereas Mrs Van der Elst had worked her way up from servant to millionairess, Alice had slipped down from being the daughter born into an affluent family to a life of domestic service.

Even though Alice felt at once that her employer was cool towards her, she asked Mrs Van der Elst for help. She told her about a concentration camp called Dachau where terrible things were happening to her son. Mrs Van der Elst listened to her story and said she would write a letter to Hitler. This horrified Alice, who thought such a move would put Karl in an even more precarious position. Looking back, however, she was convinced that the letter was never written: "Death would have been sure for him then." In her view, Mrs Van der Elst was "enormously wealthy, enormously fat and enormously crazy."[29]

*

It was a grey November day when Karl arrived in Dachau.[30] He and the other new arrivals were forced to stand to attention in the cold for seven hours. Then three photographs were taken of them and their heads shaved. In 1939 Karl wrote:

All the work was done by the non-Jewish prisoners. They wore dark striped suits, some with red triangles on their jackets; they were political prisoners. They were all very nice to us comrades. One asked me how old I was. He said, "Don't be afraid, boy, keep your humor, and fight it through. Be glad you are a Jew. You will be released much earlier than we are." Then he gave me a bite of bread.[31]

Karl estimated that around 12,000 Jews and 8,000 non-Jews were imprisoned at Dachau. Today we know that after the November pogrom in 1938, about 11,000 Jews from Austria and Germany were taken to the concentration camp, which was already overcrowded.

We were prohibited to talk with Aryan prisoners. But we always found ways to come in contact with them. I never saw finer people than these. Every profession was represented there from the simple worker to the university professor. From them we learned that preparations for our arrival had been started three weeks before von [sic] Rath was shot [...] We, dressed in nothing warmer than a pajama suit, had to march and stand outside according to the daily routine. Snow storms and icy rain came. People died on an average of 30 a week during the rollcalls and while marching [. . .] There was a hospital and two S.S. doctors, but it was impossible to get into this hospital unless you had a fever of 103 to 104 degrees, and then it was generally too late.[32]

The nights were as terrible as the days:

> [We] fell into the straw. We had to lie in bed like sardines in a can. It was so narrow that if you turned, ten others had to turn, too. All the night searchlights went round and round. We were allowed to write twice a month. One postcard with ten lines, one letter with 24 lines. The first postcard was dictated. It started, "I am healthy and in good spirits." Naturally all mail was censored, and the answers were half postcards, or letters with lines cut. People at home were careful with their letters, but the censors were bored and had their fun cutting postcards up so that you couldn't read them.[33]

The man who had arranged for Karl's deportation to Dachau was called Franz Novak; he had been a Nazi from the very beginning. In 1934 he had taken part in the failed putsch against Dollfuss and was subsequently stripped of his Austrian citizenship. Like many Austrian National Socialists, he saw the Anschluss as an opportunity for revenge. At last he could get even with those in Vienna who had stood in his way, and Jews and socialists were right at the top of his hit list. In autumn 1938 Novak was working for the office for Jewish emigration, which was under the SS and housed in Palais Rothschild in Vienna. Although the office had accelerated emigration to begin with (not without having first taken the assets of those wanting to leave), its tactics changed after the November pogrom. Male prisoners were transported from Vienna to Dachau. Novak's time had come. He impressed his commanders by tirelessly sending packed carriages to the concentration camp. His inexhaustible talent for organisation and his high success rate delighted his superior Adolf Eichmann in particular. He would later take Novak to Prague, to open another office for Jewish emigration there, based on the Viennese model. As the historian Eva Holpfer has shown, in Prague Novak worked his way up to become Eichmann's "transport specialist".[34]

One of Novak's Dachau transports contained the famous Austrian satirist Fritz Grünbaum. Grünbaum was already sixty when he arrived at Dachau, and therefore had a much poorer chance of survival than a young man like Karl. Although Grünbaum was not in good health from the outset, many of his witticisms from Dachau have been preserved. When once again food was rationed, he said, "If you can't afford it, you shouldn't keep prisoners."[35]

It would not have been long before Karl found out that the famous Grünbaum was in the camp. In his 1939 report on Dachau he mentions no names, however, to avoid putting anyone in danger, but writes simply: "I met a lot of former Austrian government cabinet ministers. There were people from every place in Germany. One heard every dialect spoken there [. . .] During the time I was there transports came every day from the 'freed' Sudetenland."[36] As with Karl, Grünbaum's friends did all they could to get him out of there. Friedrich Torberg wrote to a Jewish journalist:

> According to the latest news that [Grünbaum's] wife could send abroad from Vienna, there is one opportunity to save him: he must be procured an affidavit as well as [. . .] a work contract for the USA. It is a quite flagrant case of gratuitous harassment by the Nazi authorities, who are trying to make the usual practice – immediate evacuation of Reich territory as a condition of release – particularly difficult for him, and so have stipulated further that G must, as they say, "give a guarantee to leave for America without delay".[37]

Who in America was going to give a sixty-year-old cabaret artist a work contract? In this respect Otto had it slightly easier with his twenty-one-year-old brother. Otto and Torberg would meet after the war – both were keen on the same woman[38] – but in 1938 they had a much more serious problem, that of trying desperately to get someone out of Dachau. Cobbling together money to buy a prisoner's freedom seemed to be one option, but until now it has been hard to ascertain how often this happened, and how likely were the chances of success. Even the bureaucracy-obsessed National Socialists did not keep a record of such income and those receiving bribes certainly wouldn't have kept notes about under-the-table payments. In any case, Grünbaum's wife would no longer have had the means to pay. Although Fritz Grünbaum came from an affluent family of art dealers and had owned a large collection of Egon

Schiele paintings as well as some by Dürer, everything had gone. The Nazis had entirely looted the family possessions and made some good foreign exchange transactions with them.[39] Even if Torberg and his American friends had managed to organise money or a work contract, it is doubtful whether the authorities would ever have permitted Grünbaum to emigrate. He had been a witness to Nazi art theft, and furthermore his sharp tongue would have seriously damaged the regime abroad. In the end Grünbaum was so badly tortured that in 1941 he tried to take his own life, and ultimately died from the consequences of this suicide attempt.

Karl was not famous, and he had Otto and the Dodsons, who left no stone unturned in their attempt to free him from Dachau. In January 1939 the miracle happened:

But one morning came when I heard my number called out. I was released. I couldn't believe it, it was too sudden. I cried like a little boy and couldn't stop. At 5 o'clock in the afternoon the commander came and made a speech to us who were leaving. His last words were: "If any one of you dares say a single word about this camp while you are in Germany, we will bring you back here, and I promise you, that you won't get out of here a second time. If you say anything abroad, it makes no difference to us because no one will believe what you tell about your experiences in camp." [. . .] We marched out of the camp, accompanied by two storm troopers.[40]

Karl had to change trains several times before arriving at Willy's in Vienna. He must have looked terrible – shaven-headed and emaciated – but Willy was extremely relieved to see him again. He immediately sent a telegram to Alice and went shopping. Over the next few weeks Karl would live with him rent-free, and Willy looked after him as best he could. Every day Karl had to leave the apartment to register at the local police station. He now had one month to leave the country. The first letter he wrote after his release was to Alice:

Friday evening

Dear Mother! At the risk that this letter doesn't get to you (seeing as the telegram I sent to you immediately came back) I'm writing you the first letter I am able to write. I arrived in Vienna yesterday morning. I'm in good health! Naturally, I feel terrible for making you all so dreadfully worried and causing you so much trouble. It really wasn't negligence on my part, but fate. It is impossible to describe what Robert [Urbach] and all other relatives here, as well as Bobby [Otto] in the USA, have done to bring me back. I have very little news of you and I hope for a more detailed report soon. I have a medical examination on 15th February. On 17th I'll probably go to Rotterdam [. . .] I'm sorry not to write more, but I cannot. The change is too sudden, I'm too nervous still. I'm shaking too much from the shock. Hopefully it will get better soon. Many kisses, Karli[41]

In the meantime, Otto was busy arranging Karl's emigration:

We've taken every possible step and I hope you'll soon be well enough to enjoy life again. Everybody is constantly asking about you and your Viennese friends, and they hope to be able to do something for them all soon. The American consulate has been informed via Senator McNary[42] and I hope I can send you a welcome letter from him. I'll send money soon.

Affectionately, Otto[43]

Karl was one of many prisoners suddenly released from Dachau in early 1939. As all prisoner files were destroyed,[44] the only evidence of him in the Dachau memorial archive are his prisoner number, 28194, and the dates of his internment and release.[45] Decades later all manner of theories as to why Karl was released were still circulating in the Urbach family. One popular version concerned his cousin Anni, the daughter of Marie and Ignaz Urbach, who had taken his life when his bank was on the verge of collapse. Anni was a very attractive Viennese woman. Because her mother was "Aryan" and supposedly knew people with connections to the party, it was claimed that Anni used her feminine charms on a high-ranking Nazi official who took pity on her, leading to Karl's release.[46] It is unsurprising that this narrative became a family legend at the end of the 1970s, as it is strongly reminiscent of the television series *Holocaust*, in which Meryl Streep sleeps with an SS officer to save her Jewish husband. It is rather unlikely that Anni was able to exert much influence from Vienna, however; the truth was probably much more prosaic. When Karl vanished, Otto engaged the services of the Viennese lawyer Dr Hardt, who could prove that Karl now had an affidavit and permission to emigrate, and it is possible that this triggered his release. It may be that Hardt had to pay a bribe too, as suggested by this letter from Otto to Karl in February 1939:

> Yesterday I received a cable from Poldi [their Czech cousin Leopold] in which he tells me that the lawyer fee for you comes to 1,500 dollars. I don't have this amount and right now I don't know what I can do to get the money together. I don't know if the bill is from Dr Hardt or someone else. It seems unlikely that Dr Hardt would charge such a crazy amount.[47]

In the end Otto or Poldi must have managed to get hold of the money. It would be the last help that Poldi could give to his favourite cousin Karl. When Hitler occupied Czechoslovakia in March 1939, the Czech patriot committed suicide.

The Jewish Community in Vienna gave Karl a generous subsidy for his boat ticket,[48] and on 17 February 1939 he was finally able to board the train for the Netherlands. He really liked Holland: "The whole country seemed to express freedom and liberty. It was hard to understand that people could be nice again – nice to a Jew."[49] From Rotterdam he sailed with the Holland-America Line, and during the weeks he spent at sea he felt as if he were in one of those elegant Fred Astaire films he had seen in Paula Sieber's Palastkino:

Dear Mother!

I received your lovely letter from Tuesday [. . .] This is my first day on board ship and I'm sitting in the smoking room after an extraordinary breakfast. You won't believe it, but there's another K. Urbach travelling with me in the cabin, the nephew of Professor Urbach from Prague. We laughed at how we found each other. The five days I spent in Holland were wonderful. I was in The Hague and Amsterdam too, and in truth I felt sad to have to move on, but one marvel follows on from another. Life is great again. You ask me what I went through. Hell. Nothing else can happen to me in life, because it cannot get any worse. But I am not able to write in detail about all those terrible things. My brain turns to a mush whenever I think about it. Maybe it will be different later [. . .] Most of the passengers are emigrants, and I haven't yet had the opportunity to get to know anyone apart from Kurt Urbach [. . .] I am very happy that you seem to have found what you wanted [Alice had received an offer to run a Jewish children's hostel] and that you are happy. Although the salary is absurdly low, that isn't so important if you're happy. If things are tight it shouldn't be too hard to send you a few dollars. I am deliberately not writing about the future, let's see what comes. [The main thing] is that we all want to be together [. . .] I still cannot believe that I'm free, it really is a wonderful feeling. The only bad thing, really terrible, is the many who have remained behind.

All the best, Karl[50]

Suddenly Karl was a young man again; he simply wanted to block out everything that had happened to him. And sometimes he succeeded. Shortly before the ship docked in New York, he wrote to Alice:

6th March 1939

I have eaten and am eating huge amounts, and I really am recovering very quickly here. My hair has grown a little more so now one cannot tell where I have come from, although I'm proud of Dachau. For the fact that I survived it [. . .] Life on board is ideal, of course. Cinema, games, dancing, flirting, reading. I have not been bored for a minute [. . .] Kurt Urbach and I have been flirting at every opportunity. Everybody knows the two Urbachs on board [. . .] Everything is as one sees it in a film [. . .] But leaping from one continent to another is like a fairy tale [. . .] The atmosphere and the company on board the ship are great and relaxed, there is no stuffiness [. . .] Yesterday there was a very beautiful Purim celebration on board. The Dutch and the Americans (Christians) joined in, as did the captain and the officers. It felt good. The room was decorated with the US flag and the Dutch and Jewish national colours. Oh, how good it is to be free again. I just have to get used to it again, for I am constantly surprised that I can move freely.[51]

Like all immigrants, Karl first stepped onto American soil at Ellis Island.[52] The Viennese actor Leon Askin describes in his memoir how confusing he found the place. He recalled old newspaper photographs showing masses of shabby, poor people. In his mind Ellis Island was chaotic and dirty, and so he was surprised to see how orderly everything was, and that people were constantly cleaning around him. What struck him most of all, however, was to find a Jewish policeman there. He had never seen that before; back home a Jew would never have been able to become a police officer, and Askin concluded that he had arrived in paradise.[53]

After spending a few days with Otto's friends in New York, Karl took the bus across the country to Portland,[54] where Otto arranged for his Reed College friend Frances Murphy to interview his brother. He was determined that the world should find out what was happening in the concentration camps. In the battle for American public opinion, it seemed particularly important to emphasise that it was not only Jews who were being incarcerated by the regime. Karl had been impressed by the courage of the political prisoners in Dachau, and this was included in the article. Murphy anonymised the text to avoid putting anyone in danger. But even though the article filled an entire page of the *Oregonian*, the state's leading newspaper, it had little effect. Several other American newspapers published eyewitness reports at the time, but they were powerless against the influence of the American isolationists.[55] These included rich men on the America First Committee, like the aviation hero Charles Lindbergh and the automobile king Henry Ford. Both were convinced anti-Semites who believed that, with their horror propaganda, the Jews were trying to force America into another war. The Prussian crown prince Wilhelm had expressed this view back in 1933 in the *Herald Tribune*, and the isolationists were happy to align themselves with this illustrious mouthpiece for the National Socialists.[56] Because of such propaganda and the pressure of the isolationists, America neither raised its immigration quota nor developed a rescue plan, as Great Britain had with its "domestic permits". The idea of an American Kindertransport failed too.

Karl soon found work as a roofer and auxiliary fireman to finance his studies at Reed College, and tried to forget the concentration camp. It was only in 1969 that Franz Novak, who had organised Karl's and Fritz Grünbaum's deportation to Dachau, was finally sentenced to five years in prison by an Austrian court. Adolf Eichmann's "transport specialist" showed no remorse.

10: THE WINDERMERE CHILDREN

"On the Continent people have good food,
in England they have good table manners."
George Mikes[1]

In January 1939 Mrs van der Elst decided that her attempts at slimming could not succeed while she had a pastry chef like Alice working at Grantham Castle. The risk of her secretly slipping into the pantry at night was simply too great, and so van der Elst decreed that the Viennese woman had to go. Alice was not particularly bothered by her dismissal. Viennese cuisine was by now very popular in Britain, and emigrants who dropped the word "Austria" into their job applications had a good chance of finding work. Suddenly Viennese cooks were everywhere. One advertisement read: "Pastry Cook (Viennese) looking for position. Experienced cook." Another ran: "2 Austrians want situation as cook and parlourmaid. Small family. No rough."[2]

An authentic Viennese star cook like Alice found another

job straight away, of course, this time working for Lady Eden, a sister-in-law of Anthony Eden. The Eden family had no reservations about Jewish refugees. On the contrary, Anthony Eden had rejected the British policy of appeasement, resigning as foreign secretary in 1938. In Alice's eyes, Eden seemed to be one of the few politicians who understood that you could not negotiate with a "band of gangsters" like the Nazis. Working for his sister-in-law was for Alice an honour, but soon afterwards she was poached by a London doctor's family on an even better deal.[3] Living in London seemed to her a very attractive proposition, for in March 1939 the Austrian Centre in Westbourne Terrace had opened its doors in the capital. Besides Austrian "food and drink at the cheapest prices", you could read German books there, have your shoes resoled inexpensively, and above all attend lectures. For a small entrance fee, one could listen to emigrants who back home were luminaries in their fields giving talks on art, science, music and literature.[4]

In her free time Alice went to the Austrian Centre as often as she could. After the horrors of recent months, her situation seemed to be gradually improving. She had a secure job in London, Karl had been liberated, and her brother Felix had the prospect of a visa for Britain too. Despite this she felt guilty; her sisters Karoline, Sidonie and Helene were still stuck in Vienna.[5] Alice was keen to do something more useful than cooking for rich Londoners. She recalled the information brochure from Woburn House, which read:

> *Above all*, please realise that the Jewish Community is relying on you – on each and every one of you – to uphold

in this country the highest Jewish qualities, to maintain dignity, and to help and serve others [. . .] Use your energies and special skill to help those even more unhappy than yourself – the lonely Refugee Children, the Aged and the Sick, in your neighbourhood.[6]

When she received an enquiry as to whether she would be willing to run a hostel for refugee children in Newcastle, she wasted no time thinking about it.

Leo Rapp was a boy from Munich. When he came to Britain his mother packed such practical items as Lederhosen, pillowcases and shoes that were several sizes too big. Most importantly, however, Frau Rapp was keen that Leo should continue his schoolwork in Britain, and so she packed several textbooks and dictionaries as well as some measuring callipers. And she included an album of family photographs in case he felt homesick.[7]

There was nothing particularly striking about Leo's luggage. Only the outsize shoes suggested a protracted absence, and then there were also two unusual items in the suitcase: a phylactery and a prayer book. Not only did Frau Rapp want Leo to study while abroad; she also hoped that he would not forget his Jewish faith.

It is estimated that 1.5 million children died in the Holocaust. Leo Rapp was lucky. He was one of the 10,000 boys and girls who were able to escape to England. Whereas the USA accepted only 1,400 unaccompanied children between 1934 and 1945, Britain responded more generously. On 21 November 1938, twelve days after Kristallnacht, the House of Commons decided to allow Jewish children to enter the country without a visa. Thanks to the involvement of British and Dutch individuals, the Kindertransport could now begin. The story of this rescue operation has often been told;[8] amidst all the tragedy it is a success. The majority of these children were later to make something of their lives. Almost all set off on careers and started families.

We know the contents of some of their suitcases because they had to be itemised on printed forms. One boy brought some colourful playing cards depicting the Brandenburg Gate and various German landmarks. Other children packed their favourite cuddly toys, as in Judith Kerr's famous novel *When Hitler Stole Pink Rabbit*. Many toys went missing over the years, but hardly anyone lost their family photographs. They reminded the children of two key things: that their parents loved them and fervently hoped they would be able to embark on a better life. And so the children just had to plough on. To give up was not an option.

All the same, it would be naïve to assume that these children had a straight path to a normal life; in fact the opposite was the case. The war years were an emotional roller coaster, and some children were occasionally afflicted by severe psychological problems, which their foster families and carers had to deal with. Alice and Paula Sieber were among these care workers; they could hardly have chosen a more difficult job.

According to Peter Sieber's research, the idea for the refugee hostel came about after Kristallnacht in November 1938, when Woburn House asked Jewish communities in Britain to take in persecuted children from Germany and Austria. A small neighbourhood group in Newcastle saw the appeal and acted immediately. They were led by Mr Summerfield, a Jewish jeweller with a shop in the city. He was a completely ordinary man who did something extraordinary. He founded a private children's home overnight, helped by his wife and friends in Newcastle: Rita Jackson, who was already working for the Women's Voluntary Service; Mrs Rita Freedman and her husband Dr Wallace Freedman; Nolly and Ike Collins; and Mrs Wilkes. The families lived only a few streets apart, and the planning took place in their sitting rooms. They were an energetic group who wanted to make things happen quickly and informally; they did not even bother to take minutes of their meetings.

Their first step was to appeal for donations in local synagogues. With the help of two rabbis they were able to raise enough money to rent a house in Tynemouth: 55 Percy Park. The small town of Tynemouth lay outside Newcastle and was therefore cheaper, but even so Percy Park was not in good condition. Peter Sieber described how the committee members asked all their friends and acquaintances for help: "Artisans were found to bring the house up to standard, adapt it for so many people, decorate it, make sure it could be heated [. . .] Members of the community brought everything they could spare, vans belonging to Jewish-owned businesses took it to Tynemouth."[9] These items included curtains, rugs, twenty beds and cots, bedclothes, and cutlery and crockery marked with the letters M and F (*milchig* and *fleischig* – dairy and meat), for the home was to be run along kosher principles. Although Newcastle had suffered badly from the economic depression of the 1930s, the committee managed to collect enough food supplies, clothes, coats and shoes for the children.

When the renovations were completed, they had to decide whether the house would take in boys or girls. At the time, a mixed children's home would have been regarded as morally unacceptable, so long discussions ensued as to who most urgently needed help. Back then many unemployed young girls had to fend for themselves on the streets of Newcastle. Summerfield's group feared that the same might happen to the Jewish refugee girls, and in the worst-case scenario they could be abused. The decision was taken, therefore, to offer a home to up to twenty-four girls.

But who would take on the task of running the hostel? Nobody in Newcastle was going to volunteer for such a post. The committee asked Woburn House in London for advice and was told that there were several immigrants who might be suitable for the job, but nobody more so than Alice Urbach. Rita Jackson travelled to London to meet Alice, and the two women hit it off at once.[10] The minimal salary represented a pay-cut, but Alice recalled the advice from the Woburn House information booklet and said yes.

It was an ambitious appointment to say the least. Apart from her cookery skills, Alice had no relevant experience for such a job. Although Otto had sometimes made her despair, she had a very idealised notion of children and imagined that girls would certainly be easier to look after than her unruly son had been. Her only concern was over the size of the group, and so Alice asked the committee if she could bring another carer with her – her old friend Paula Sieber. After having fled from

Vienna, Paula was in a bad state mentally. Like all Jewish cinemas, her Palastkino had been Aryanised immediately after Anschluss. According to *Kinojournal*, by October 1938 fifty-five Viennese cinemas had already been given to "deserving party comrades". By December of the same year Aryanisation was complete save for two cinemas.[11]

With the expropriation of her cinema, Paula was deprived of her only source of income, but this was merely one of her struggles in Vienna. What crushed her the most was the November pogrom. Plunderers had broken into her apartment in Schreyvogelgasse, smashing objects and forcing her to pack her bags. She then had to overcome a number of obstacles before she was able to emigrate with her son Peter. But her elder sister Selma, with whom she had run the cinema, stayed behind. After such traumatic experiences Paula would have given anything to lose herself for ever in the fantasy world of a British cinema, but Alice would not allow Paula to give up. Although aware of her friend's traumas, she was convinced that Paula needed a new purpose and could be invaluable to the children's home. She knew her as a proficient businesswoman and organiser, skills that would surely come in handy. Alice proposed that Paula would look after the administrative side, while she would be matron.

Both Paula and Alice were capable women who had learned to work hard, but from today's perspective they appear completely unsuited to running a home. Neither had ever looked after a group of children, let alone undertaken any relevant study or training. This would prove a shortcoming, as the children they now had to care for were frightened and deeply unhappy, having been wrenched from familiar surroundings to live in a country whose language they didn't understand. With their naïve enthusiasm, Alice and Paula thoroughly underestimated the challenge, as had the Newcastle committee. Mr Summerfield and his friends had assured them that their help would only be needed temporarily. In a few months the parents would come to fetch their children and the hostel would be closed. In summer 1939 nobody imagined that these "few months" would stretch to seven years.

Peter Sieber was seventeen when he arrived in Newcastle with his mother. Being a boy, he was not allowed to stay in the hostel and instead had to live with one of the committee families nearby. Despite this he gave Paula and Alice as much help as he could. In his report Peter Sieber lists all the girls who came to the hostel in summer 1939.[12] One of them was nine-year-old Lisl Scherzer from Vienna. Now Alisa Tennenbaum, she lives in Israel and a picture of the children's home hangs on the wall of her sitting room. She talks with enthusiasm of her time in England, although her route there was anything but straightforward.

Lisl's parents owned a grocery in Vienna. Like Karl, Lisl's father Moshe Scherzer was sent to Dachau in November 1938. At the end of January 1939 he was released on condition he leave the German Reich within a month. Lisl describes the horror of seeing her father when he returned from the camp: "A thin man with no hair. I thought, this is not my father. He was crying." But Herr Scherzer gritted his teeth and secured Lisl one of the hotly contested places on the Kindertransport programme. On 22 August 1939, together with many other children from Vienna, she was on a train heading for the Netherlands, from where she took a boat to Harwich. After another rail journey she got on an underground train for the first time in her life. When Lisl finally arrived at King's Cross, a member of staff from Woburn House was waiting for her. The lady gave her some fruit, put her on another train and told her to get out at Newcastle.[13] Until that point Lisl had been travelling in a large group of children, but now she was on her own. She felt frightened, and she got into a panic on the train:

> My mother had given me a dictionary, English–German, but I didn't know where to get off and began to cry. A man sitting opposite me went down the whole train and asked everyone, "Can you speak German?" [. . .] I could not speak the language and did not know how to thank him. He found an old lady and a priest and they said to the man, "Why are you shouting for someone who speaks German?" And he said, "This little girl is sitting here crying all the time and needs to speak German." And the lady understood me. And I asked, "What is Newcastle? I have to get off at Newcastle but the train does not stop." And she said, "You got on the train in London and Newcastle will come up in an hour." They were very nice and they were heading to Edinburgh but they got off at Newcastle just for me and found the people who were to pick me up.

Paula Sieber was waiting for Lisl and the two took a taxi to Tynemouth: "I was in the taxi and came to a street and it was all dark. I was shivering and scared, I thought they might just have invented this hostel and kill me and throw me in the river. But all the girls were standing at the entrance to greet me."[14] Lisl was relieved to see other children. Alice had baked her best biscuits to allay the girl's fears, and Lisl soon calmed down. But the biscuit trick didn't work with all the children. Peter Sieber notes how difficult the first few weeks were for newcomers: "Some could not stop crying [. . .] The older ones were mainly silent [. . .] Several had nightmares and Alice Urbach and Paula Sieber were up much of the night in the first weeks."[15] The nights were hard, but the days were scarcely better. The children were permanently waiting for news from their parents: "Every morning's post was a ritual of hope and disappointment."[16]

On 29 August 1939, just a few days after the arrival of the last child, Hitler issued his territorial ultimatum to Poland. Britain had promised military support to the Polish government and everyone could guess what might happen now. The radio had been on permanently at the hostel since 29 August. Looking back, Peter Sieber writes: "The children and the matrons with parents and other close relatives still in Germany did not eat, not sleep."[17]

On 1 September Hitler invaded Poland and Britain had to respond. Despite the tension, Alice tried to give the hostel a touch of normality. Lisl's tenth birthday was around the corner and Alice planned a special celebration. In her cookbook she had written extensively about which cakes, ice creams, waffles and sandwiches were ideal for children's birthdays: "Young people have an astonishing capacity for eating sandwiches." She had also emphasised the importance of decoration: "A colourful, festive table, a little present for each child [. . .] and a well-thought-out programme of entertainment will create the best atmosphere."[18]

In the end the entertainment had to be cancelled, but everyone remembered Lisl's tenth birthday on 3 September 1939. At 11.15 Prime Minister Neville Chamberlain gave a short speech on the BBC, in which he explained that Hitler had not responded to the British demands to withdraw his troops from Poland. For this reason Great Britain was now at war with Germany. Shortly afterwards sirens wailed up and down the country, a deafening sound they would all soon get used to. Lisl's memory of the day begins with the sirens:

> All of a sudden sirens go off. I said, "Oh, it's music for my birthday!" And Ruth said, "Are you stupid? These are sirens." I had never heard sirens in Vienna [. . .] The matrons said, "Girls, there is a very important announcement on the radio from the King, come down and listen." And it was the speech that England is now at war.[19]

For everyone at the home it was a catastrophe. Only a few parents had managed to escape to Britain – Lisl's and Helga's fathers, and Ilse's and Edith's mothers.[20] The parents of the other children, as well as Alice's and Paula's sisters, were now trapped.

Everything changed at the hostel after Lisl's birthday. Initially the British were expecting a German invasion, and both Alice and Paula were gripped by anxiety over this. They got rid of all the German books and ordered the children to tear up their letters. If the Nazis came, there should be nothing to betray that the girls were from Germany and Austria. It was an eccentric overreaction, for if Wehrmacht soldiers had in fact turned up in Newcastle they would hardly have been taken in by Paula's and Alice's thick accents (not to mention the children's few broken words of English). The British, however, were not only alarmed at the prospect of invaders; they were also unsettled by the Germans already in the country. Any one of them could be a spy. Every German and Austrian had to anticipate, therefore, being interned as an "enemy alien". For Alice this was not a problem; the Home Office gave her an exemption because her two sons lived in America and she was an "anti-Nazi".[21]

Decades later Lisl recalled the panic that dominated those days: "We are now enemy aliens. Only speak English [outside the hostel]. One English lady [. . .] came in the afternoon to teach us English."[22]

Not every German refugee received such intensive English tutoring. In 1941 the London exile newspaper, *Zeitspiegel*, set up a prize for the best "refugee English" jokes. As an example, it provided this exchange, which is reminiscent of the well-known dialogue in *Casablanca*:

"How much the cauliflower?"

"Sevenpence."

"Such much? Too much! For sevenpence I can become a cauliflower round the corner!"[23]

Humour aside, Alice was determined that "her" children should not speak English like this. Although she still made grammatical errors herself, her English vocabulary was extensive. She insisted that the children start attending an English school only a few days after their arrival. Not many people at the time were aware of what is today known as the "immersion method" – being plunged fully into a different language and culture. Alice had come across this idea at her Viennese language school, but the children found it taxing. Dasha, who was from Czechoslovakia, felt particularly out of her depth. Paula Sieber spoke a few words of Czech, but none of the other children did. Now Dasha had to learn English very quickly, and nobody was able to translate the words into her mother tongue. Lisl too was disoriented. On her first day at Priory School in Tynemouth she did not understand a single word:

> The first lesson was geometry, I did not understand anything. The teacher comes to my desk, I had not written anything. The teacher pulls me up by my ear and puts me in front of the class, she has a cane and says give me your hand. But a girl gets up and says to the teacher, "She came with the people from the home," and the teacher puts down her cane. And she said, "Your address?" I say, "55 Percy Park." She embraced me and later helped me with my lessons.[24]

Alice was very keen that her charges should not become outsiders, and she aimed to do all she could to integrate them. She always returned to point 5 of the Woburn House information booklet: "The Englishman [. . .] values good manners far more than he values the evidence of wealth. You will find that he says 'Thank you' for the smallest service."[25] Alice attached great importance to good English manners and dressing smartly. The children should never look scruffy and down at heel. Paula Sieber taught them to mend holes in their stockings

223

straightaway, and she was forever patching up items of clothing. For the time, the children were always dressed immaculately.

Apart from the Newcastle committee, the girls were also visited by official Jewish aid organisations who opened files on them. These have been accessible since 2018.[26] They shed light, for example, on how often the children were asked about their physical and mental condition. The file on Margot (b. 1924) goes through to 1947. Her father was a butcher in Frankfurt, her mother a housewife. Her health was judged to be good, but she was anaemic and had to drink certain tonics. As she was the eldest girl at the home and desperate to be with girls of her own age, it was arranged for her to meet other refugee girls from Danzig (now Gdańsk). Over the years Alice and Paula got in touch several times with the Jewish Refugees Committee to address problems of individual children. At the same time they had to fight for the hostel's survival.

The winter of 1939–40 was dreadfully cold. The pipes burst in the old house in Tynemouth and the entire place was flooded: "Mrs Urbach and Mrs Sieber worked hard with all of us to try and clear up the damaging floods," Ruth later wrote, "but it was obvious that we could not remain in the house."[27] Without heating or running water the children had to be housed with families in the area. Ruth was so unhappy with where she had been placed that she ran back to Alice and Paula a few days later. The two matrons took her in and finally managed to get the heating working again in the house. All the other girls could return now too, but the harsh weather led to another problem: the children caught whooping cough and flu. To reduce the risk of infection, the matrons now placed great emphasis on hygiene. In her cookbook Alice had written: "All the housewife's work is aimed at combating three enemies: hunger, cold and dirt."[28] A fourth enemy soon appeared on the scene. No matter how clean the hostel, it could not prevent the children bringing back lice from school. Under protest they had to put up with being given short, boyish haircuts.

The lice were bothersome, but things became really critical when one of the girls contracted diphtheria, and soon half of them were in hospital.[29] Because she had been married to a doctor, Alice was able to spot illnesses quickly. Max may have been a lousy husband but he'd imparted basic medical knowledge to his wife, which was now invaluable. After the diphtheria had passed, Alice also saved a girl with a ruptured appendix.[30]

She often found herself calling for an ambulance, but the children's emotional problems were harder to diagnose than a tummy ache. Alice's guide in the labyrinth of raising children were the theories of her Viennese acquaintance, Anna Freud. In 1936 Anna Freud had started a kindergarten for working-class Viennese children. Her timing proved to be poor. After Anschluss she had to flee to London with her father and start from scratch again. She founded a new institution, the Hampstead War Nurseries, which took in the children of single mothers living in the East End of London.[31] When war broke out Anna Freud was also one of the experts who advised on how best to evacuate children from bombed cities to the countryside. Should they live with foster families or in homes? Freud's position on this was clear. "Taking children from parents and 'billeting' them like soldiers is to be decried," she said. In her view, boys and girls ought to be housed in school groups, separated by ages.[32] Following this advice, Alice and Paula divided "their" children into three groups: big, medium and small.

Another advantage of accommodating the children in groups was, according to Freud, that they had better eating habits. She had not been aware of any eating disorders in her nursery, whereas she gauged they were fairly common when children lived with families. Alice had a similar experience. Some children in her home later developed neuroses, but there was never any incidence of eating disorders.[33] In her cookbook Alice had emphasised how important it was to eat together: "A meal is often the only occasion when all family members come together and this brief period should be a restful pause in the family's daily life."[34]

Alice attached particular importance to breakfast. Every morning she served the children Swiss muesli, a speciality unknown in Britain at the time:[35]

> It is extremely important that children have enough time for breakfast, and that they don't leave home without it for fear of being late. Many cases of so-called school nerves, where children throw up a breakfast that has been eaten in haste, or refuse to eat at all, could be avoided if the children had sufficient peace and time for this first important meal of the day.[36]

The Aga cooker that Alice used became the focal point of the house, even earning its own nickname: "Jo". For the girls, Jo became another family member and they collected wood to keep him going. Alice spent many hours every day standing at Jo, and was pleased to see the older children develop an interest in cooking. Once a month some of the older girls were allowed to help out. Lisl was especially lucky as her turn came on a Thursday, which is when they baked yeast cake. To this day Lisl still bakes yeast cake on Thursdays. Cooking and eating together were important for the girls.

Another rule of Anna Freud's adopted by Alice and Paula was to involve the parents as much as possible. In her studies Freud had discovered that children in homes who were regularly visited by their mothers were better adjusted than others. During the war many of these mothers worked long shifts in factories, nonetheless Freud encouraged them to come by as often as possible. She also made great efforts to find male role models for the children. As the fathers had been conscripted into the army, or had left the family for other reasons, Anna persuaded the air-raid wardens and other men in her neighbourhood to spend time with the children.[37]

Alice tried something similar. Four of the children at the home had parents who lived in England. Lisl's father served in the Royal Pioneer Corps, and Alice invited him to come to dinner at the home as often as he could. Lisl was proud of him: "My dad said, 'I am the only father so write me all the names of the girls and their birthdates and I'll bring them a present.' [. . .] He was a father for all twenty girls."[38]

Helga's father became involved in the children's daily lives too. When a nearby hotel was seeking a chef, he applied for the post. He had never cooked in his life, but Alice managed to prepare him perfectly for the interview with a crash course.

He got the job and was able to continue visiting the girls.[39] Ilse's mother Margarethe also tried to keep in touch with her daughter. In Vienna she had attended one of Alice's cookery courses, and this proved to have been worth it in every respect. She would later tell her granddaughter that she'd survived because of her baking skills. She got a job in service with the affluent Shand Kydd family on Hayling Island, where she baked her way through the war.[40]

Despite the adverse circumstances, the adults tried to give the children at least some sense of stability, and this was partly why they resolved to find another location for the children's hostel.

Newcastle was home to industrial plants vital to the war effort, and these became targets for the German Luftwaffe in summer 1940. Now the sirens wailed every night. One of the young children at the hostel, Lore, recalled how they used to be carried, half-asleep, into the air-raid shelter in the cellar. Between July 1940 and December 1941, four hundred civilians were killed in the "Newcastle Blitz". Alice, Paula and the Jewish Committee decided to evacuate the entire hostel to Windermere in the Lake District. Their new address was like the famous home of Winnie-the-Pooh — not the "Hundred Acre Wood", but "Southwood, The Wood, Windermere".

It would be hard to find a greater contrast in Britain than the industrial city of Newcastle and the small town of Windermere in the Lake District, a tourist paradise where people allow themselves to be transported back to the 19th century by reading the Lakes poets. Although the girls were not familiar with the poetry of William Wordsworth or Samuel Taylor Coleridge, they did know Winnie-the-Pooh. They didn't care that Pooh and Christopher Robin lived in a wood in Sussex; they believed their wood in Windermere and Pooh Bear's were one and the same. No sirens wailed in Windermere, and the house they now lived in was not dissimilar to Christopher Robin's: a large, enchanted villa close to the wood. Rhododendrons bloomed by the entrance and all the bedrooms looked out onto a large garden with a little stream flowing through it. Eighty years on, Lisl still describes the house with a certain owner's pride, talking of the large veranda, the dining room and living room, and how each child had their own bed and desk.[41]

The children immediately set about exploring the area, going for walks and swims (not all the girls enjoyed this – Ruth described how she almost drowned in Lake Windermere). The film buff Paula Sieber saw to it that they could go to the local cinema as often as they liked. During the day they attended nearby St Mary's Church School, which was free. "When the older ones got to the age of fifteen," Lisl says, "the people came from the committee and they said we don't have money to send 20 of you to university [. . .] Start thinking what you want to do when you leave school."[42]

This was not unexpected. The Woburn House information brochure said that boys would mainly be trained in "agriculture and handicrafts", while girls' training would focus on "nursing and domestic service". The brochure then advised: "Please do not expect these young people to be trained as doctors, dentists, lawyers, professors etc. There are already far too many Professional men amongst Refugees for the needs of today."[43]

The refugee children in Windermere. Lisl Scherzer is in the back row, second from right

It was a bitter disappointment for the children at the Windermere home not to be able to continue with a formal education. Some of them came from solid middle-class families, and in normal circumstances they would have gone to a Gymnasium, comparable to the grammar school with its emphasis on academic learning. In England and Wales,[44] however, schooling was only free until the age of fourteen. In 1938, 80 per cent of children in England and Wales left school at this age, and only one in a hundred could embark on university study – thanks to private schools or grants. Although a new bill was brought to Parliament in 1944, proposing free schooling until the age of eighteen, this law was not enacted until after the war and so refugee children couldn't benefit from it. Most had to leave school like the majority of their English and Welsh counterparts.

Some girls, Ruth for example, found relatives who financed their continued education. Elfi and Lisl were not as lucky and both began an apprenticeship. Whereas Elfi felt unhappy about this, Lisl looked forward to learning a practical job. Paula had taught her how to sew and she wanted to become a dressmaker. Alice, who had always urged the girls to study hard, was horrified at the premature end of their school careers. In the early 1930s, as a member of the Austrian Women's Party, she had championed women's rights, and all her life she would regret not having gone to university. She admired women like her sister Helene, who had studied, and of course Cordelia, Otto's friend from Reed College. And now, instead of learning foreign languages and maths, "her" children had to cycle to Windermere to do apprenticeships. By now Alice knew only too well what a life in a badly paid job felt like. In 1941 she turned fifty-five and the physical strains and responsibilities of recent years had left their mark on her. Alice's hair had turned snow-white, and even though outwardly she appeared to be brimming with energy, she was worn out. She never stopped thinking of Vienna and her former life.

Homesickness afflicted everyone in the house and the children suffered most. With each year of the war, the likelihood that they would ever see their parents again decreased. Alice and Paula believed that these fears were best countered by suppressing them, but this would prove a fallacy. During the war the girls developed worrying patterns of behaviour, beginning with Marion. She was one of the older girls in the group and had arrived at the home deeply traumatised. When asked a question she would often fall silent mid-sentence and appeared to be miles away. Alice thought she might be suffering from "petit mal", the term used back then to describe the bouts of absence that occurred in epileptics. Paula and Alice did not know how they could help Marion, and were relieved when the girl showed an interest in a secretarial course. To improve her concentration she was allowed to work alone every afternoon in Paula Sieber's office. After a few days Paula noticed that money was missing from the office. As there were other cases of theft in the house at the time, they questioned Marion. She admitted to having stolen the money, and when asked what she'd done with it, she simply said that she had burned it. However bizarre this sounded, the matrons believed her. They knew that Marion wasn't trying to fill her pockets, but was severely traumatised. Alice looked back on this episode in the 1970s:

Some of my protegées were as young as four years of age, without parents whom they would never see again as all those poor people met their fate at the hands of the Nazi murderers. So with the problems which befell those suddenly bereaved of their parents, their homes and sense of security – swindling and difficulties came up! I would say that most of the children behaved normally as long as they had letters from their parents. As soon as the letters stopped, the last ones mostly saying, "Mummy and Daddy have to go on a long journey," the girls developed many neurotic habits. One, who was always rather shy, started at the age of eight the habit of bed wetting [. . .] Another one, a fine and well brought-up girl from a good family, about fifteen years old, suddenly became a thief – she stole money, soap, writing paper – anything she could lay her hands on![45]

Several children had already complained about Marion's thieving, and so the matrons now had to deal with it. They contacted the local doctor, and on his advice Marion was sent away for psychiatric treatment. Her file shows that her "absences" stopped in 1943 and, to Alice's delight, she could start training as a nurse. In 1944 Marion obtained a British passport and after the war emigrated to Australia.[46]

In her research Anna Freud discovered that older children often experienced an "idealisation of lost parents" which resulted in an "increased difficulty for upbringing". She saw a particular "danger in adolescence when there are no parents to fight against".[47]

The younger children dealt with the trauma of separation from their families in other ways. Lore was another girl who preoccupied Alice and Paula a great deal. Born in 1933, she and her older brother Walter came from a lawyer's family in Königsberg, and though they had an uncle in London, he could not take them in. Lore suffered from homesickness, but to begin with received Red Cross letters from her parents. Years after the war she described how she often had fits of anger in Windermere and was sent to bed, where she cried herself to sleep. She would cry at the slightest thing and then withdraw with her doll into a make-believe world. When the Red Cross letters stopped in 1942 her mental state deteriorated rapidly and the bed-wetting began.[48]

Alice and Paula tried all the methods of the time to cure Lore of her bed-wetting. They stopped giving her anything to drink before bed and woke her up during the night to take her to the loo. Alice, Paula and the other girls washed her sheets. When the situation did not improve, however, Alice called on Anna Freud for help. In the 1970s she said of this visit, "I met Anna [Freud] in England [again] with one of our girls. She was a shy child, who celebrated her sixth birthday with us. I took her to London and she was asked if she didn't like it at the home, if she'd like to go anywhere else. She said no, she wanted to stay. Nothing worked."[49]

Paula and Alice were stumped by this seemingly insoluble problem. All the same, Lore didn't want to leave the hostel after the war. The Jewish Committee was able to locate relatives in New Zealand and paid the passage there for her. Lore wrote letters to Alice from New Zealand, mentioning one day that she had spent the night at a friend's house. Alice immediately understood and asked if the "problem" was now solved. "Yes," Lore replied, "I'm fine now." This news must have come as a huge relief to Alice. In the 1970s she proudly talked of how all the girls later went on to begin normal lives: "Nearly all the girls did well at school, and all my charges are now married and they send me pictures of their babies – for whom I have a feeling of an 'honorary grandmother'! Some of the girls live in New York and they make me feel welcome in their homes."[50]

Alice kept the letters and photographs all her life. One picture of Elfi and Ruth carried the dedication: "In kind remembrance of Elfi and Ruth, forever grateful."[51] On the back of a photograph she gave to Elfi, Alice wrote in 1940, her English grammar still a little shaky: "In the hope, you shall remember me – as I will do always and ever, yours Alice Urbach."[52]

In the 1990s Peter Sieber sent a questionnaire to all the girls still living about their time at the hostel. Most of those who responded believed that Alice and Paula had done their best in the circumstances, but two were critical of the matrons.[53]

Dorit Whiteman also sent out questionnaires for her book *The Uprooted*. These went to a far larger group – "children" who had lived with families as well as in hostels. Her survey also reached three of the Windermere children. One girl mentioned Alice and Paula only in passing: "They were OK." One was quite negative about the matrons: "I did not like either one. The cook was round and chubby, the other one very severe." The third child, by contrast, really liked Alice: "I was very fond of her. I stayed in touch with her till she died. My husband and I visited her in 1979 [. . .] I have her book *So kocht man in Wien!* It is one of my treasures, as are the last letters she wrote to me." Dorit Whiteman knew at once who the round cook was:

> Aunt Alice, a distant great-aunt of mine. I had no idea that she had ever been a matron in England. I do remember her visit one hot July day in New York, when she was already in her eighties. She came to teach me the art of cookie baking. She baked the whole day while a friend of mine and I wilted in the steamy kitchen after a mere three hours; Aunt Alice continued her lesson for another three [...] It could, of course, be that all three descriptions of Alice by the Kinder are correct. Perhaps her bouncy manner did not suit every personality. Perhaps she formed a better rapport with one type of child than another. Perhaps she did not know how to respond to one child's particular problem. The different descriptions of her are illustrative of the different impact the same person may have on different personalities.[54]

Alice (left) and Paula gave each of the children a photograph to remember them by

11: UNLUCKY FELIX

"They can certainly do rain!"
anonymous emigrant[1]

Like Alice, Felix had also undergone a sharp social decline. After the maltreatment he had endured in Viennese prisons he finally arrived in Britain in May 1939. Alice found him accommodation close to the children's home, at 78 Oakwood, Blackhill, Newcastle.[2] The house belonged to the Quakers, who had supported the Kindertransport programme and also helped adult Jews.

Their shared experience of fleeing the Third Reich brought Felix and Alice closer together. As children both had tried to combat their feelings of inferiority. Felix described how they had suffered under their overpowering father: "Our father was strict, harsh and had a razor-sharp mind, our mother was tender, sentimental and romantic [. . .] Sometimes when I have a conflict to resolve inside myself I think: Now my father is quarrelling with my mother. It was the strictest, most middle-class milieu [you] could imagine."[3]

Like Alice's marriage, Felix's career had been arranged by his father. After studying business in Hamburg and London, Felix, who would have preferred to study languages, worked in the family business in Cairo.[4] In the First World War he spent four years fighting with almost no leave. The death of his father in 1920 and the demise of the Mayer family firm liberated him, and for the first time Felix was able to decide for himself how he wanted to live. In 1922 he married a young Viennese woman by the name of Helene Pollatschek, and when their son was born five years later Felix was happy for the first time in his life.[5] Although he was still working in commerce, he wrote poetry and books of riddles in his spare time. All his manuscripts were destroyed in the pogrom of November 1938, but later Alice was able to recall a few of the riddles: "When I disappear there is hatred, love, war and peace, there is everything that exists in the world. When I appear everything is finished. You think I'm a ghost, a dream, oh no, you can touch me, I am real. What am I?"[6] The answer: a theatre curtain.[7]

Felix was grateful to have found refuge in Newcastle in 1939, but he could not stop thinking about his wife Helene, who was still stuck in Vienna. He was permanently tormented by the idea that he had abandoned her, and his only comfort was that he could at least now visit his twelve-year-old son Thomas, who was at boarding school in England.[8] Covering the school fees was difficult. Felix couldn't find work in Britain and only survived because he was supported financially by Alice and the Quakers. He had turned fifty-five in 1939, and nothing reminded him of his old life in Vienna. Alice suspected that the downward social mobility was harder to bear for a sensitive man like Felix than for her; she at least still had an income. Whenever she was able to leave the children's home for a few hours, she tried to cheer up her brother by telling him anecdotes. But by May 1940 this was no longer enough. Felix later processed the events in a novel which was never published. He wrote it in German, and apart from the names of the characters he changed virtually nothing in the chapter about 1940. The story of "Georg Bauer" reflected exactly what happened to Felix in 1940:

It was rainy for the first third of the month. But today, 10th May 1940, the sun came out first thing this morning. It was still early and water dripped from all the leaves in the large garden behind the big house in Gateshead, which the Quakers kept as a hostel for refugees. Everybody in the house was still asleep. Suddenly two police cars pulled up and a number of officers got out. [They] made their way into the house and woke the drowsy residents [. . .] In one room on the first floor three refugees were asleep: a middle-aged man from Vienna, an elderly man from Prague who used to be a teacher and a young man from Hannover. They quickly got dressed [. . .] and went downstairs. When the first of them entered the room one of the policeman said, "You are being detained."[9] The man being addressed, the one from Vienna – Georg Bauer – shrugged; he couldn't take this seriously.

Soon all the residents – around two dozen of them – were assembled. The police sergeant (who seemed embarrassed and clearly found the whole thing distasteful) explained briefly that they had to pack essentials into a small case they could carry, for they were all going to be taken away. They had fifteen minutes. He didn't answer the questions they put to him. All he said was that they'd find everything out in due course. Numbed by this unexpected turn of events they all hurried to pack. Some ladies from the committee that had founded the hostel appeared [. . .] They told the men under arrest [. . .] that they believed they were friends of Britain, not Nazis, and that they hoped to see them all again soon. The ladies gave each of them a small amount of money. Then all the men were loaded into cars and driven away. Their first stop was the police station, where each was given a brief interrogation and had to empty the contents of his pockets onto the table. Bauer put his possessions into two piles: penknife, matches and razorblades in one; the rest of his belongings in another. He pushed the first one towards the policeman.

"How did you know that?" he asked with a smile.

"I'm an old jailbird," Bauer replied, smiling too.[10]

In truth Felix had been well acquainted with "prison etiquette" since the November pogrom. This time, however, there was a major difference. In Britain he wasn't a prisoner, but an "internee", and nobody was threatening to kill him. All the same, the situation was anything but pleasant. Paula Sieber's nineteen-year-old son Peter had also been detained. Felix and Peter were amongst the 30,000 Austrians and Germans interned by the British as enemy aliens in May and June 1940. For Alice and Paula these arrests were another psychological blow, and it was a long time before they were able to discover how the two men were faring.[11]

Younger internees generally coped better with the situation than the older men. The twenty-two-year-old bon vivant Frank Marischka described his experiences as an entertaining adventure. He brought along his accordion and sang his favourite songs, much to the delight of the other internees: "Wien, Wien, nur du allein" (Vienna, Vienna, only you) and "Ja, das Studium der Weiber ist schwer" (The study of women is indeed hard).[12] As the grandson of the famous librettist Viktor Léon, Franz knew what he was singing. Felix, who was now fifty-six, was less relaxed about internment. His alter ego Georg Bauer

paced up and down the room for hours, always wandering the entire length of it. He couldn't believe that the English, these quiet, sensible, well-meaning people, could have suddenly resorted to such a drastic, wrongful and unwarranted measure. "The Nazis locked me up three times and now it's the turn of the English," he thought. "Don't they see I'm their friend? It's a breach of trust."[13] And he couldn't compose himself. Like all the others he was anxious and unsettled that they weren't allowed to see any newspapers and thus had no idea what was going on in the world. They knew that the Germans had invaded the Netherlands and Belgium [but] what had happened in recent days? Surely it concerns us just as much as it does the English. Even more, in fact. Is there nobody who can spell this out to the stupid Home Office? That's what everyone thought [...]

There were plenty of rumours going around [. . .] On one occasion Rosenfeld came up to Bauer and told him he'd received a package from an English friend. In this package were a pair of shoes stuffed with an old newspaper [. . .] It was a copy of the *Daily Mail* with the headline: "Intern the Lot!"[14]

Now Bauer understood what had happened and he thought, "A clear case of mass hysteria. Very un-English. Ah well, I suppose it is wartime."[15]

Felix/Bauer saw how charged the mood was when he was transferred to Liverpool with other internees:

They were told to get out and stand in line, bayonets pointing at them again [. . .] The train [of internees] caused quite a stir. Seeing the bayonets, the public must have assumed that we were all [. . .] dangerous saboteurs and they behaved accordingly. They shouted loudly and cursed the internees, street urchins ran alongside them, jeering, and they weren't far off from having bricks thrown at them. The whole thing resembled a Roman victory parade. The men weren't led directly through the city, but via a circuitous route. The intention must have been to put on a show for the public. After about an hour they reached their destination, which would have taken only fifteen minutes had they gone straight there. They marched into a large hall, apparently a sort of warehouse. Bauer approached the nice officer [. . .]

"Excuse me, Sir, but what we've just experienced was the most un-English behaviour I've ever seen."

The officer nodded. "I agree, it was disgusting, but not our fault. The local police are responsible. They'd promised us buses to transport you. We will report the incident to our superiors."

That's English too, Bauer thought, typical English fairness. The internees were assembled in the large hall and the commander stood in the centre of the semicircle they had formed. He was a major – elderly, slightly portly with a friendly, jovial face. To the general astonishment of everyone present he began his speech in good German [. . .] It was clear that this kind, sympathetic man knew who was standing before him and that felt good. As ever the soldiers escorting us took their cue from the commander.

The commander guessed how desperate they were for news from the outside world:

From the makeshift office we all of a sudden heard the wireless that the commander had *supposedly* forgotten to turn off. It was the BBC news service, not in English but in French, which *supposedly* the commander couldn't speak [. . .] A breathless silence took hold in the hall, but when the arrest of Oswald Mosley was announced a cheer erupted. Then the wireless was switched off.

For Felix and his fellow internees this news came as great relief. The arrest of the Fascist leader Mosley (and his icily beautiful wife Diana Mitford, a friend of Hitler) showed quite clearly that the British were no longer going to tolerate their own Fascists.

As the internees hadn't heard any news up until this point, they could not know that Prime Minister Winston Churchill had also begun to weed out the pro-German appeasement politicians in his party. But the Jewish refugees remained in custody and were shunted from one camp to another. The accommodation, as described by Felix in his manuscript, was very poor, with "straw sacks on the bare earth and nothing else. When someone found a rusty nail at one point and knocked it into the wall to hang his coat up, word went around that he had a furnished apartment."

What Felix endured here with admirable stoicism was Warth Mills near Bury, Lancashire. From other reports we know that conditions were utterly dire. The building was infested with rats, and instead of lavatories, two thousand men had to share a few buckets.[16] In Huyton, a similar makeshift camp in Lancashire, four internees killed themselves and two more made failed suicide attempts.[17]

Over the course of the following months Felix met a number of camp commanders, not all as sympathetic as the one who had turned on the news for a few minutes. A less astute commander had apparently watched the internees march past and then said, "It's funny. I'd never have thought that there were so many Jews amongst the Nazis."

Felix/Bauer needed anecdotes like this to distract him from the agonising thoughts of his wife. In his story he tries to describe his fear, without getting sentimental:

A small group of writers had [. . .] gathered and soon a lively, witty conversation was in full flow, which would been more at home in Vienna's Café Central than an

English prison camp. But the cheerfulness was only superficial [. . .] Those who were married felt very unhappy; nobody knew what would happen to their families. According to the news that some had received, the women were still free. Perger[18] asked Bauer if his wife was in England too.

"She's still in Vienna, sadly."

"Oh no," Perger said. "Why?"

"You know I had to get out as quickly as possible. But I was only able to get a permit for myself. Someone in London had made a mess of her application, so I had to leave by myself. But we do have a joint affidavit for America. So I'm waiting here and she's waiting in Vienna. Of course I did everything I could in London to get a permit for her too, but in wartime it's really difficult. They made it pretty clear to me that if she were in some neutral country it would work. But how can I get her to a neutral country?"

"Do you hear from her?"

"Yes, via Sweden and sometimes even via New York. Quick connection, isn't it? So far, touch wood, she's just about alright, thank God."

Apart from this conversation Felix/Bauer tried to avoid burdening his friends with his private concerns. The only thing that really interested them all was the general war situation:

As the prisoners were still cut off from all news, Perger plucked up courage and asked a kindly lieutenant if the news from the war was good at least. The lieutenant replied, "No, I'm afraid not. The news isn't particularly good. But we didn't expect any good news for the first five years."

So long as there was British humour, there was hope. Felix had gradually rediscovered his faith in the British, but not everyone shared his trust. Many of the internees could not get over the fact that they had been locked up. Even Dr Schmidt, the Christian camp leader in Felix's manuscript, sometimes had his doubts:

It was not the fact of being locked up, not the miserable living accommodation or the pitiful food that offended [Dr Schmidt] but the fact that he had been locked up by the English. "I've been in the country for fifteen years, I love this country, its people and shouldn't want to live anywhere else. I have an English wife and the English don't have a better friend than I. So why?"

"Try looking at it differently," Bauer said. "Imagine a man living for many years in marital bliss with his sensible wife who one day has a terrible hysterical fit and claims that he's trying to kill her. Does he file for immediate divorce or wait quietly, affectionately and with patience until she comes to her senses again?"

Dr Schmidt was grateful for this answer and became friends with Felix/Bauer. In the camp, however, there was also a pastor (Felix calls him "Pastor Harms") who was a fervent National Socialist and kept spreading false information. He claimed, amongst other things, that the "British government and the royal family had fled to Canada [...] The anti-Nazis were furious at Harms, but they refrained from bringing the matter to the attention of the English."

Felix/Bauer was relieved when one day he heard that they were all being transferred to the Isle of Man.[19] The British government had fenced off with barbed wire a group of hotels, guesthouses and a mini golf course, sixty houses in total.[20] The accommodation marked a steep improvement for the internees:

> The young ones stormed ahead to get the best rooms [...]
> Bauer was lucky to secure a bed to himself; most had
> to share a double with someone else [...] Although the
> house and rooms were primitively furnished, at least it
> felt somewhat humane [...] Some of the rooms even had
> running water.[21]

The painter and writer Fred Uhlman, another internee and author of *The Reunion*, was less impressed: "To save on blackout material, someone had the 'brilliant' idea to paint the windows blue and the light bulbs red, with the result that during the day it was as dark as in an aquarium and looked like a brothel at night."[22] Franz Marischka was on the Isle of Man at the same time as Uhlman and Felix, and remained jolly, as ever. One of his best memories concerns the hospital there. To obtain a sick note you had to get hold of some urine from a certain Jonathan Silbermann. Silbermann was diabetic and had come up with the business idea of selling his urine in little bottles. Few could afford this "Silbermann tincture", but if a prisoner was lucky it might even accelerate his release on account of serious diabetes.[23]

Because they were both from Vienna, Franz Marischka and Felix may have been accommodated in the same house. The internees were carefully placed in homogeneous groups to avoid arguments. The biggest group on the Isle of Man were

the German and Austrian Jews, followed by the eastern Jews,[24] but there were also houses for Catholic priests, Protestant pastors [. . .] and then there was a house where the real Nazis lived [. . .] They were uninhibited and felt themselves to be the victors. Swastikas were put on show and one of the Nazis even went so far as to threaten Perger, saying that he would see to it that Perger was executed. If anyone tried to tell the British officers about such machinations he was summarily dismissed. It was the job of the internees to keep order amongst themselves. It was indicative that Pastor Harms was one of the first to be released. Only much later were those being released asked whether they had seen any suspicious goings-on.[25]

When it came to postal censorship the British did not differentiate between interned Nazis and Jews either.[26] But even the best censors couldn't spot everything. Felix's alter ego Bauer managed to describe the meagre rations thus: "The food here is as good as it is plentiful and often reminds me of that grand establishment in Stein." No British censor could know that Stein was home to Austria's largest prison.

But the inmates were less concerned by the poor food and more by what would happen in the event of an invasion:

Nobody knew whether, when and where the Germans would choose to invade. Should an invasion occur, it was not out of the question that there would be a landing on the Isle of Man. A deputation was sent, therefore, to the commander, who promised that the prisoners would be sent away in good time if such a threat was imminent. Everyone was very pleased about this; nobody wanted to shovel coal in Newcastle under the supervision of the SS.

Felix/Bauer overestimated the prospect of a German invasion – and he underestimated the capabilities of the British:

> As time went on imprisonment became ever more oppressive. The internees would stand by the barbed wire on the side of the camp that gave them a view of the promenade, gazing out longingly. In the morning they watched the soldiers doing drill on the beach, but never got the impression that the English army would be properly prepared and in time. Everything looked very dilettante. Bauer's friend Perger joked bitterly, "It will get better. The English have decided to switch over to firearms." They were always overwrought; one careless word could unleash a vicious quarrel. They found it hard to be cooped up with the same male company all the time. The sections of the barbed wire where there was a good view of the promenade and the women wandering past were always crowded.

All of them longed for tenderness. One of the internees found a little kitten that everyone adored. For days they thought about a suitable name. "Internida" made the short list, but in the end they agreed on "Re-Lieschen", playing on the German diminutive for Elisabeth and the English word "release".

To keep their minds occupied, they listened to talks and lectures. Fred Uhlman describes how proud the men were that thirty of the internees were professors from Oxford and Cambridge, all of whom tried to outdo each other: "What if Professor William Cohn's lecture on Chinese theatre clashes with Egon Welleszen's introduction to Byzantine music? [. . .] Perhaps you would prefer to hear Zuntz talk about the Odyssey or Friedenthal about Shakespearian drama."[27] The most famous artist amongst the internees was the Dadaist Kurt Schwitters. His talks seemed particularly timely, as everyone was now "leading a surreal life. After all, what could be more Dadaist [. . .] than two thousand 'enemy aliens' praying for the victory of 'our gracious King George VI and our gracious Queen Elizabeth'?"[28]

Felix's situation turned out to be more Dadaist than anyone else's. In the camp he had a namesake, another Felix Mayer who would play a key role in his internment story. The two men kept being mixed up, beginning with them receiving the wrong letters. When the young Felix was deported to Canada, the old Felix remained in the camp and thought no more about his namesake. In the meantime, however, Alice and the Quakers had managed to get a British MP to champion Felix's case and put pressure on the Home Office. What happened then is described again by Felix as his alter ego Bauer:

The MP wrote that Bauer should be released within days. Bauer waited, full of impatience. Then another letter from the MP arrived which said that Bauer's release had been instructed. Bauer waited impatiently, for a week, then another, then a month. In vain, for nothing happened. And one day he heard to his amazement that his name-sake, the young man who had been deported to Canada, had been brought back and released. Bauer was livid, naturally, cursing furiously about the mix-up in names that must have happened. He wrote again to the MP, who promised to investigate. But many more months would pass before the error was cleared up [. . .] From now on Bauer was known in the camp simply as "the man who has no right to be here".

When Felix had been interned for almost a year, he had to put up with being transferred to another camp on the Isle of Man:

The internees took their leave of the friendly officers and marched up the hill to the other camp. It was a bad swap. The other camp was ruled by the strictest discipline. The men felt bitter that the new commander looked down on them with scorn and treated them badly. It was reported, for example, that he once used the expression: "Feeding time for the Jews". Harsh punishment was meted out for the slightest misdemeanour. In the past, it was said, the commander [. . .] had been entrusted with leading the Black and Tans (a particularly brutal English unit) in the Irish uprising and evidently he hadn't moved on. The accommodation was dire too. One man joked he had running water in his room. This was true, when it rained

[. . .] Bauer only had to spend two weeks in this camp, then came the long-awaited release. He found it hard to leave all his nice comrades behind, he was almost embarrassed at having been favoured, but he was delighted when he boarded the boat in Douglas and suddenly there were no guards to be seen. Then the boat left the port and he was free.

Felix was released on 14 March 1941. After a year in internment camps, he could now finally see his son Thomas and sister Alice again. Without Helene, however, he still felt only half a person. Bauer experienced it thus:

He'd heard from his wife a few times now; her letters were not at all reassuring. She had written to him via Sweden, cleverly coded, that the situation was getting ever worse [. . .] He heard nothing for a long while after that, then came another letter via Sweden. The message was so encrypted that no matter how hard he tried Bauer couldn't understand it, much to his despair. But at least she was still alive and free.

Then Felix/Bauer received a less ambiguous missive:

It was a farewell letter. Not in so many words, but it was full of despair and resignation. The question was whether she would get out in time. Although her number ought to come up in the next few days, as the American consulate had told her, if this didn't happen really, really soon, it would be too late and she would have to go to Poland. She'd already had a summons from the Gestapo. And thus she took her leave from him.

Bauer felt as if he'd received a terrible blow to the head [...] He had to do something, he felt the urge to shout, his helplessness was driving him into a rage [...] What to do? What to do? He had an acquaintance at the American consulate in London and paid him a visit. Yes, it was true, the American consulate in Vienna was going to close in the next few days.[29] He shook Bauer's hand and waited for him to leave. But Bauer just stood there in disbelief. He couldn't think, he was rooted to the spot, aware only that something hurt, hurt like hell, something couldn't be true, something had to be done, there was something that humanity mustn't allow to happen. Placing a sympathetic hand on his shoulder, the consular official said, "Where there's life, there's hope. I believe in miracles and you should try to believe in them too." Bauer left, a forlorn man. I'm not going to survive this, he kept thinking. What was there worth living for? So I can watch Hitler being strung up? The truth is, he's won; he's beaten me at any rate.

Felix had been an unlucky man since 1938. But the miracle he could not believe in now happened. A telegram arrived from his wife with the words. "Saved. Embark tomorrow New York. Kisses."

Helene obtained her visa just as she was about to be deported to the east, and only days before the American consulate in

Vienna closed. In May 1941 she embarked for America.[30] Alice and Felix celebrated this miracle royally. Even though her brother and his wife had to wait a further three years before they could finally see each other in New York, each knew that the other was safe. So in the end unlucky Felix had a spot of luck after all.

But there was one feeling he could not shake off altogether. He continued to long for Vienna. In 1942 he sent Alice a poem in which he described his thoughts.[31] Nowadays it might sound sentimental, but at the time Alice learned all the verses by heart. It described exactly what she felt.

Homesickness

Once more I would like to stand on the Kahlenberg
And gaze at the city, the Danube, the Marchfeld in
    the distance.
Once more I would like to be at the Heldenplatz
Once more stand by the Donnerbrunnen.
Once more hear the sound I have missed,
Of the good old dialect from back home,
When through an open kitchen window from across
    the courtyard
A Viennese girl sings *Gassenhauer*.

Once more I'd like to wander through the suburbs,
Where the low buildings stand, tired and grey,
Like old friends, I know them all well.
Familiar too those I've never seen.

Oh, a Vienna winter! Snow-covered streets,
The sun shining warmly from a blue sky.
No Viennese can or ever could
Forget you, my beloved Vienna!

[...]

Now I sit at the tables of strangers
Hear foreign sounds, break foreign bread.
Of course I am grateful to this people
Who offered me refuge in a difficult time.
The people are good, only the country is dark,
I need warmth, I need sun, light –
It remains a foreign land, a foreigner I remain,
For old trees cannot be transplanted.

Once more I would like – but why the lament?
What is dead is dead, there is no resurrection.
My child is young and in time will learn
To see this foreign land as his own.
The world is big and people are everywhere,
There is no country where the sun has never shone.
But none can replace my homeland,
For only in Vienna can I live and breathe![32]

12: AN AMERICAN TURNS UP

"I am the sword,
I am the flame."
Heinrich Heine

Alice dreamed of a miracle similar to that which had blessed
Felix and his wife. She could not imagine what it was like to
miss a spouse, but she longed to see her sons again. Sometimes
with Paula Sieber she would imagine the reunion with her
children. And then, in 1944, something unexpected happened.
A man in American army uniform turned up in the Lake
District. Outwardly he reminded her a little of the actor David
Niven. Like Niven he smoked a pipe, sported a thin moustache
and moved with the insouciance of a man who could no longer
be surprised by anything. In front of Alice stood her eldest
son, Otto. Alice had not seen him for almost nine years, and
despite his nonchalant air she would have been able to pick him
out of any crowd. When they'd last said goodbye he had been
a rebellious twenty-two-year-old who hated Vienna and was
desperate to get out of the city. His instinct had been correct.

His arrival wasn't just a boon for Alice, it was also proof that the war against Nazi Germany was about to turn. Otto had arrived in Britain in 1944 with 500,000 other American soldiers to support the Allied invasion. He was fortunate not to be one of the troops who landed in Normandy on 6 June; their chances of survival were reckoned to be relatively slim. As Otto had a pilot's licence he worked for the US Air Force, where he'd been assigned to the Strategic Bombing Survey, a commission investigating the impact of the air raids on Germany. This made sense, given his close acquaintance with bombardments. After his experience in Shanghai in 1937 he knew how it felt to be on the side of the victims.

The Strategic Bombing Survey was situated in Teddington, near London, and thus almost 300 miles away from Alice. Even today a railway journey from London to the Lake District takes three and a half hours, and in 1944 the trip must have been much more laborious. The trains were packed with soldiers, and because of the lack of space the public was urged to avoid making gratuitous trips. Everywhere there were posters asking reproachfully: "Is Your Journey Really Necessary?"

It certainly was as far as Otto was concerned. He didn't care how long it took to get to Alice. He had to see her before he was sent to Germany.

Alice would have loved to tell all the children at the hostel about Otto, but she was only too aware that some of the girls already felt neglected. What would they say if her son now turned up? Would it elicit even more envy? The situation was emotionally charged as it was. All the children were waiting for that one moment when a family member appeared, anyone who might have managed to escape the National Socialist regime. It was a dream that became more improbable with every year of the war. Alice therefore kept it to herself that her eldest son had arrived in Britain. At least, none of the children was later able to recollect having seen Otto in Windermere, and it is only from her writings that we know he visited her and what this meant to Alice.[1]

Otto looked older, but despite his calm air Alice must have suspected that his inner restlessness remained. He was clearly eager to get going again, only now it was something other than a spirit of adventure that drove him on. This war had become his war, and he had many reasons to fight it.

Otto had acquired American citizenship in April 1944, after nine years and via a tortuous route. In return he had to declare himself prepared to die for the USA. This was not such a bad deal as, apart from the American passport, he had another – highly emotional – reason to sign up for the arrangement. Entry into the army finally gave him the chance to resist. Many Jewish emigrants later said how they longed for nothing more than to fight against the National Socialist regime: "I was seriously asked by my superior if I'd have a problem fighting against the country of my birth," one Jewish soldier said. "I just laughed. I didn't want to be sent to the Pacific [. . .] I wanted to fight in Europe."[2]

For Jewish soldiers the fight against Hitler was a very personal war. Even emigrants who otherwise would never have willingly picked up a gun were determined to join the army. The aesthete Victor Brombert, who became an eminent scholar after the war, wrote that he was enthusiastic, but his enthusiasm wore off on Omaha Beach.[3]

Like all American soldiers, Brombert and Otto wore a so-called dog tag around their necks. This displayed their personal identity number, blood group and also their religion. Jewish soldiers were allocated an "H" for Hebrew, which unsurprisingly horrified the German and Austrian exiles amongst them.[4]

The letter was not just a symbol of their otherness; in combat it could have lethal consequences. Prisoners with an "H" were immediately shot by the Germans. Without the "H" a Jewish soldier could hope to survive in a prisoner-of-war camp (although he would have to fear that in a thorough body search they would notice he was circumcised). In view of the substantial risk of ending up a prisoner of the Germans, Jewish soldiers could decide whether they wanted to have the "H" or another religious affiliation on their dog tag. The British army did not give them the choice. Every Jewish soldier was summarily declared to be an Anglican and, as a further precaution, German emigrants were assigned English first names and surnames (Franz Marischka, for example, who by now had been able to leave the Isle of Man, became Francis Marsh).[5] Such pragmatism did not exist in the US army.

We do not know if Otto decided for or against an "H" on his dog tag, but as he was soon working in the army under a codename we can assume that in 1944 he was already passing himself off as a Catholic. Although he never left the Jewish community, his religious affiliation was always given as "Catholic" in German registration documents, even after the war.[6] He never said when his supposed conversion took place, but there is no doubt he rehearsed his Christian identity well and quickly learned a few prayers by heart. He was going to need them.

There were many things Otto couldn't talk about when he was reunited with Alice. "Careless Talk Costs Lives" warned the posters that hung in countless public buildings. Members of the army were not permitted to discuss classified work with family members either. Alice knew, therefore, that she shouldn't ask Otto about his work in America or Britain, but she was curious. And she was a Jewish mother who expected to be kept informed. She had heard, for example, that Karl's Viennese friend Hermann Bondi was involved in research essential to the war effort.[7] Was her son doing something similarly exciting, perhaps? Otto had to disappoint her. He couldn't compete with Bondi, who at a secret location was refining British radar technology and later became a Cambridge professor and was knighted.[8] What Otto worked on always stayed under the radar.

According to the scant army documentation relating to Otto that has been released, he joined the US army in New Hampshire on 11 January 1943. We still don't know for sure precisely what he was doing before he visited Alice in 1944. Over the course of his army career he had two personnel numbers: one as a simple soldier, and later a completely different one as an intelligence officer in the Counter Intelligence Corps (CIC). Research has been made all the more difficult because Otto had a namesake – a CIC man by the name of Captain Rudolf Urbach. On several occasions Rudolf appears in places where Otto was also deployed (in America, Germany and later Japan).

At first glance one might assume that Rudolf Urbach was Otto's alias, but he was a real person. He was born to a Jewish family in Duisburg in 1908, and thus was five years older than Otto.[9] The two Urbachs were not related, but they seemed to have used the fact they had the same surname to work jointly on projects.

Their cooperation must have begun in Colorado back in 1943. Rüdiger von Wechmar, prisoner-of-war at Camp Trinidad in Colorado and later a West German diplomat, was sure he had met Otto as an interrogation officer. In his autobiography he describes encountering Otto when he arrived in Colorado: "[We were working] with the officers of the American commander, including First Lieutenant Urbach, who I met again in Germany after the war when he was representing the American firm 3M there."[10]

Otto did in fact later work for 3M and he knew Wechmar well, but was it really Otto whom Wechmar recalled in Colorado? To date we only have photographs from there showing Rudolf Urbach.[11] Perhaps Wechmar was mistaken, or Rudolf and Otto were already working as a team. At any rate Otto was well acquainted with the countryside around Camp Trinidad, near the Rocky Mountains. Before the war he had considered building a ski hotel there.

Despite its spectacular location, Trinidad was anything but a place of rest and relaxation. It consisted of long rows of barracks that had to be erected in a very short time to accommodate the first wave of German prisoners-of-war. Until then the British had been obliged to shoulder this burden alone; now they were supported by the Americans. The US army had scarcely any experience of dealing with POWs, and they were initially overwhelmed by the task. But they remembered a special weapon they could now deploy. In no other country were there so many immigrants who understood the language and culture of the enemy. These former citizens of Germany and Austria could understand and analyse far better than any psychologist what their former compatriots were thinking. They made the ideal interrogation officers.

The Austrian cabaret artist Georg Kreisler later summed up his work for the American army in one sentence: "Anyone who could speak German, Italian or Japanese was sent for reconnaissance."[12] The majority of emigrants were trained at Camp Ritchie in Maryland. The journalist Hans Habe, a "Ritchie Boy", wrote:

Camp Ritchie [...] at the foot of the Blue Ridge Mountains was the strangest army camp in the world. Here everything was surrounded by secrets; half of the pupils went around in disguise. Entire companies marched in German Wehrmacht uniforms, Japanese snipers – they were American–Japanese – perched in the boughs of trees, and in one part of the camp fake SS officers exercised. We studied day and night: scouting behind enemy lines, interrogation of prisoners-of-war, reading aerial photographs, counter-espionage, ethnology, psychological warfare, news analysis [...] The daily news bulletins relayed over a loudspeaker during mealtimes in the canteen were played in fifteen languages.[13]

A creative bunch was assembled here. Men from Viennese theatre, such as Marcel Prawy and Ernst Haeussermann, or people who became famous later, like Henry Kissinger and J.D. Salinger, were trained as intelligence officers at Camp Ritchie and similar institutions. Before they were deployed in Germany they could try out their interrogation techniques on German soldiers in American camps. One of these was Camp Trinidad, and it was there in 1943 that emigrants like Rudolf (and probably Otto too) first met Rommel's soldiers taken prisoner in Africa. Now the roles had been reversed: defeated Nazi officers came face to face with their former victims. But the Jewish interrogation experts never revealed their German backgrounds. Rudolf Urbach, for example, pretended to speak German with an American accent,[14] an essential disguise for accessing the right information. The Geneva Convention stipulated that prisoners-of-war had only to disclose their personal details. But of course the Americans tried to get much more out of them. This called for creativity – and who better to offer this than imaginative coffee-house men of letters?

In Fort Hunt, for example, a prisoner-of-war camp where the most violent Wehrmacht soldiers ended up, they came up with what was known as the "Russian treatment" – an effective method for making inmates talk. Because of their lack of cooperation, they were told, they would have to be handed over to Russian liaison officers. A Russian-speaking emigrant would then put in a scintillating performance as this "liaison officer". At Fort Hunt they listened in to the prisoners' cells, and thus we know today what a Nazi radio operator by the name of Heinrich Speyer told his comrades about interrogation by the "brutal

Soviet liaison officer": "And the one who called himself Commissar put a hand on my shoulder as he was going and said, 'Ivan Ipanovitch [advises] you to sign.' [. . .] Then he said, 'You'll feel the full force of Russia. We'll burn your eyes out with spotlights.'"[15] We can assume that the radio operator gave in.

Although there were fewer fanatics in Camp Trinidad than at Fort Hunt, here too the ardent National Socialists terrorised those prisoners who disparaged Hitler. Among the latter was Otto's acquaintance Rüdiger von Wechmar. His opinions were not without danger, for there were repeated attempts at murder of "traitors" like him, and the camp leadership felt compelled to protect those prisoners critical of the National Socialist regime. As late as May 1945 German officers in Camp Trinidad were still planning to kill disloyal compatriots.[16]

If von Wechmar was right and Otto really did work in Colorado, he would have been able to learn in 1943 what he later perfected in occupied Germany: identifying true zealots from the mass of nominal supporters.

Otto was not, therefore, allowed to talk to Alice about his work when he finally saw her again. But there was one question she certainly wanted an answer to. She had heard nothing from her three sisters in Vienna – Sidonie, Karoline and Helene – since 1942. She knew that in 1941, by emigrating to America, Felix's wife had escaped deportation to Poland at the last minute. There were many rumours circulating about the camps in the east. Was it possible to survive them? Did Otto know more about them? Those were the hardest questions she could ask him.

Some years after the war Anna Freud was asked why her elderly aunts had been murdered. "The Nazis wanted their apartments," she replied.[17] Once they had them, the next logical step was to dispose of the witnesses to the theft. Like Anna Freud's aunts, Alice's elderly half-sisters Karoline and Sidonie had also been homeless since 1938. To begin with they lived with friends, then in mass accommodation. The last address they had together was the synagogue in Müllnergasse in 1942.[18] They might have survived the war if Baldur von Schirach had not become Gauleiter of Vienna in 1940.

Von Schirach's American mother, Emma Middleton von Schirach, wrote enthusiastically after her son's appointment as Gauleiter: "Yes, I am mighty proud of my boy, and he has his head and hands full [...] A huge amount he has to do. He wants to make Vienna the leading city in culture, music etc. etc., and it seems to have started well."[19] Schirach's most significant cultural act was to deport Austrian Jews to their certain deaths, among them the sisters of Sigmund Freud and Alice. Sidonie and Karoline were deported from Müllnergasse to Theresienstadt on 14 July 1942. This transport consisted of 1,009 people, 950 of whom were killed and 59 survived the war. Sidonie and Karoline's names appear one more time on transport lists. On 21 September 1942, Sidonie's birthday, she was sent to Treblinka with her sister and other elderly people. This Theresienstadt–Treblinka transport carried 2,002 people, only one of whom survived.

Otto was unaware of all this at the time, yet he suspected that his aunts' chances of survival in the camps were minimal. There was little hope too for Alice's younger sister Helene and her husband.[20] Their last known address is the Łódź (Litzmannstadt) Ghetto.

In the nineteenth century, Łódź was an emerging industrial city, a magnet for the rural Jewish population. You went to Łódź to find entertainment or a good income. In Jewish jokes the city became a sort of "promised land". The Jewish librettist Fritz Löhner-Beda alluded to it when he wrote the 1915 song "Rosa, wir fahr'n nach Łódź" ("Rosa, we're going to Łódź"), with music by Artur Marcel Weray. Löhner-Beda's output was legendary; he wrote an incredible number of operetta texts and hits such as "Ich hab mein Herz in Heidelberg verloren" ("I lost my heart in Heidelberg") and "Dein ist mein ganzes Herz" ("My heart is all yours"). His Łódź song, however, would have a bizarre afterlife.

In January 2019 the comedian Wolfgang Trepper presented a satirical programme on German television.[21] He played himself, a grumpy guy looking back nostalgically on his childhood in the 1970s. At one point he fulminates against the ghastly German "Schlager" music of this time, picking on Vicky Leandros's 1974 hit "Theo, wir fahr'n nach Łódź". The text of this new song was even more banal than Löhner-Beda's original:

> Theo, we're going to Łódź.
> Get up, lazybones
> Before I lose my patience.
> Theo, we're going to Łódź
> Where we'll have a big party
> That will allow us to forget the world.
> Theo, we're going to Łódź.

The song isn't exactly a musical gem, and in the programme Trepper gives it both barrels:

Theo, we're going to Łódź! Like hell we are! Theo didn't want to go to Łódź. *She* was the one who wanted to [. . .] If you fancy going to Poland in the middle of the night then do it on your own, you silly cow! What is there in Łódź? Nothing, nothing ever happened in Łódź. Have you ever passed a travel agent's and seen a sign saying: *Shopping in Łódź*? Bugger all happens in Łódź, that's the problem, nobody wants to be there. Nothing of any significance has ever happened in Łódź, Łódź is as dull as ditchwater.

On this point Trepper could not be more mistaken, as during the Second World War quite a few significant things happened in Łódź. And when "Theo, wir fahr'n nach Łódź" became a hit in Germany in 1974, not even thirty years after the war's end, there were still many Wehrmacht and SS soldiers who knew all too well what had happened in Łódź back then. None of them had any interest in making it public knowledge. In the Łódź Ghetto about 43,000 people died of cold and malnourishment between 1940 and 1944. For most deported there, it was a stopover on the way to Auschwitz or Majdanek.

In 1974, when "Theo, wir fahr'n nach Łódź" became such a success, nobody asked how many people had been killed in Łódź. Not even the writer of the original song, Löhner-Beda, could comment on the new lyrics. He was beaten to death on 4 December 1942, after a director of IG Farben had reprimanded him for working too slowly.[22] For the Schlager music industry, Löhner-Beda's death had the advantage that the lyrics could be rewritten and now Vicky Leandros was going to Łódź.

*

Alice knew nothing of the precise circumstances of Helene's murder. Otto had decided to spare her the details. He could not, however, prevent Alice from finding out after the war what had happened to Karoline and Sidonie. They were gassed together. Alice mentions this in her memoir in just a few words, writing that the two of them clung together in death.[23] Of course there is no proof of this embrace, but it was of some comfort to her.

And maybe it was even the truth.

13: CORDELIA'S WAR

"Reed stayed very much with me,
and what training I had in using my brain
and examining what I was being told
was very useful in working in the intelligence world."
Cordelia Dodson[1]

There was something else that Otto refrained from telling his mother in 1944: Cordelia Dodson would soon be arriving in England too. Otto could not mention this to Alice because she would have insisted on seeing Cordelia again. At their first meeting at Café Sacher back in 1937, Alice had totally underestimated the young American. Now she knew that Karl would not have survived without Cordelia's help. She owed her a great deal, but Otto was unable to bring the two women together in 1944. Apart from a few colleagues, nobody could know about Cordelia's trip to London. It belonged to her secret life.

If Cordelia had not been witness to the Anschluss of Austria, she might never have worked for the American wartime intelligence agency, the OSS. As she later said herself, this experience influenced the rest of her life: "I learnt to hate the Nazis from that time on."[2] After returning to America in October 1938, there was nothing she could do to begin with. She was a mere student who knew that most Americans were opposed to military engagement in Europe. Even when war broke out in September 1939 Cordelia had to accept that her compatriots were unwilling to support Britain in her fight against Hitler.

She continued to study German, French and psychology at Reed, all the while hoping that public opinion would change. When the Japanese bombed Pearl Harbor on 7 December 1941, and the US declared war on Nazi Germany a few days later, she had just completed her studies. The mood did finally shift and Cordelia immediately went to Washington, finding her first job at the Pentagon, the headquarters of the US Department of Defense. Like Otto and her brother Daniel,[3] she was officially with the Air Force, and her most important intelligence task was to translate information about the German Luftwaffe into English and assess it. Cordelia's excellent analyses proved useful, but after three years of desk work she was desperate to be sent to Europe in an operative role. Since March 1944 rumours of invasion had become increasingly persistent. More and more of her friends were being transferred to Britain and Cordelia was certain that she too could be more effective there than in the safety of Washington.

On 6 June 1944 she, along with millions of other Americans, listened to President Roosevelt's radio address: the invasion of Normandy had begun. Cordelia had been working long enough in the Pentagon to know that the initial casualty rate would be

Cordelia Dodson at her Reed College graduation, 1941

very high, and she could no longer bear to stay in the US. There was a job posting that suited her perfectly: "Secretary and assistant to the chief of X-2 Branch. The position will involve considerable responsibility in analyzing and processing reports of X-2 nature, using own judgement and initiative to a large extent. Excellent knowledge of French and German is required."[4]

The OSS head, William Donovan, had established X-2 in 1943 to provide liaison with the British.[5] Inside the OSS, X-2 was known as the "elite within the elite". Cordelia wanted this job above all else. Her references were impressive; she was backed by her boss E.R. LeRoy, F. Peters, E. Barnhart and of course Dexter Keezer.[6]

Notes from Cordelia's job interview described her thus: "Single, no dependants, intelligent, very good impression, businesslike". Her salary was set at 2,600 dollars per annum.[7]

Now Cordelia could embark for Europe. But when she arrived in London in November 1944, she did not recognise the city. She had heard about the bombings, of course, but the reality was considerably harsher than expected. The pulsating capital she had known as a student in the 1930s no longer existed. The people looked careworn, wore threadbare clothing, and rubble and bomb craters were everywhere. There had been more air raids from January to May 1944, and the population had grown war weary. In affluent, safe America, Cordelia had been able to buy food any time. She was also used to reliable heating and electricity. This was rarely the case in London, and she had to sit in her office in overcoat and gloves, wondering where she might find something to eat for the weekend.

But before she could adjust to the conditions in Britain she was assigned to go to Switzerland in December 1944. Nobody told her what she was needed for there, but there was a change in how she received her salary. Until then she had been paid regularly, like all other employees, but from 1 December the money came from a secret account. This "slush fund" was intended to conceal who she was working for in Switzerland.[8] He was a man who played a relatively glorious role in the war, but an inglorious one later as director of the CIA: Allen Dulles.[9]

The New York lawyer Dulles was not a man of nuance. He had little interest in psychology and cultural differences, but he was smart enough to surround himself with people who could explain what was going on in the heads of his opponents (and allies). His best OSS agents were those who had spent time abroad and understood other countries. This was true of Cordelia.[10]

On her way to Dulles, Cordelia would also make herself briefly useful as a "tour guide". Her tour group was anything but usual, however, consisting of German prisoners-of-war who had been turned and were now going to be smuggled back into Germany for the purposes of espionage. The man who had prepared these operations was Cordelia and Otto's friend Peter Viertel.[11] After the war Viertel would write a hard-hitting screenplay about one of these "tourist" missions; the film *Decision before Dawn* became a global hit in 1951.[12] Cordelia later remembered all the things that went wrong on her mission.[13] The plane was rickety, and had the pilot not been so experienced they would never have managed to land in Lyon in such weather conditions. The city was considered safe – it had been liberated in September 1944 – but nerves were on edge. Cordelia didn't regain her composure until she had delivered her German prisoners-of-war and finally made it over the Swiss border. Here there were no blackout regulations and she could once again drive through the night with headlights. It was close to Christmas and the brightly lit houses radiated Swiss prosperity and style. She enjoyed the normality to the fullest: "We dined at an elegant restaurant where the martinis were served in proper glasses, not paper cups, and the napkins were real linen, not Kleenex."[14]

Even more exhilarating than the martinis was her new mission. Two days before Christmas 1944 she reported for service at 23 Herrengasse in Bern. Number 23 was a grand building that had been extended several times since its construction in 1690. On the nameplate beside the bell it read: ALLEN DULLES – SPECIAL ADVISOR TO THE AMERICAN AMBASSADOR. Allen Dulles had not rented the building out of historical interest, but because it had a separate entrance through which visitors could come and go discreetly. He had also arranged for the streetlights outside the house to be defective, with good reason: both the Swiss intelligence and all enemy intelligence services were interested in the identity of his visitors.

Cordelia first worked with Paul C. Blum, one of Dulles's most important advisors. Fifty years later Cordelia recalled their time at Haus Silberhof: "We each had a typewriter [. . .] I think Paul accepted the fact that we were going to work together and that he'd have to make the best of my bad typing [. . .] One of the chief problems was burning our own trash. We had no central place to dispose of classified material."[15]

Although Switzerland was officially neutral, Cordelia soon learned that this neutrality differed from region to region: "In

Zürich they were very pro-German. The Germans had managed to establish a sort of illegal Nazi party in Switzerland. The Swiss police were trying to identify these people they considered traitors [. . .] They wanted to know what was going on. So did we." Occasionally the situation became farcical. The opposing parties would dine in Bern's most elegant hotel, the Bellevue Palace. The OSS would sit in one half of the room, and Heinrich Himmler's Security Service (SD) in the other.[16] Such proximity had its advantages. Cordelia helped Paul Blum recruit a female SD agent,[17] but she was also involved in one of his most important projects: uncovering the channels by which Nazi functionaries were trying to rapidly smuggle gold into Liechtenstein, Spain and South America before the end of the war.[18] Blum had various informants in the banking and business world and trusted nobody outside his team: "We were a small group working closely together," Cordelia said later, "and we drank more than we ought to have."[19] But they were successful: in September 1946 Blum, Cordelia and their OSS colleague Hood were promoted for having uncovered Nazi gold.[20]

Cordelia not only worked on Blum's projects, but directly for Allen Dulles too. He was interested in her student days, in particular her visit to Italy in 1937.

Karl and Cordelia's friendship had begun in a Viennese railway station on 9 April 1937. Karl recorded exactly the train Cordelia took: Venice–Trieste–Klagenfurt–Semmering–Vienna. He had not asked her what she'd been up to in Italy; he must have assumed that Americans always did the same things there: visiting ruins, churches and museums. Cordelia had indeed done all of these, but away from the tourist track she had also paid a visit to the parents of her fellow Reed student, Emilio Pucci di Barsento, for the simple reason that she was curious.

At Reed, Pucci and Otto had awakened Cordelia's interest in both skiing and European politics. The two men descended the mountain in similar rapid style, but when it came to politics they had very different points of view: Otto warned against Fascism, Pucci defended it. Cordelia was keen to observe both sides.

The Puccis were one of the oldest noble families in Italy and had lived in the Palazzo Pucci in Florence since 1480. When Cordelia met Emilio's parents in 1937 she learned that he'd had an English governess as a child, and as a teenager had been enthusiastic about the American societal model as well as Italian Fascism. This was a contradiction he was never able to fully resolve. To take part in sporting events, he joined the Fascist youth organisation Opera Nazionale Balilla (ONB) when he was fifteen, and later, as a student in Milan, he became a member of the Gioventù Universitaria Fascista (GUF).[21]

After her visit to Italy, Cordelia was convinced that Otto's criticism of Fascism was justified. But if Pucci lost out to Otto politically, he came out on top romantically. All her life Cordelia found the Italian extremely attractive: "he was a slender young man, very graceful, and a good athlete. He skied, fenced, danced beautifully."[22] And she wasn't alone in her view. Few female students at Reed would ever forget Pucci, perhaps because he was not the monogamous type: "Some women were just delighted to see him again and others wouldn't come within 10 feet of him," a fellow student recalled.[23]

Pucci's professional career would prove to be even more

interesting. After handing in his final dissertation at Reed in 1937 – entitled "Fascism: An Explanation and Justification"[24] – he travelled across Asia, only returning to Italy several months later. According to the statements he later gave to OSS, it was now that he saw the dark side of the regime for the first time: "I discovered that I had idealised Fascism, while I was abroad, and now, confronted by the corruption, the lack of responsibility, and the incompetence that was obvious in all governmental dealings, I felt a very severe disillusion."[25]

But Pucci remained an Italian patriot and trained as a fighter pilot. On a skiing trip in 1938 he met and befriended Mussolini's children. He was drawn in particular to the eldest daughter, the married Edda Ciano, with whom he had an intense affair. Edda was only four years older than him, sporty and attractive. In Italian society she was known as a "modern" Fascist who was 100 per cent behind her father. At her wedding to Count Ciano in 1930 she had given the Fascist salute for the cameras. Through Edda, Pucci even managed to have a private audience with Mussolini in summer 1943.[26] But his hope of telling the Duce about corruption in the Italian air ministry remained unfulfilled. Pucci returned to the front. In 1943 his nerves were already so shredded that he could only fly if he dosed himself up with the drug Pervitin beforehand.[27]

Still in London in 1944, Cordelia came across the name Pucci in an encrypted dispatch. She told her superior officer that she had known Pucci as a student at Reed and that she had visited his parents in Italy in 1937. She was then tasked with establishing contact with him.[28] Pucci and Edda Ciano possessed something that the Americans were keen to get their hands on: the diaries of Edda's husband, Count Ciano, Mussolini's former foreign minister. One of OSS's assignments was to gather as much material as possible for future trials of war criminals. The diaries were seen as potential evidence, as rumour had it that Ciano had written down all his conversations with the German foreign minister Joachim von Ribbentrop and several other Nazi bigwigs. In 1943 Ciano had fallen out of favour with Mussolini and been imprisoned. His wife Edda had broken with her father too. She now kept her husband's diaries hidden and tried to use them as a bargaining chip to secure his release. Pucci was helping her as best he could, and this was the information that Cordelia had seen in the dispatch. It was just like the Pucci she had met at Reed.

In all likelihood there are few men who would put their life on the line to save their lover's husband. But Pucci was no average man, and Edda Ciano was anything but an average wife. At the beginning of 1944 the two of them almost persuaded Himmler's SD agents to bring about Ciano's release – in return for the diaries. But when Hitler was informed of the deal, he stopped it in its tracks. On 11 January 1944 Ciano was executed in Verona on the orders of his father-in-law Mussolini, and Edda told her children the news in a most unusual way: "Grandpapa had Papa shot."[29]

The only person who continued to stand by her in this messy situation was Pucci. After the deal failed, he took Edda and her children with sections of the diaries to the Swiss border, but was captured by the SD. In his secret report for OSS he described his "interrogation" by the SD:

It is not my intention to make a detailed description of how I was tortured. Torture is such a humiliating experience in itself, that just talking about it, is, in some way, a humiliation. I only shall say that on that day I was tortured for 8 hours. My skull was fractured in different places, one of my ear drums was blasted, and they practiced that nasty form of suffocation they attain by drowning a person until he becomes unconscious.[30]

The SD changed their tactics, however. Pucci was sent to Switzerland where he was to persuade Edda to hand over the diaries. His belief in Fascism now definitively destroyed, Pucci immediately tried to make contact with the Allies on arrival in the country. The British had no interest in him, and after this setback he suffered a nervous breakdown and was admitted to a Swiss hospital where they noticed his serious injuries. Only now did Allen Dulles appoint Cordelia as Pucci's handler. After everything he had been through Pucci was understandably delighted to be visited by Cordelia in a Swiss sanatorium. The sight of her speeded up his recovery and Cordelia was pleased to see him too: "He and I won a dance contest at Zermatt, above and beyond the call of duty! We skied, relived college memories, discussed the Italy that Pucci saw collapsing under Fascist rule as we relaxed in front of a roaring fire at one of the resort chalets."[31]

The relationship flourished and progress was made in the procuring of the diaries. Pucci said he was prepared to go to Italy to fetch the rest, but by now some of the material was in the hands of German intelligence. Thanks to Pucci, Edda Ciano still had five volumes. She too was in a sanatorium under the surveillance of Swiss intelligence.

Pucci did his best to persuade Edda to hand over the diaries, and ultimately she consented to receive Dulles in the sanatorium. After lengthy negotiations the two agreed that 1,200 pages should be secretly photographed and later published as a book. The result of this deal was a major PR coup for the Allies. The international press printed extracts from the diaries, and they were used as evidence against Ribbentrop at the Nuremberg Trials.

The Ciano diaries represented only a modest proportion of the incriminating material the OSS and CIC made available to the prosecutors at Nuremberg. In some cases awkward compromises had been struck to access the material, but it did help to convict some of the worst Nazi criminals.[32]

Cordelia could be happy with the part she played in getting hold of the diaries. The dance performance in Zermatt had certainly been worth it.

14: ALIVE!

"The day is ours,
the bloody dog is dead."
William Shakespeare, *Richard III,*
cited on 1 May 1945 on the BBC

On 5 May 1945, as Lisl Scherzer was cycling from the children's hostel to the dressmaker's where she worked, she bumped into the postman. Not imagining he might have anything for her, she kept pedalling energetically. Soon afterwards she was busy altering a customer's seam when Ruth came storming into the shop and said, "You've got to come home right now. There's a telegram for you!" This put Lisl into a panic. Her father was serving in the British army, and the fear that something might have happened to him – in the last days of the war – made her rush back to the hostel: "The matrons were already waiting for me with a cup of tea and a sedative."

Alice and Paula took Lisl into a separate room and handed her the telegram. It was from Sweden and addressed to her father, who'd given the children's home as his contact address.

Lisl was relieved to read his name as it meant that nothing had happened to him. She opened the envelope and read:

Stockholm. 4th May Sherzer.
Your wife saved; Arrived here Red Cross transport from Germany.

Even as an elderly lady Lisl would weep for joy when she spoke about the moment she realised her parents had survived.

I was the only one with a dad[1] and now I have a mum! Nineteen girls are standing behind the closed doors, the ladies are sitting with me and the telegram and I hear "Why does she not come out and tell us who the telegram is from?" How can I tell them my mother is alive I am the only one with a dad and a sister in Palestine, they have no-one. I go out and tell them. And they say how nice perhaps we will hear something as well. And they never do.[2]

Over the coming weeks Alice and Paula would often have to fetch the sedatives from the cupboard. Apart from this telegram, only bad news arrived at the children's home after the war ended on 8 May. Alice was so worried about the mood in the house that she censored the newspapers and switched off the radio as soon as the news came on. She asked the older children not to turn up at the cinema until the main film began, because beforehand they would show Pathé News, which reported on the week's events. The children had been allowed to watch it throughout the war, but now there were reports about concentration camps too. When Alice heard that an entire film would be shown about the liberation of the camps, she strictly forbade the girls from going to the cinema at all. Peter Sieber described what happened then: "One of the oldest sneaked out and went to the cinema. When the newsreel came on, she fainted. The cinema staff comforted [. . .] her. The local policeman kindly brought her home in his patrol car."[3]

What Alice and Paula had anticipated for years had now become a reality: they weren't running a children's home but an orphanage. Together with Jewish aid organisations they sought out distant relatives of the girls, but several children did not want to leave the hostel, and for a long while Alice and Paula remained their only parental substitutes. From a file that the Jewish Refugees Committee continued to update even after the war, we can see what happened to a Margot H., who was keen to stay at the hostel even though she reached the age of twenty-one in 1945. The entries from the post-war period are a combination of tragedy and banality:

- 14/7/45: [. . .] The name Bela H. has been found on the list of people from Bergen-Belsen [. . .] wondering whether it is the same person as Margot's mother Bella H.
- 16/7/45: To Margot giving her the above information, and telling her that we shall let her have further news as soon as possible.
- 1/11/45: From Mrs Urbach to say that Margot has got engaged and wants to get married soon. To Mrs Urbach

informing her that Rabbi Neuman will get in touch with her regarding technical questions.

- 26/2/46: [Margot] has given up job to help out hostel. Move back to NE, will then look for job in London. Wants tonsils out before going south. Jewish hospital has confirmed need for operation, and will see about doing it. Engagement broken off.
- 12/4/46: Visited Margot in hospital. She is fairly comfortable.
  [...]
- 3/6/46: From the North Western Council passing on a Red Cross message for Margot, giving the information that the two people she enquired for were deported, probably to Riga, on 22/11/41.[4]
- 6/6/46: To Mrs Urbach sending this message, and asking her to tell Margot.
  [...]
- 9/8/46: [Margot] has found a very good job with a hairdresser in Stamford Hill.
  [...]
- 16/4/47: Margot is engaged to be married to Nathan D., who is at the moment in His Majesty's Forces. He is a Jewish refugee and a former member of the chibbutz. In view of the engagement Margot is not anxious to hurry up her emigration to America [...]
- 29/5/47: Miss Jacobs rang to say that Margot will definitely be considered for a dowry.[5]

The hostel was not, therefore, shut down immediately in 1945. On the contrary, according to Peter Sieber it was turned into a sort of stopover for children from other houses. Alice and Paula looked after a total of forty girls up until October 1946.[6]

Anna Freud too seems to have remembered Windermere and Alice's work. Freud worked with aid organisations who, after the liberation of the camps, brought a group of child inmates to Britain. From Alice she knew how soothing the landscape of the Lake District could be. The children from the camps were now also housed near Windermere, in the hope that they might at least achieve some physical recovery in the beautiful countryside. The group lived on the Calgarth Estate. Paula and Alice warned the girls to keep away from the concentration camp boys. This was not simply for moral reasons. Lisl remembered being told by the matrons, "You don't know what they went through. Don't talk to them." But Lisl ignored this; she and the other girls met the boys queueing up at the cinema: "It didn't take long before each one of us had a boyfriend!"[7]

Although they had agreed never to abandon their charges, when the Jewish Committee had raised enough money in 1946 to send the girls to distant relatives, Paula and Alice could once again think of their own futures. Paula wanted to stay in Britain, but Alice was dreaming of a new beginning.

In Auschwitz there was a name for the place where everything existed in abundance: Canada. If anyone asked how they might get hold of a musical instrument for the women's orchestra, the answer would come back: Canada. Here "Canada" referred to the warehouses storing everything that had been taken from the prisoners – their warm coats and the valuables they hid inside them. Canada became a synonym for prosperity, a place all the inmates dreamed of.[8]

Although Alice's fate cannot be compared to that of her sisters in the camps, there was a place she dreamed of too. It lay right beside Canada and was called the United States of America. It wasn't just the prosperity that attracted her; more importantly, it was the new home of her sons and her brother Felix. Alice was desperate to be reunited with them, and emigration to America became her great dream. Being a new American citizen, Otto could now act as full guarantor for her, but the Dodsons also helped to accelerate the process. The wealthy William Dodson worked in Washington and his statement was ultimately decisive. He gave a detailed explanation to the immigration authorities of how commendably Alice's sons had integrated in America:

When the Anschluss took place and the Nazis began abusing all people having Jewish blood, my children appealed to me to help get Karl Urbach out of Austria and into America. This I did and agreed to sponsor him in this country [. . .] We cooperated in getting him placed in colleges where he could finish his education [. . .] After graduating from Reed College he went to Northwestern University in Chicago for a technical course in chemistry [. . .] He has been a remarkably intelligent, thrifty and energetic young man [. . .] His brother, Otto Urbach, went into the Air Force of the United States and is now in

Europe with either this or some other United States agency. He has also been highly patriotic, energetic and aggressive.[9] [. . .] I have never met the mother of the two young men but my three children did get acquainted with her in Vienna. They found her an expert dietician and she was employed at various times in Vienna and London in this capacity [. . .] So far as my young people have learned [. . .] the mother was very capable and a high-grade woman [. . .] In view of [her] advancing years, both sons earnestly desire her to come to America where they can support her after she has finished her work.[10]

Dodson's statement made an impression on the authorities and Alice was able to book a crossing to New York. On 16 September 1946 she boarded the *Queen Elizabeth* in Southampton. The liner was named after the wife of King George VI, who had launched it before the war, but the planned luxury crossings of the Atlantic had never taken place. The ship was converted for troop transports, and it wasn't until 1946 – with Alice on board – that she had her "maiden" sailing as a commercial passenger ship. Alice enjoyed every minute of the crossing. She was particularly excited that the captain was Sir James Bisset, who as a young officer had helped rescue passengers from the *Titanic* in 1912.[11] Over the last few years Alice had had plenty of opportunity to observe who stepped up in a crisis and who failed. Travelling with Bisset felt reassuring, and she arrived safely in New York.

At the time, elderly or infirm immigrants into America were picked out at Ellis Island and sent back, irrespective of the fate awaiting them in their countries of origin, whereas those who looked fresh and fit for work had nothing to fear. Photographs of Alice disembarking in New York in 1946 show an exhausted woman straining to smile. Her hair is snow white and she's dressed plainly. She would not have made much of an impression on the immigration officers, and if Alice hadn't been able to show her letter of recommendation from the influential Dodsons she might not have been waved through so quickly. She was only too aware of this, and was particularly ashamed of her shapeless, rough overcoat: "When I arrived in New York my sister-in-law [Felix's wife Helene Mayer] came to pick me up and the first thing she said to me was, 'Your coat looks like it's from the Salvation Army!'"[12]

It was a brutal but accurate observation. Clothing was in abundance in America, and yet it was still rationed in Britain. By now there was not a single item of clothing in her possession Alice could be proud of. After all the years of frugality she had almost forgotten the emphasis her family had placed on dressing smartly. As the Mayers had made their fortune in textiles, there was an unwritten rule for all family members: the men were to wear immaculate suits, the women elegant skirt suits and matching hats. Every stroll through Vienna was an exhibition; you didn't go out as a private individual, but as a representative of the firm. Although those times were long past, Alice resolved to take more care over her appearance now that she was in New York. In America this seemed possible even with little money. The department stores were overflowing with goods and Alice could scarcely believe that she was seeing such beautiful things again. Her sister-in-law Helene did not earn much, and even Felix struggled along in poorly paid office jobs, but both managed to avoid letting their poverty show.

Later Alice would live very close to them in New York, but in 1946 there was only one thing on her mind: to be together with Karl again. He was studying at Northwestern University in Chicago and Alice travelled to see him. It must have been a strange reunion. In her mind she still pictured a shy twenty-year-old, but Karl was now twenty-eight and had been through a lot. Imprisonment in Dachau, keeping his head above water in America with casual work while also completing a PhD in record time in Chemistry, a subject crucial to the war effort. These experiences had boosted his confidence and finally he could study what he most wanted to: medicine. After all the years apart, they longed to live near each other again. Karl secured Alice a job as a dietary advisor in a large Chicago hotel and she started all over again, learning the ingredients and units of measure of a foreign country.[13]

While Alice was overwhelmed by the plenitude of clothing and food in America, Otto was in Germany experiencing the opposite. He saw the hunger of the population, the bombed-out cities and the piles of corpses in the liberated camps. His intelligence colleague, the journalist Hans Habe, described encountering Germans again in 1945:

I met all [. . .] types [. . .] cowardly opportunists, who only yesterday were preaching hanging on to the bitter end and now were avidly dusting off their English; brave resistance fighters who made no attempt to curry favour with us; incorrigible Nazis who tried to postpone the inevitable with minor acts of sabotage; nationalists who were indifferent to the destruction of their country that had bled dry; patriots longing for peace.[14]

It was a dismal mixture of human ruin, and it comes as no surprise that most of Otto's comrades were keen to return to their civilian careers as quickly as possible. After what he had witnessed in the concentration camps, Otto was planning no such return. Once again Alice's sons differed from each other: Karl tried to forget it all by leading a normal life – he would not allow the Nazis to determine his future – whereas Otto never built the ski hotel he had dreamed of in 1938. Everything he would do in the next thirty years was in some way determined by the war.

Like so many men of his generation, Otto never discussed his feelings. Only his objective intelligence reports, housed in the National Archives in Washington, give an indication of what he witnessed in post-war Germany. One document written in 1946 achieved international notoriety: the Odessa report, about the organisation of former SS soldiers. It became the springboard for years of research and was later fictionalised by Frederick Forsyth in his novel *The Odessa File*, published in 1972.

In early 1946 Otto started working in Stuttgart, region 1 of the Counter Intelligence Corps.[15] The CIC was not as elitist as Cordelia's OSS, but it carried out similar tasks. Originally founded as a counter-espionage agency, in destroyed post-war Germany it had to undertake a large number of policing jobs – from black market controls to hunting down war criminals. Some of these war criminals had gone to ground in the Displaced

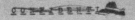

HEADQUARTERS
COUNTER INTELLIGENCE CORPS
UNITED STATES FORCES EUROPEAN THEATER
Region I (Stuttgart)
APO 154

Sub-Reg. Stuttgart
3 July 1946

MEMORANDUM TO THE OFFICER IN CHARGE:

SUBJECT: Subversive Organization of Released SS Prisoners "ODESSA"

1. Information received at this office indicates that there exists an underground organisation of released SS prisoners who have passed through the Auerbach Entlassungslager. The permanent staff of this camp consists entirely of higher SS personnel, and it is believed that the lower SS ranks passing through this installation are influenced by that permanent party of SS officers. *Ev. F-6*

2. It is reported that upon mentioning the code word "ODESSA" special food privileges and special consideration can be had in the AugsburgnGerman Red Cross, diagonally across from the Main Railway Station at Augsburg. A particular Red Cross helper, who was on duty at 0900 hours on 8 June 1946, upon being told that the men who approached her knew the cover name "ODESSA", gave them extra bread and coffee although she had turned ed down other released PWs only a few moments before. *Ev. F-6*

3. Discription of this Red Cross worker is as follows:

       Name: unknown
       Age : 28 - 30
       Height: 168 cm.

4. It is suggested that this personality be carefully investigated by the CIC Sub-Region concerned and that information about this "ODESSA" movement be obtained by inside investigation of the SS Entlassungslager, Auerbach, near Grafenwoehr. Ev. F-6

                                    OTTO R. URBACH
                                    Special Agent CIC

APPROVED:
       CLAYTON L. HOLOGON
       Special Agent in Charge
       Sub-Region Stuttgart

CONFIDENTIAL

Otto's Odessa report on the organisation of former SS soldiers

Persons (DP) camps, where chaos prevailed. Here, former concentration camp inmates could encounter SS officers pretending to be refugees. They had no papers, or falsified ones, and gave accounts that nobody could verify. Profiteering and all kinds of criminality were the order of the day, and the DP camps became known as hotbeds of violence. Otto and his CIC colleagues had the thankless task of trying to establish who was telling the truth and who was lying. For this reason the CIC regularly infiltrated the camps with its own people (mainly German emigrants) to access information. The same method was also used in the prison camps where SS men were incarcerated. It was about one of these camps that Otto wrote the famous Odessa report in 1946, which was purely routine, one of hundreds written daily by CIC agents. Otto described Odessa as the codeword of an underground organisation. But over the next few weeks new information would come to light. An Odessa organisation emerged in British-occupied Hamburg, and in Bavaria the CIC planted an informant in Dachau prison camp. Following the liberation of the concentration camp inmates, SS men were now imprisoned here. The Dachau informant picked up rumours suggesting that an escape organisation by the name of Odessa was organising papers for emigration to Argentina.[16]

The name "Odessa" itself was a puzzle. Otto believed it stood for "Organisation der ehemaligen SS Angehörigen" (Organisation of former SS members), but as SS officers were known for their particularly macabre humour, Odessa could well have had another meaning. In autumn 1941 Romanian troops under German leadership had murdered about 25,000

Jews in Odessa – an act of which the SS were very proud. Whatever the story behind the name, the purpose of Odessa seemed pragmatic: to obtain supplies for like-minded men and to organise escape routes. In late 1946, the CIC discovered that former SS men responded with great flexibility; new networks now existed with entirely different names.[17] The methods were also perfected over the years. One of the last (known) aid organisations for members of the SS is "Stille Hilfe" (Silent Aid). It was supported by Heinrich Himmler's daughter Gudrun until her death in 2018. "Stille Hilfe" provided SS criminals with legal assistance and comfortable accommodation in old people's homes.[18]

Otto's CIC report from 1946 remained classified until 2000. Despite this, the name Odessa became known as early as the 1960s, thanks to the books written by the Nazi hunter Simon Wiesenthal: *Ich jagte Eichmann* (I hunted Eichmann) and *The Murderers among Us*. After his incarceration at Mauthausen, Wiesenthal pledged to track down Nazi war criminals and their networks. One of these was Adolf Eichmann who first went to ground in Altaussee in Austria, then spent five years hiding in Germany before taking flight to Argentina in the early 1950s. Living underground like this could only be made possible by a dependence on a large circle of supporters and sponsors, and it was by looking for such networks that Wiesenthal came across Odessa. He passed on the information to the Reuters journalist Frederick Forsyth, who embellished it in the writing of his novel.[19]

Of course, people often asked Wiesenthal how he had found

out about Odessa. He never revealed his source, only saying that it was a successful German industrialist.[20] In fact there were many CIC members who had good reason to tell Wiesenthal about Odessa. Otto, who had been working in Austria since 1949, could have been one of them. Like Wiesenthal, he did not want the hunt for war criminals to be shelved. But this is precisely what his CIC superiors seemed to have decided should happen. Victor Brombert described how at the end of 1945 he watched as local Nazi officials were released, including those he had only recently tracked down and arrested. His commanders believed that these men were "indispensable for running things".[21] That was perhaps one reason, but another, less pragmatic reason was that the American intelligence service was never a homogeneous group and included officers who had no scruples about cooperating with Nazis. Not all of them possessed the same moral compass as Cordelia Dodson, and Brombert even considered some of his superiors to be unequivocal anti-Semites.

And there was a third reason: the hunt for Nazi war criminals lost priority because a new enemy had appeared on the scene: the Soviet Union. The Cold War had begun, and compromises needed to be struck.[22] Brombert responded by returning to civilian life, later becoming professor of French literature at Princeton. But Otto remained in the CIC, which had many disadvantages. To be able to continue working in Germany he needed permanent camouflage. Emigrants were seen as traitors, and to begin with they were despised even more than "authentic" Americans or Brits. In 1954 the first Gestapo chief Rudolf Diels described German emigrants as "whistle-blowers" for the Nuremberg trials. They had spread propaganda abroad against

Otto (centre) with a Major in the US army in 1946 or 1947

the Fatherland and "prompted German prisoners-of-war to betray military secrets".[23] Diels's arguments come across today as particularly hypocritical as he himself offered his services to the CIC. In post-war Germany there were many Rudolf Diels types, and perhaps that's why Otto chose Mr E.W. Stone as his first alias in Stuttgart.[24] The name was apposite for his state of mind back then; once he had encountered these criminals, he wanted a heart of stone. He was not going to let anyone upset him again.

But the reason his heart did not turn to stone was a woman by the name of Wera Friedberg. Beside her beauty, there were a number of reasons why he fell in love with the twenty-year-old actress. Wera herself believed it was pure chance:

In 1946 I got my first job at the Staatstheater in Stuttgart. I was hungry, all of us were hungry all of the time. There was a black market in Stuttgart,[25] where I went with some of the family silver. At my second attempt to do a deal I was caught and was taken to the CIC station. The American officer there, one Mr Stone, gave me a long lecture about the dangers of the black market. He said I had no idea about what went on behind the scenes and I should never go there again. I swore eternal regret and managed to make it just in time for the evening performance. Two days later the first packages arrived. They were handed to my landlady, wonderful, large food packages. We could hardly believe our eyes and started eating with gusto. But there was no note. No sender, nothing. I knew, of course, that the packages could only be from

Mr Stone, and when I finally managed to thank him all he said was, "It's nothing. I do it for anyone who is hungry." He didn't seem to have much interest in me, and I just gave him a ticket for the theatre.[26]

Wera was thirteen years younger than Otto, engaged to be married, and she lived for her job. Before allowing himself to be drawn into this futile affair, Otto checked her family for Nazi Party membership, as a precaution. Every day, as Mr Stone, he interrogated Nazis, and by now he had heard endless variations of "amnesia" and wanted nothing to do with these people personally. To fall in love with a girl who came from a Nazi family would have aggravated his nightmares (and without doubt upset Alice).

Otto had been struck, however, by Wera's surname "Friedberg". It sounded promising. Apart from being the name of a few small towns, Friedberg was also a common Jewish surname. Although Otto only had a vague recollection of his History lessons, he knew that there had been a Jewish minister under Reich Chancellor Bismarck: Heinrich von Friedberg in the ministry of justice. It was so unusual that it had stayed in his memory. This Friedberg had made it to the very top, to the inner circle of government, and to Otto's delight Wera happened to be related to him. Heinrich von Friedberg's father was a merchant by the name of Israel Friedberg, whose children had gone far despite their Jewish background.[27] Heinrich became Prussian minister of justice and his brother Eduard a successful Berlin industrialist. Wera was from Eduard's side of the family. He was known by his descendants as "Schrauben-Ede" (Screw

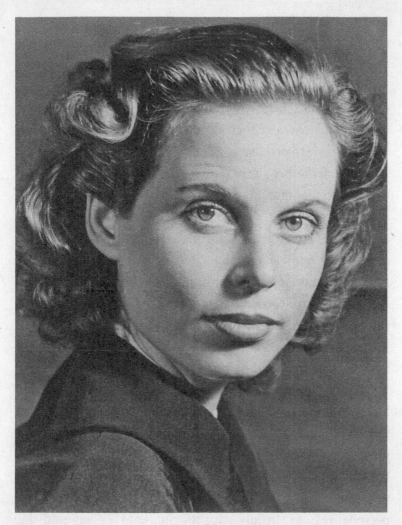

The actress Wera Friedberg, later Frydtberg, in 1947 or 1948

Ede) because he had invented particular types of screws for the new railway lines. After "Schrauben-Ede" died, no other family member would show any technical competence. The Friedbergs focused on becoming a middle-class Protestant family. But this was of little help when the Nuremberg Race Laws came into force and Wera's father, as "mixed race, second degree", was no longer able to practise as a doctor.[28]

It was her father's experiences that Wera was now able to translate to the stage. She had not given the nice Mr Stone just any old theatre ticket. As the youngest member of the ensemble at the Württembergische Staatstheater in Stuttgart, she had to appear in a number of productions simultaneously, but one role meant more to her than others. She played the daughter Ruth in the anti-Nazi play *Professor Mamlock*, which tells the story of a Jewish doctor who is booted out of his clinic in 1933 by the National Socialists. One by one his old friends abandon him, his daughter Ruth is humiliated at school and Professor Mamlock falls into the hands of the SA. They tear his clothes, hang a sign around his neck identifying him as a Jew, and finally drive him to suicide. Friedrich Wolf's play had been a great success in the Soviet Union and America in the 1930s. In Germany too it was performed in several theatres right after the war. The role of Ruth was important to Wera for very personal reasons. In July 1946 the *Stuttgarter Zeitung* said she was "likeable and honest as Mamlock's daughter", although the critic noted that the play was already "outdated":

And yet it cannot do any harm if one of these sad episodes from the reign of evil is held up to the mirror once more.

Wera as Ruth with Herbert Herbe as Professor Mamlock in Friedrich Wolf's play, Staatstheater Stuttgart, 1946

There is definitely a certain tragicomedy in the fact that, at the Stuttgart premiere, enthusiastic applause broke out at a number of points in the play as if at a political meeting, probably from those people who kept very quiet when taking a combative stance was fraught with danger.[29]

On this point the critic was surely right. It is possible, however, that Mr Stone was one of those applauding wildly. Otto fell in love with Wera because it was hard not to love her. But he may also have fallen in love with her because she was Ruth Mamlock.

15: RETURN TO VIENNA

"I have to pass withering judgment
on this city –
Vienna is still Vienna."
Alfred Polgar after a visit to Vienna
at the end of the 1940s.[1]

In her new American clothes Alice stood out from the rest of
the Viennese population in 1949.[2] But it wasn't just her clothes
that attracted attention; there was something about her that
every local noticed at once. She still spoke with her charming
Viennese accent, but her old self was gone; she now had the air
of an emigrant. The Austrian Ernst Lothar, another emigrant,
described in his barely fictionalised novel *Die Rückkehr* (The
Return) how he found Vienna and the Viennese after the war:
"Mountains of rubble amongst what had been spared [. . .]
Windows covered with cardboard, shop windows boarded
up with wood. Almost nobody on the street, the few you saw
were hollow-cheeked and unbelievably shabby."[3]

The once magnificent mansions of the Ringstrasse were now

just bombed-out shells. In Lothar's novel, the emigrants who have returned from America stand horrified beside the ruins of the State Opera and hear a passer-by comment, "Look what the Americans did!" No hint of self-reflection; the Viennese were as wrecked as their buildings. And they hated the well-fed exiles who suddenly turned up in their city: "Why've you come over from England if you don't like it here?" they snarled.[4]

A dislike of the emigrants was only exceeded by a hatred for the Russians. Like Germany, Austria was divided into four zones, and Vienna was in the Soviet zone. The access roads and stations were controlled by the Soviet occupying authority, although Vienna itself was an island, divided into five sectors: British, French, American, Soviet and an international sector covering the city centre. The administration of the city centre passed from one of the Allied Powers to the next on a monthly basis, a system which often led to verbal and physical confrontation.[5]

In 1949 Vienna was firmly in the grip of the Cold War, and so it was no coincidence that Alice should be visiting her son Otto there. The city was at the centre of a war of espionage in which Otto and Cordelia had assumed new roles.[6] The two made a good team even though they now had other partners. Otto had married Wera in November 1947 and Cordelia was engaged to her OSS colleague William Hood. Like all Americans they lived in the American sector, which encompassed the 7th to 9th and 17th to 19th districts. It cannot be an accident that of these districts Otto should have chosen Döbling, the 19th, to live in and that he rented a yellow villa at 30 Hasenauerstrasse.[7] Number thirty resembled a building from his childhood. Only 450 metres away, at 5 Linnéplatz, Otto used to visit his rich grandparents and marvel at Sigmund Mayer's extensive library.

When she arrived in Vienna, Alice was immediately struck by the symbolism of the address. In summer 1949 she was back in her home city for the first time in more than eleven years, to visit Otto and Wera. But this was not the only reason for her trip.

Alice was searching for something, although she would not have been able to describe exactly what. She had been working in Chicago for almost three years now, and she felt enormous gratitude towards Britain and America, which had given a home to her and her sons. Nonetheless the countries remained foreign to her. Many emigrants experienced a similar ambivalence. When the writer Annette Kolb was asked how she felt living as an emigrant in America, she said, "grateful and unhappy".[8] Alice knew exactly what she meant.

She found it difficult to break definitively with her Viennese background and she strolled around the city on her own, revisiting the places from her past, while her daughter-in-law rehearsed new plays at the Theater in der Josefstadt and Otto played his own, dangerous form of theatre.[9] Alice was alone with her memories. She looked for a synagogue, but only the temple in Seitenstettengasse was left standing. It had been spared a torching in the 1938 pogrom because the neighbouring houses in the narrow street would have caught fire too. "When I stood outside it," Alice said, "I just cried because I thought of all the weddings there and everyone who'd perished because of Hitler."[10]

She went on, past Café Landtmann and Paula's old apartment at 3 Schreyvogelgasse. The building now looked more sombre than it had before the war. Only a few metres away, at number 8, they had just finished filming *The Third Man*. Alice could not know that the writer of the screenplay, Graham Greene, had regarded the city similarly, as a derelict Moloch full of opportunists.

One day on her wanderings through Vienna, Alice passed a bookshop. In 1949 shop windows in Austria had little on display, but one title immediately caught her eye. She went in and picked up the book. Surely that was her cookbook, wasn't it? Her text, her photographs? But there was an unfamiliar name on the cover: Rudolf Rösch. At that moment all kinds of thoughts must have shot through her mind: the memory of 1935, when she first held the large volume in her hands and celebrated the launch with her friends; the three years that followed, during which the book became a bestseller, with readers even approaching her in the street; and then 1938, when suddenly she could no longer be its author. She had kept a copy with her since leaving Vienna, and the children in Windermere had learned to cook from it.

After Alice saw Rösch's name on the cover she could think of nothing else. This book must be given back to her, at least. She had lost three sisters in the Holocaust, compared to which the loss of a cookbook was a trivial matter. And yet for Alice it represented all the injustice and humiliation of the last few years. By reclaiming the book, she intended to regain control over her life after all this time.

But what exactly had happened to her cookbook? Alice knew that Ernst Reinhardt had died in 1937, but she didn't know how the publishing house had fared in the Nazi era. To this day, the information remains contradictory. Ernst Reinhardt Verlag claims it suffered in that period. To celebrate its centenary in 1999, the publishing house organised an exhibition in the Munich Literature House, where "a large amount of correspondence from the 1930s and 1940s" was displayed to "[give] an impression of publishing under the repressive measures of the National Socialist regime". The exhibition insisted that "a definitive order to close down was given and the publishing house found temporarily exile in Basel."[11]

Several points here are misleading. A number of books were indeed confiscated, but Hermann Jungck rapidly adapted the business to the new circumstances. On 28 June 1938, the chamber of industry and commerce declared: "Our enquiries have revealed that sole proprietor Hermann Jungck, publisher in Munich, is a Swiss national and of [Aryan] blood. According to our information no Jewish capital is involved in the Ernst Reinhardt company in Munich."[12]

The claim that Ernst Reinhardt Verlag had found "exile" is incorrect too. Exile is a word used for victims of political and "racial" persecution. The publishing house, on the other hand, continued to trade successfully under the National Socialist system. A major reason for Jungck's *moving* to the safety of Switzerland in 1944 may well have been the air raids on Munich. Jungck's Swiss passport and large amounts of foreign currency enabled him to go to Switzerland at any time, unlike the rest of the population. This luxury was otherwise only the privilege of high-ranking Nazis in wartime.

Another reason given for the move to Basel was the "order

to close down" in 1944. This sounds dramatic, but again the context is decisive. In 1944 all publishing houses were ordered to shut down. In Goebbels's total war there was a shortage of paper, and it was no longer to be "wasted" on printing books. The Germanist Christian Adam has shown that this order to cease production was used by a number of publishing houses after the war to present themselves as victims of National Socialism.[13] They claimed their activity was "prohibited in the Nazi era". The phrasing suggests resistance and ensured that no further questions were asked.

It is hardly a surprise that publishing houses in the Nazi era behaved no differently from other businesses. Desperate to survive, they adapted to the regime. When in 1937 and 1938 Hermann Jungck used front men as authors for Paul Wessel and Alice Urbach, he could have claimed with some justification that he had no other choice. It was not possible to publish books with Jewish authors' names, and taking them off the market would have financially damaged the publishing house. Therefore – Jungck could have argued after the war – he had to use the front man method for the period. But he continued to use it thereafter too. Hermann Jungck's real culpability begins only after 1945. He is a classic example of what Ralph Giordano called the "second guilt" of the post-war years.

In 1945 Jungck must have believed that Alice Urbach and Paul Wessel were dead. Neither had any savings. How could they have survived six years of poverty, illness and bombing?

But then Wessel turned up again out of the blue. The irritation Hermann Jungck must have felt comes through in every line of his 1974 history: "I suddenly received a fifty-page handwritten letter from Dr Wessel sent from England, describing what had happened to him, claiming he was the sole owner of the copyright to the series and declaring the three-way contract invalid, it having been signed only under coercion."[14]

This letter must have been awkward for Jungck for several reasons. He had just re-established Ernst Reinhardt Verlag in Basel, and in the longer term he planned to continue running the business from two cities: Basel and Munich. One of the publishing successes making this financially possible was a reprint of Wessel's physics book. As Juncgk writes, it was "snapped up" by students.

Now Paul Wessel wanted his rights back, including those relating to the study series he had conceived. He was absolutely right to state that the volumes had been his creation: "Outline, brief revision, exam questions and answers." Frau Riederer von Paar, on the other hand, had simply been used as a front.

Jungck refused to accept this argument, however. In a head-on riposte he focused on portraying Wessel as incompetent. It was a tactic he would later use with Alice. He claimed that Wessel had only "borrowed" the key ideas of his book – parts had apparently been lifted from predecessors Jungck did not care to identify. Moreover the series had been completely updated by the co-editors, while Wessel's work in the 1930s had been extremely slipshod and cost the publisher a lot of money in corrections. Jungck gave the impression of being morally outraged by Wessel's letter,[15] claiming that it had damaged Frau Riederer von Paar's reputation: "Even though she'd stood up for him during the Nazi era. I found his attitude so reprehensible that I refused to cooperate with him any further."

It did not stop there, however. The rest of Jungck's account sounds confused; he claims to have given Wessel back the copyright for the series, which then appeared in a different form in Reinhardt Verlag.[16]

Jungck makes no mention here that there was a Spanish translation of Wessel's physics book from which the author ought to have earned his share. After the war his anger at the "reprehensible" Wessel seems to have been so great that Jungck goes so far as to describe how he dissuaded other publishing houses from working with the penniless author:

On one occasion I was called up by a publishing house in Lucerne to which Dr Wessel had offered his physics book. According to the author, the book's sales had been excellent, so why was I giving away the copyright? My answers were slightly evasive. Was he not a nice man, then? I couldn't deny that. Afterwards the publisher in question clearly decided against taking on the rights.

It is unclear when this conversation took place, for Wessel suffered a heart attack soon after the quarrel with his unrelenting publisher. This does not seem to have had much of an influence on Jungck, who wrote in 1974: "Dr Wessel died in Switzerland soon afterwards [...] He got caught in a snowstorm, through which he struggled with the last of his strength to reach the pub. He then died from the heart failure this induced."[17]

In 1974 Hermann Jungck also goes into detail about Alice's book. He writes: "Because I could no longer sell the cookbook in

Austria after the war, and sales prospects in Germany were too poor, I gave an Austrian publisher a licence and it was this edition of the book that came into Frau Urbach's hands when she was on a visit to Vienna."[18] Despite the supposedly "poor sales prospects", Jungck continued to sell the book through Reinhardt Verlag in Munich and also licensed it to an Austrian publisher. In 1954 *So kocht man in Wien!*, "in a splendid gift ribbon", cost twenty-two marks in Germany.

What Jungck writes about his meeting with Alice cannot be true either:

> Around 1948, financially one of the most difficult periods for the publishing house [. . .] Frau Urbach suddenly turned up at the offices in Basel wanting to speak to me. She claimed that because her cookbook had continued to be printed under another name, as she had learned, she had suffered losses for which she was now demanding compensation.[19]

This meeting cannot have taken place, because in April 1953 Alice wrote to Jungck: "I would very much like to take the opportunity to meet you in Switzerland and finally have the pleasure of making your acquaintance. I would be very grateful if you would let me know where and how this might be possible.[20]

In Jungck's mind, however, a "meeting" had taken place in the late 1940s, at which he claimed he had told Frau Urbach that she no longer had any rights to her book because "she had secured and been paid a one-off fee and thus had not suffered any financial losses; besides, she admitted herself that the title came from my uncle."[21]

As has already been shown in Chapter 8 ("Book thieves"), in 1938 Alice had – under duress – signed a declaration in which she surrendered all her rights.[22] In Jungck's eyes this "arrangement" continued to be legally binding – as he had argued with Wessel.

In his version of the story Jungck also neglects to mention that Alice's cookbook became a bestseller in 1935, and in early 1938 had just appeared in its third edition with a print run of 25,000 copies. Instead, he presents only Rösch's book as a success and gives the print runs for the editions that carry his name: December 1938, 1st edition, 10,000 [this figure is wrong as the Rösch version didn't appear until 1939];[23] June 1939, 2nd edition, 16,500; June 1940, 3rd edition, 11,300; March 1941, 4th edition, 12,000.

In his 1974 history Jungck devotes a surprising amount of space to this affair. At the end of his demolition of Alice, he describes how the negotiations continued at their alleged meeting:

Now she claimed that her personality rights had been infringed. The recipes were mainly hers, but there was no mention of her name. I said this could be redressed; I would be happy to see to it that future editions of the book would appear under both names: Urbach and Rösch. She (understandably) wanted nothing to do with this and eventually left in a temper.[24]

Did Jungck really make Alice this offer? When her story became known in 2020, Reinhardt Verlag found in its archive eighteen letters that Alice had written to Jungck in 1954 and which painted a very different picture. Alice first made contact in 1950:

> Dear Herr Jungck
>
> We have not been in contact for a long time, have we? I would be very interested to know how you are – professionally and personally! A long while ago you kindly promised to send me two manuscripts of the vegetarian cookbook and the one on Viennese baking. I've never seen these two creations of mine in print.[25]

By way of an answer Jungck first sent her his publishing catalogue. Alice replied:

> I was very interested in your new books and new editions, although seeing *So kocht man in Wien!* made me feel very strange. Can I now get my rights back to this title?[26]

Jungck's responses have not survived, but he seems not to have answered her question, for two years later Alice asks again: "Can't you do anything to restore my name? After all, it is *my* work!"[27]

Jungck must have claimed that National Socialist laws gave him no other choice at the time. Alice was sympathetic to this and wrote:

Thank you for your friendly letter. I already knew why my original book could no longer be published, but I think it would be only right and proper to mention my name [. . .] The changed book [Rösch's] is nowhere near as different as you think [. . .] If you would be so kind as to send me a copy I would be interested to look through it to see whether the new addition contains more changes. Also, I have never set eyes on the vegetarian and baking cookbooks.[28]

Jungck then appears to have played for time. Alice was now sixty-six. When she finally got hold of the vegetarian cookbook after much toing and froing, she saw that once again Rösch's name was on the cover. She wrote straight to Jungck: "How I'd love to see my name mentioned as the author!!"[29]

Now Alice encountered Rösch's name everywhere. In 1953 she was back in Vienna and sent the following to Jungck:

The Aryan edition of the book is in the window of every bookshop. You can imagine that it breaks my heart, especially when every bookseller says: This is the most popular cookbook, people hardly ever ask for or buy anything else. I also went to Singerstrasse where funnily enough the director said, "So there really is a Frau Urbach." He thought I was just a name or a phantom.[30]

Singerstrasse was home to the offices of the Zentralgesellschaft für buchgewerbliche und graphische Betriebe (ZG). Until the Anschluss in 1938, ZG had been selling Alice's book in Austria.

Although the new director seemed to have heard of the Aryanisation of the book, he did not feel in any way responsible. Jungck too remained unyielding. His claim that he offered to publish the book under both names is as fictional as his account of their meeting in the 1940s. In the last extant letter Alice sent Jungck she mentions a much more modest offer: "Regarding a mention of my name in the Foreword of a new edition, there is no way I can commit myself right now."[31]

Alice had finally realised that Jungck would never restore her as the author of the work. Their correspondence ends in 1954, although amongst Alice's papers there is a letter from 1980 that yet again deals with her fight for the cookbook. Alice had found out that in the 1950s the publisher Gerlach und Wiedling had acquired a licence from Hermann Jungck to publish Rudolf Rösch's *So kocht man in Wien!* Now she asked her daughter-in-law, Wera, to find Gerlach Verlag and give the people in charge there this letter:

Mrs Alice Urbach   4 April 1980
40 Camino Alto
Mill Valley, CA 94941

To Gerlach + Wiedling Verlag, Munich
    I am the author of the cookbook *So kocht man in Wien!*, which was published by Reinhardt Verlag, 11 Isabella-strasse, Munich, in 1934.[32]
    This same book was Aryanised in 1938 under the name Rudolf Rösch. Herr Jungck, the nephew and successor to Ernst Reinhardt, promised to have the book

published under my name again, but he didn't keep his promise. My question to you is: Do you still have one or two original copies of the book? I would <u>happily</u> pay for them!

My daughter-in-law, Frau Wera Urbach-Frydtberg, will be in contact with you soon – if you still exist.

Yours,

Alice Urbach

When Alice wrote this letter in 1980, Gerlach und Wiedling Verlag did in fact no longer exist, having been wound up in 1976.[33] So Alice's request came four years too late.

Jungck must have anticipated that this affair might rear its head again. In 1970s' West Germany, awareness of the crimes of the Nazi period gradually changed. It would be another couple of decades, however, before historians addressed the topic of Aryanisation and began to investigate how publishers acted in the Third Reich.[34] In his jubilee publication from 1974 Jungck helped to control the narrative, and indeed he was successful in this until his death. When in 1999 his heirs published a new history, they simply resorted to omission, neglecting to make any mention of Alice's story in the new version. Without giving further explanation the following title was included in the publication list: "Urbach, Alice, *So kocht man in Wien!* Later editions see Rösch, Rudolf."[35] The editions of the cookbook from 1939 were then listed under the name Rösch.

The 1999 text does contain an interesting snippet, however. Jungck had claimed that the firm had been going through its "most difficult time financially" when Alice made her claims.

Alice's 1980 letter to Verlag
Gerlach und Wiedling

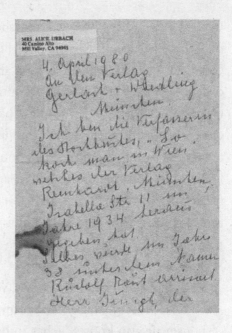

But according to the new volume, the company already had a publishing licence in 1949 and was financially secure.[36] Jungck could certainly have given Alice a share of the profits of her own book, therefore. But although Jungck had met the ghosts of his past – like Ebenezer Scrooge in Charles Dickens's *A Christmas Carol* – he had decided against purging his sins. He continued to be the sole earner from Alice's book. In 1966 he granted one last licence, this time to Forum Verlag. The cover was made to fit the post-war years of prosperity. It showed a juicy roast next to a colourful fruit salad. The blurb played on the German meaning of Rösch (crisp):

> As every good housewife knows, Wiener Schnitzel has to be crisp [rösch], and golden brown. And as every good housewife also knows, it has to be the "Rösch", for this standard work has become a classic which, with more than 2,000 recipes, is without equal. More than 90,000 copies sold speaks more clearly than any praise for the high quality of its contents. For many years Rudolf Rösch was a head chef in Vienna, and his recipes are testimony to great expertise and a wealth of experience.[37]

German academic Christian Enzensberger wrote about the most famous Alice in world literature: "In the lands through which Alice wanders, people die the death of embarrassment and having to remain silent; nobody is murdered, they are muzzled; and no throats are cut, but people are cut off."[38]

Like Lewis Carroll's Alice, Alice Urbach also took journeys into the absurd, in which Jungck played a leading role. He had muzzled her in 1938, and in the 1950s he cut her off. What chance did she have to fight back?

She seems to have toyed with the idea of hiring a lawyer,[39] but it would have been a drawn-out process and emotional torture for her. In his history Jungck portrays Alice as an incompetent writer and cook whose book supposedly needed modernising. In court he would have argued along these same lines.

At the time this sort of defamation was commonplace. In a similar case in the early 1950s, Herbert Cram, the boss of de Gruyter Verlag, was particularly deceitful. He resisted claims for restitution from Georg Stilke, the former owner of the publishing house Stilkes Rechtsbibliothek. As a half-Jew, Stilke had no Aryan certificate and was therefore expelled from the Reich chamber of culture in 1938. He was then forced to sell his publishing house, which Cram acquired within a week at a favourable price. When Stilke sued for compensation in 1949 he stoked Cram's anger. At the time, Cram claimed, Aryanisation had been a normal business procedure and he had paid Stilke a good price.[40] He also doubted that the plaintiff had been in mortal danger under the regime. Not only did Cram's lawyers question Stilke's persecution as a half-Jew, they also formulated counter-demands.[41] After four years, which for Stilke were agonising, a settlement was reached in 1953.[42]

We cannot assume that Alice knew of this case, but her belief in legal certainty had utterly vanished in 1938. She also suspected that most judges and lawyers in West Germany and Austria were the same as those in the Nazi era. Why would people like that help an insignificant Jewish author achieve justice?

In Austria, especially, it seemed futile to hope for a fair trial.

Post-war advertisement from Ernst Reinhardt Verlag for the books of
the "highly experienced chef" Rudolf Rösch

An old Viennese acquaintance of Alice's was Elsa Pollak, daughter of the Jewish publisher Moritz Perles. In 1925 Alice had published her first cookbook with Perles. The publishing house was Aryanised in 1938 and several members of the Perles family died in concentration camps. Ella Pollak survived in America and hoped for restitution after the war, but the opposite happened: "The heirs [. . .] were instead handed down a fine payable to the financial directorate."[43]

Even though the Nazi era was over, Alice knew that the other world through the looking glass still existed.

16: NEW BEGINNINGS

"I like to be in America,
OK by me in America.
Everything free in America—
For a small fee in America."
West Side Story

"The Riviera" is a thirteen-storey apartment block at 790 Riverside Drive in New York. Built in 1911 in Beaux-Arts style, it comprises 199 apartments. The name "Riviera" is misleading, for the building stands in a stone desert, far from palm trees and sandy beaches, and the New York winters can be brutally cold. Only the property prices are reminiscent of the French Mediterranean. In 2020, for example, apartment 5b was on sale for 1,325,000 dollars.[1] When Alice lived in the neighbouring apartment 5c in the 1950s and 1960s, the rent was still around sixty dollars a month. The price increase is due to the shortage of living space, but perhaps also because of the romance of Woody Allen's New York or the film *Shame*, in which Brandon, alias Michael Fassbender, lives out his sexual fantasies in the very same building.

Alice would have been shocked by both the fantasies and the prices. When she moved into 5c, the Riviera was seen as neither chic nor shabby. The apartments were of different sizes, and the most desirable had views of the Hudson.[2] Many of the building's residents were Jewish. The Riviera is in Washington Heights, a district of New York where a large number of emigrants lived, including so many from Frankfurt that the area was occasionally referred to as "Frankfurt-on-the-Hudson" or – in defiance of the Nazis – the "Fourth Reich".

Alice was now experienced at adjusting to new places; she had been moving around for sixty years, after all. Some of these moves had been voluntary, others against her will, and not all had been defined by upward mobility. The family's move in the 1890s from Leopoldstadt to Döbling had been a great success, but for Alice the poverty of Ottakring during her married years soon followed. The cookery school in smart Goldeggasse symbolised her – far too short – resurgence, and the billets thereafter were even more austere than Ottakring: the attic room in Grantham Castle, her maid's quarters in London, and the spartan, ice-cold room in Newcastle. The enchanting house in the Lake District provided the first improvement in a while. Then, in Chicago, Alice became acquainted with soulless American apartments, so she was happy to move to New York, which was far more colourful. An area like Washington Heights had more interesting residents than the Midwest, and many here had gone through the same experiences. The life journeys of her doctor, bookshop owner and grocer were all similar. In

England Alice had always had to spell her name; in Washington Heights that wasn't necessary: "Here, in the States, I still very frequently meet some woman immigrant from the old country, who when she hears my name says, 'Oh, Mrs Urbach, I have never seen you before, but when I emigrated to America I brought your book over with me, for I have always treasured your recipes.'"[3]

Thanks to this fan following Alice rose to the status of minor celebrity in the area. Washington Heights housed both successful and far less successful emigrants, who would bump into each other in restaurants and nod knowingly. Everyone was aware, for example, that old Herr Rosenfeld had been a famous lawyer in Vienna.[4] Now he had to take on temporary work, but there was an unwritten law that he be treated with the same politeness as he had been accustomed to before 1938.

Older academics were rarely able to follow on from their former professional success, but they did everything they could to enable their children to study. Academic status still counted for a lot. Alice told everyone in Washington Heights that her son Karl was a Doctor of Chemistry, while her elder son Otto had fought in the war as a First Lieutenant, and still had "a good position" these days.[5]

Ever since her arrival in America, Alice had been hoping to get her cookbook translated into English. To this end she found one of the best literary agents, Franz Horch. Horch represented many émigré writers in the US, such as Franz Werfel, Erich Maria Remarque and Thomas Mann. Like Alice, Horch came from Vienna and had some understanding of food.[6] He was

Alice and Otto, 1948 or 1949

also interested in representing the writer of a cookbook, but there were two obstacles. First, Hermann Jungck was unwilling to give Alice the translation rights.[7] Second, there was a rival project. *Wiener Küche (Viennese Cooking)*, by the Austrian Olga Hess, was in the process of being translated. In 1913 Olga Hess published *Wiener Küche* with her husband Adolf, and received many awards throughout her life (she died in Austria in 1965).[8] In America too she got there first, as Horch died unexpectedly in 1951, before he could sell Alice's book project. One year later *Viennese Cooking* appeared, and thus the American market for Austrian cookbooks was sated for the time being. That it should be the "Aryan" Olga Hess rather than the exile Alice Urbach who succeeded in America was an irony of fate. Even though she never let it show, Alice took the defeat to heart. In moments like this she must have asked herself: Why do I always lose? My homeland, my sisters, my book and my career too.

Many exiles asked similar questions. Some despaired, others suppressed their bad memories or swore eternal revenge. Most experienced each of these emotions over the years. Alice's standard tactic was suppression, and this is especially evident in the recorded interview she gave in the 1970s, in which she endeavours to evade all the unpleasant topics such as the Holocaust or her emigration. The way she tries to deflect from her real experiences by way of anecdotes, riddles and poems seems almost manic. Very occasionally, in an aside, she touches on the events of the Nazi era, only to skate over them and recite a Löhner-Beda poem. She is as entertaining as Torberg's Tante Jolesch, and you might think she's trying to prevent the people she's talking to from having nightmares. But nothing could have shocked the two women Alice is conversing with. They too were Jewish emigrants, ten years younger than Alice at most, and they had their own traumatic family stories and experiences. All the same, Alice does not speak out about the important things, which may have been for reasons of self-preservation. Not thinking or talking about them meant keeping the pain at bay for as long as possible. And Alice managed this for a very long time.

One method was to surround herself with lots of people. She shared the New York apartment with a Viennese acquaintance, Margarete (Grete) Klemperer, and began to give parties.[9] The best were on her birthday, 5 February. She would transform the sitting room into a replica of Demel's famous patisserie, a paradise of colours and aromas. Lashings of colourful pastries, tiered birthday cakes and spicy Viennese specialities would cover every table and surface. The small apartment would be crammed with guests who never wanted to leave, and the success of these parties reminded Alice of the great cookery exhibitions she had organised in Vienna. She spent a lot of money on these celebrations, often more than she could afford. She had not worked since her seventieth birthday. In November 1956 she summed up her financial situation for the Austrian assistance fund:

I'm a widow, I'm 70 years old and no longer able to work. I draw my social security of $61 per month, a small widow's pension from Vienna, about $8 per month, a small old-age pension from England ($14 per month) [...] My two sons support me to the extent that they can. I don't think I fall into the category of "needy" but into the category of those who cannot work because of their age.[10]

Those 83 dollars are the equivalent of about 750 dollars today. Alice was able to have so many parties only because of the financial support she received from Otto and Karl. Keen to be independent, she now toyed with resurrecting her career.

In the 1960s a food writer had risen to fame on US television, and everything she did, Alice believed she could do much better. The name of this rival was Julia Child. As a slightly eccentric, middle-aged cook, Child brought something entirely new to the American kitchen: the art of French cuisine. In her show she entertained millions by nonchalantly pushing pots and pans around and chatting about her cookery training in Paris. Even today Americans revere Child as a culinary idol. Alice did not share their enthusiasm. She studied Child's programme "The French Chef"[11] in great detail, unable to understand why the Americans so admired someone who trivialised French cuisine. What was praiseworthy about that? Alice believed Julia Child to be overrated and felt something had to be done about it.[12] But unlike Child, Alice had no influential society friends to support her cooking career, and it was a while before she came up with a plan.

By now Karl had married the Berlin emigrant Lilly Mendelsohn and was running a hospital in San Francisco. In 1969 Alice followed him there, and at the age of eighty-three she entered an old people's home in a picture-postcard setting, which she found deadly boring. Once a week she cooked for mentally impaired people at a charitable institution, which gave her the idea that she wanted to teach again.[13] Her career had begun in a cookery school and it should end in one. The Judith Ets-Hokin Culinary Institute was the most celebrated of these in San Francisco. Alice went to see the owner and introduced herself: "I might look old," she said, "but I am a lot of fun. There are a lot of cooking schools here, but not a Viennese one. Wouldn't you like one?"[14]

She was hired immediately and threw herself into the work.[15] She had always enjoyed teaching and could spend hours in a hot kitchen without tiring. Moreover, Alice was on a mission, which she explained to the *San Francisco Examiner* with the following words: "You have *strange* food here in America." As far as she was concerned that had to change. At around the same time she wrote to one of her Windermere children, Ilse Camis: "There is poetry in a good dish. Whenever you come across one, think of me, the champion of good food."[16]

Alice's mission was highly contagious. In San Francisco she excited a new generation with her style of cooking, including many young women who, apart from the recipes, wanted to hear Alice's life story. Thanks to the cookery school she had a number of interviews with journalists who found it fascinating that an emigrant over the age of ninety should still be teaching. In every interview Alice mentioned "her third child", the cookery book that Rudolf Rösch had taken from her. But although all these conversations were published and her daughter-in-law Wera contacted Reinhardt Verlag again in 1980, still nothing happened. The publishing house kept silent, even when Alice began to appear on American television. One of her young friends had written a long letter to the Public Broadcasting Service (PBS) about a wonderfully entertaining woman still giving lessons at ninety-five.[17]

At the end of the 1970s PBS aired the talk show *Over Easy* for older viewers, the perfect programme for Alice. Stars like Eartha Kitt, Gloria Swanson or Omar Sharif came on to discuss their careers and ageing, and when Alice was invited to appear on the show she sparkled as the oldest cookery teacher in America. The programme was filmed in San Francisco, and so she was able to appear several times. *Over Easy* didn't turn Alice into another Julia Child, but she did get recognition for her work. For her this was imperative, as right at the end of her life, when she was ninety-seven, her memories caught up with her. For almost forty years she had managed to suppress the fate suffered by her sisters, and now she was suddenly thinking about them all the time. In these moments, which became ever more drawn out, not even her best pupils could distract her.

When the doctor filled out Alice's death certificate on 26 July 1983, he gave the cause of death as "generalised atherosclerosis", and in the box for "other conditions contributing but not immediately related to the cause of death" he wrote: "depression".[18] Despite the depression Alice was keen to be useful to the very end; she bequeathed her body to the medical faculty.

There is a neurological phenomenon, occurring particularly in children, that doctors call "Alice in Wonderland syndrome". Patients suddenly see their surroundings as much larger or smaller, they hallucinate, perceive time differently and become highly sensitive to light and noise. Some of these symptoms are similar to migraine attacks and it is suspected that Lewis Carroll himself suffered from such attacks. In a similar vein, Alice Urbach's experiences can be perceived as being of greater or lesser magnitude; she herself saw the loss of her cookbook as something momentous. It was symbolic of everything she had lost, and because Jungck refused to restore the book to her after the war, he robbed her of the opportunity to be successful as a cookery writer in her home country. But from another perspective Alice's story is a minor one, because she was only one of millions of women who lost their livelihoods as a result of persecution and the war. What was stolen from her was "merely" authorship, and although research into the Aryanisation of books is only in its infancy, it could be argued that the stealing of a book is not as significant as the theft of a large Jewish firm. What is shocking, however, is that the thieves who profited were not merely party bigwigs, but perfectly ordinary people. The publisher Jungck did what many did, Nazis as well as non-Nazis. It was only in 2000 that the German financial authorities released Aryanisation documents listing the names of countless beneficiaries like Jungck. The names of the officials involved are now known too. In some cases the same officials who dealt with the expropriations even processed (and delayed) the applications for restitution after the war.

In an interview she gave in 1980 Alice said, "My book had a fate."[19] She would have been surprised to learn that there would be a further twist in this fate. When the German edition of *Alice's Book* appeared in autumn 2020, the *Spiegel* journalist Eva-Maria Schnurr wrote about Alice's story.[20] The management of Ernst Reinhardt Verlag subsequently issued a public apology: "After the war Alice Urbach suffered from the fact that her work did not appear in its original edition with her name. We consider the behaviour of the publishing house back then to have been morally indefensible."[21]

Alice's granddaughters were not seeking financial compensation from the publisher, but they achieved something far more important. Within a few weeks the rights to *So kocht man in Wien!* were made over to them, and Ernst Reinhardt Verlag reprinted the 1935 edition. German and Austrian libraries have been sent a copy of the book free of charge.

Almost forty years after her death, Alice is once again the author of *So kocht man in Wien!*

Wiener Semmelknödel in San Francisco: 92-year-old Alice with
her pupils

AFTERWORD

Karl Urbach married the artist Lilly Mendelsohn and they had two children, Katrina and Daniel. He called his son after Daniel Dodson. To Alice's delight, Katrina became a paediatrician.

Karl died in 2003 in San Francisco.

Cordelia Dodson married her OSS colleague William Hood in 1950. The two worked – with and without Otto – in Vienna, Berlin and Switzerland. Owing to the CIA's restrictive archival policy we will never find out exactly what Cordelia did after the war. She died in 2011 in Maine.

The files on **Otto Urbach** are also still classified; only the memories of his colleagues provide some clues to his intelligence work after 1948.

Because his favourite name Katrina was already taken, Otto called his daughter *Karina*, to the bewilderment of his family.

Otto died in 1976 in Brussels. His wife Wera Frydtberg enjoyed a long career in film and the theatre. Alice's favourite film of Wera's was *Wir Wunderkinder*, in which she played an emigrant called Vera. It won a Golden Globe in 1960.

Felix Mayer went in 1950 with his wife Helene to Vienna, the city about which he had written that it was the only place he could breathe. After a fortnight in the Austrian capital he changed his mind. He died in 1960 in New York, and Helene followed him soon afterwards. Their son Thomas Mayer (1927–2015) became a renowned American economist.

Lisl, one of Alice's Windermere girls, is still alive. In a Franco-German TV documentary she asserts that she learned three things from Alice: independence, respect for others and a very good recipe for yeast cake.

Paula Sieber gained British citizenship after the war. But she often spent the summer holidays with Alice in Austria, where the two women had to suppress the knowledge that not many years earlier, signs had read "Jews are not wanted here".

Until her death in 1978, Paula lived near her son Peter Sieber and his family in London.

The publisher **Hermann Jungck** died in 1988, eight years after Wera had contacted his publishing house about Alice's book.

No photographs survive of Alice's murdered sisters **Sidonie** and **Karoline**. But in September 2020, together with **Helene** and her husband Georg Eissler, they were given a "stone of remembrance" outside Helene's old apartment in Vienna's 1st district, 10/12 Ebendorferstrasse.

ACKNOWLEDGEMENTS

As a child I had the fortune to meet some of the emigrants mentioned in this book. Ernst Haeusserman, Franz Marischka, Eva Haas, Curt Riess, Friedrich Torberg and Peter Viertel were emigrants who returned to Europe because they couldn't live without coffee houses. They were friends of my parents but I was too young to ask the right questions. In America I got a second chance. I met the then ninety-seven-year-old Victor Brombert, professor of French literature at Princeton and former "Ritchie Boy". He lived just a few streets away from me. I had similar luck with Alice's great niece, the psychologist Dorit Whiteman, who lives in New York. She interviewed Jewish refugee children in Britain in the 1990s and published their stories in the book *The Uprooted: A Hitler Legacy* (2001). Now in her nineties, Dorit has remained as mentally sharp as her emigrant contemporaries Renata Rainer and the only recently deceased Lilly Mendelsohn Urbach.

Essential to this book were the discoveries made by my cousin Katrina Urbach. In 2014 she gave me the letters written by my father Otto in the 1930s and Alice's cassette recording from the 1970s. Without Katrina I would never have embarked on this project.

I write in German and English but this book was translated from the original in German and I am particularly fortunate that Jamie Bulloch took on this job. Among many other things he is an expert on Austrian history and (unlike me) a great cook. This would have pleased Alice tremendously as well as the fact that my British publisher at MacLehose Press is Katharina Bielenberg. Her maternal grandfather, Fritz-Dietlof von der Schulenburg, was executed in 1944 for his involvement in the 20 July plot to kill Hitler.

Many thanks also go to my literary agent Andrea Wildgruber from Agence Hoffman (itself founded by an emigrant) for her dedication and the ideas she contributed to the book.

Nobody has a better understanding of Sigmund Mayer and the Mayer family in general than Michael Livni, who is currently revising Sigmund's memoir for a new English edition. Discovering a relation like him was such a boon.

Sarah Fisher kindly allowed me to see letters and photographs written by her aunt Cordelia Dodson, and Clara Fontana told me the best Cordelia anecdotes.

Special thanks are also due to three of Alice's "Windermere children". Lisl Scherzer (now Alisa Tennenbaum) sent me many emails and gave an extended interview for our TV-documentary on Alice. Sue Camis organised the conversation with her mother Ilse Camis in Florida (Ilse died in summer 2020), while Paula Sieber's granddaughter, Vivien Sieber, interviewed the now deceased Elfi Reinert in Birmingham. The private papers of Vivien's father Peter Sieber and his report on the children's hostel, which are held in the Wiener Holocaust Library, were a huge help. It was only thanks to Deborah Cantor, volunteer archivist at the World Jewish Relief archive, that I was able to view the files on the Kinder-transport children, which were not released until 2018. The children's names have been anonymised in this book.

I have also been helped by many friends, historians and archivists. First and foremost here I should mention the extraordinarily generous Paul Hoser, who has an answer to every question. Eva Klesse, wise friend and child psychologist, explained Anna Freud to me; Christian Bommarius, always a live wire, told me about the lawyer Max Friedlaender; and Harald Stolzenberg showed me his Vienna. Hiroaki Kuromiya studied Otto's photographs from China and explained why the pictures of landscapes say more than the piles of corpses.

The intrepid Eva Holpfer from the Jewish Community of Vienna tried with me – in vain – to surmount the high walls of Ernst Reinhardt Verlag in 2018. Thomas Boghardt, Hayden Peake and Heather Steele helped me scale different walls – the CIC material in the National Archives in Washington. For the Odessa story the writer Frederick Forsyth and René Bienert from the Vienna Wiesenthal Institute for Holocaust Studies gave me important pointers. In Austria I was helped by a number of colleagues. Wolfgang Weber from the University of Innsbruck provided me with many contacts (including Brigitte Rigele, the director of the Wiener

Stadt- und Landesarchiv, and Hubert Steiner from the Austrian State Archive). In Café Landtmann the Alice enthusiast Susanne Belovari told me the history of Jewish–Austrian cuisine. Regina Zodl and Johannes Koll from the provenance research department at Vienna University of Economics and Business found a book from Sigmund and Felix Mayer's Aryanised library and reinstated it in a special ceremony at the Jewish Museum in Vienna in June 2021. Roswitha Hammer and Dahlia Hindler arranged a "stone of remembrance" for Alice's murdered sisters in September 2020. Hannah Lessing, Secretary General of the National Fund of the Republic of Austria for the Victims of National Socialism helped us raise money for our TV documentary and her colleague Doris Macht patiently answered my many questions.

In Germany too I had fantastic support. At the Federal Archives in Lichterfelde, Robert Luther helped me look for the many Rudolf Röschs, and Cornelia Matz (Archivgeschichten) personally undertook the Friedberg research in Baden-Württemberg.

The phenomenal lawyer Marcellus Puhlemann protected me from legal pitfalls.

Parts of Alice's story are now a TV-documentary thanks to the director Andrea Oster, the producer Anna Schwarz, the editor Nina Stolzenburg and cameraman Tim Webster.

The book was written at the Institute for Advanced Study, Princeton, where I benefited from generous research grants and even more generous colleagues. Thanks particularly to Angelos Chaniotis, Kim Davis, Uta Nitschke-Joseph, Sabine Schmidtke, Kimberly Tribbett, Marcia Tucker and the great contrarian Freeman Dyson, who died in February 2020.

Telling Alice's story was an exhilarating experience, though some of the darker chapters were tough to write. That I did not have nightmares, however, I owe to Jonathan and our son Timothy – my two companions on all journeys through time.

NOTES

PREFACE

1   Otto to Karl Urbach, 5/6/1938. Otto Urbach papers.

CHAPTER 1

1   Cordelia Dodson to Karl Urbach, 2/10/2003. Cordelia Dodson papers.
2   Cited in Reed College's obituary for Cordelia Dodson, 2011. See: https://www.reed.edu/reed-magazine/in-memoriam/obituaries/december2011/cordelia-dodson-hood-1936.html
3   William D.B. Dodson (1871–1950) was the chairman of Portland Chamber of Commerce for thirty-six years. See his obituary in: *Oregonian*, 29/6/1950.
4   Cited in: Elizabeth P. McIntosh, *Sisterhood of Spies. The Women of the OSS*, Maryland, 1998, p. 176.

CHAPTER 2

1   The writer Hermann Broch who, like Einstein, lived in Princeton, is the source for this verse. See Friedrich Torberg, *Die Tante Jolesch oder der Untergang des Abendlandes in Anekdoten*, Vienna, 1986, parts 1 and 2 (first published 1975), p. 288. The Institute for Advanced Study (IAS) in Princeton, where Einstein worked, has no evidence of it, however. Thanks to the dedicated IAS archivist Marcia Tucker for her help in searching for many other sources for this book.
2   Alice Urbach, "Some Members of the Mayer Family, 1789–1957". Typed family memoir, dictated by Alice Urbach in 1957 to Charles Landstone, London, 1957. Mayer family papers.
3   It could be that Salomon's mother was just using common speech for grey horses.
4   Felix Mayer, "The Mayer Family, from Pressburg to Vienna", New York, 1960. Ten-page typed manuscript. Mayer family papers. See also Georg Gaugusch, *Wer einmal war. Das jüdische Großbürgertum Wiens 1800–1938* (Jahrbuch der Heraldisch–Genealogischen Gesellschaft Adler, Vol. 17). Vol. 2, L-R. Vienna, 2016, pp. 2254ff.

5   Alice would later get to know her grandmother Tony and described her as a "legendary character". See Alice Urbach, "Some Members of the Mayer Family", p. 2.

6   See also Adelheid Mayer/Elmar Samsinger, *Fast wie Geschichten aus 1001 Nacht. Die jüdischen Textilkaufleute Mayer zwischen Europa und dem Orient*, Vienna, 2015, p. 13.

7   Sigmund Mayer, *Die Wiener Juden. Kommerz, Kultur, Politik 1700–1900*, Vienna, 1917, p. 5. For more detail see his memoir: Sigmund Mayer, *Ein jüdischer Kaufmann 1831–1911*, Berlin/Vienna, 1926. Sigmund was proud of having been congratulated on his depiction of the ghetto by authors such as Karl Lamprecht, Werner Sombart and Lujo Brentano. See Sigmund Mayer's letter to Arthur Schnitzler, undated, c.1914. Arthur Schnitzler archive, Literaturarchiv Marbach.

8   Sigmund Mayer, *Wiener Juden*, p. 4.

9   ibid., p. 10.

10 Sigmund describes it thus: "Under the law a Jew was not permitted to own property. To buy a house he had to get a Christian to act as the purchaser and secure his rights through an irrevocable use contract […] or by some other underhand means. But even going down this route, it had not been legally possible until then for a Jew to purchase a house in the city outside of the ghetto or even consider it. After all he would not be allowed to live in it!" ibid., p. 6.

11 ibid., p. 4.

12 Sigmund's desperate portrayal of the ghetto came in for particularly strong criticism from Orthodox Jews: "[Sigmund Mayer] was the typical assimilator and his description of the Pressburg ghetto shows a striking lack of sensitivity for the Jewish life that prevailed there." Cited in *Jüdische Presse, Organ für die Interessen des orthodoxen Judentums*. No. 17/33, November 1920, p. 5.

13 Sigmund Mayer, *Wiener Juden*, p. 3.

14 Alice Urbach, "Old World – New World. The Personal Life Story of Mrs. Alice Urbach", 25-page typed manuscript, 1977, p. 2. Alice Urbach papers.

15 Eric Hobsbawm thought his mother Nelly was related to the Mayers because she called Sigmund's brother, Albert, "Uncle". See Eric Hobsbawm, *The Age of Empire: 1875–1914*, London, 1987, pp. 1–3. In fact, Albert appears to have been an uncle in name only (info from Michael Livni).

16 Rudolf Agstner, "A Tale of Three Viennese Department Stores in Egypt.

The Oriental Adventures of Mayer, Stein and Tiring", *Aufbau*, No. 9, 30/4/1999, p. 12.

17 A. Mayer & Co. was in place 828. The firm's co-founder Sigmund had left the business the previous year, however. The top places in the list were taken by "the imperial house, the high aristocracy, rentiers and bankers". See Roman Sandgruber, *Traumzeit für Millionäre. Die 929 reichsten Wienerinnen und Wiener im Jahr 1910*, p. 11; for the entry on the Mayers see p. 400.

18 Cited in Mayer/Samsinger, *1001 Nacht*, pp. 99f.

19 He wrote for the *Neue Freie Presse* for forty years, making an enemy of Karl Kraus, amongst others. In 1903 the *Neue Freie Presse* printed Sigmund's paper "Der Reichtum der Juden in Wien" ("The wealth of Jews in Vienna"), in which he tried to refute the idea that the Jews possessed a greater share of the national wealth than the Christians. The Jewish journalist Karl Kraus wrote a caustic reply, saying that it was ludicrous for someone as rich as Sigmund Mayer to spout such claims. Karl Kraus, *Die Fackel*, No. 131, February 1903, p. 22.

20 See Alice Urbach, "Old World", p. 5.

21 *Die Zeit*, 28/8/1897, Vol. XII. (*Die Zeit* was an Austrian newspaper that appeared every Saturday from 1894 to 1904.)

22 Herzl died in 1904 and was transferred from Döbling to Israel in 1949. Sigmund, meanwhile, remained in Döbling cemetery.

23 Alice's half siblings were Dr Arnold Mayer (1862–1926), Sidonie Rosenberg (b. 1865), Karoline Löwit, later Fleischner (b. 1867), Siegfried Mayer (1869–1923) and Gabriele Mayer (1872–76).

24 She was born 12/8/1850 and died 17/4/1921.

25 Alice Urbach, "Old World", p. 3.

26 Alice Urbach, cassette interview from the 1970s. Alice Urbach papers.

27 Alice Urbach, "Old World", p. 4.

28 Alice Urbach, cassette interview.

29 Alice Urbach, "Old World", pp. 14f.

30 A "well-run" house, according to Friedrich Torberg, could improve a husband's prospects of promotion. Torberg, *Tante Jolesch*, p. 64.

31 ibid., p. 25.

32 Alice Urbach, "Old World", p. 17.

33 ibid., p. 3.

34 Stefan Zweig, *Die Welt von gestern. Erinnerungen eines Europäers*, Frankfurt, 1978 (first published 1942), p. 88.

35 "A diary is found, of course the most recent one (about Emilie). Big scenes with my father." Diary entry of sixteen-year-old Arthur Schnitzler, 18/3/1879, cited in Peter Gay, *Schnitzler's Century: The Making of Middle-Class Culture 1815–1914*, New York, 2012, p. xxvii.

36 Alice Urbach, "Old World", p. 3.

37 Torberg, *Tante Jolesch*, pp. 17f.

38 Ludwig Hirschfeld, *Wien. Was nicht im Baedeker steht*, Munich, 1927, p. 241.

39 When she was nineteen Sidonie married Julius Rosenberg, who was born on 13/11/1849 in Temesvár (now Timişoara) and died in August 1938. In 1910 they lived at 13 Servitengasse in the 9th district. See the register of the Jewish Community of Vienna and (with a few mistakes in dates): https://www.geni.com/people/Sidonie-Rosenberg/6000000024633195072

40 Although Löwit set up the bookshop and publishing house himself in 1883, the business only thrived thanks to Sigmund's support.

41 Karoline married Richard Löwit in 1887 and their son Fritz Löwit was born in 1890. He soon left middle-class life and became a fervent communist. The last the family heard of him was that he was working for a communist newspaper in Bucharest in 1942. Karoline's husband Richard Löwit died in 1908. Karoline sold the publishing house, which continued to bear the name R. Löwit and now belonged to a new Jewish owner, Dr Mayer Präger. In September 1938 the "outstanding National Socialist" Erich Landgrebe took over the firm. Mayer Präger was arrested soon after the Anschluss of Austria. See Murray G. Hall/Christina Köstner, "... *allerlei für die Nationalbibliothek zu ergattern . . .*". *Eine österreichische Institution in der NS-Zeit*, Vienna 2006, p. 111. Mayer Präger was deported to Auschwitz in 1942, where he was killed on 3/11/1942. See also Iris Pawlitschko, "Jüdische Buchhandlungen in Wien. Arisierung und Liquidierung in den Jahren 1938–1945", Master's dissertation, University of Vienna, 1996, pp. 97f. In 1913 Karoline married her second husband, the manufacturer of metal goods Max Fleischner, partner in the firm Pick und Fleischner. See Felix Mayer, "The Mayer Family".

42 Anna Sacher (1859–1930) was the legendary owner of Hotel Sacher in Vienna and guardian of the recipe of the world-famous Sachertorte.

43 Interesting to note here is that they celebrated Christmas in Sigmund's house. Alice Urbach, "Old World", pp. 17f.

44 *Prager Tageblatt*, 3/7/1908, p. 4.

343

45 Alice Urbach's unofficial memoir, Alice Urbach papers in the possession of Katrina Urbach.

46 See Roman Sandgruber, *Traumzeit für Millionäre*, p. 16.

47 The official version is entitled "Old World – New World"; the unofficial one is only ten pages long.

48 Alice Urbach, "Old World", p. 5.

49 Alice Urbach's unofficial memoir.

50 Over the next few years Sigmund Mayer moved three times within Döbling. His addresses were 77 Karl-Ludwig-Strasse, 12 Lannerstrasse and 5 Linnéplatz.

51 Salten to Karl: "Dear Karli Urbach, I'm sending this advice about your rabbit by express mail. It must have fresh salad leaves, fresh cabbage, fresh small or large yellow beetroot [...] everything it eats must be fresh, not interfered with by human hands, not washed, but exactly as it grows. It is important to give it fresh food every day and as varied a diet as possible. As well as ensuring it has enough to drink, leave the rabbit in peace, try to pet or cuddle it as little as possible and do not carry it around. And see to it that it has space to run around. If you succeed in keeping the little thing alive then I will have done something good. My best wishes [...] Felix Salten." Karl Urbach papers.

52 The Habsburgs' summer palace in Vienna, built in the mid-18th century.

53 Alice Urbach, "Old World", pp. 6f.

54 Alice Urbach's unofficial memoir.

55 ibid.

56 Cited in Friedrich Torberg, *Die Tante Jolesch*, p. 92.

57 At a medical examination in 1909 Max was deemed "unsuitable", but in 1917 he was considered "fit for service". In his file he is described as a paediatric doctor. Landsturmevidenzblatt Max Urbach, AT-OeStA/KA Pers GB Evidenzen LSt MilKdo Wien Sanität 9, ÖStA.

58 Alice Urbach's unofficial memoir.

59 On these efforts see Karina Urbach, *Go-Betweens for Hitler*, Oxford, 2015, chapter 2.

60 Lillian M. Bader, *Ein Leben ist nicht genug. Memoiren einer Wiener Jüdin*, Vienna, 2011, p. 189.

61 Sissi was Empress Elisabeth (1837–98), wife of Emperor Franz Joseph I. A beautiful but introverted woman, she preferred to live her life out of the spotlight and spent little time in her husband's company. She was

assassinated by an Italian anarchist in Geneva, sealing her reputation as a romantic figure. To this day Sissi remains a major tourist symbol in Vienna.

62 Torberg, *Tante Jolesch*, p. 29.

63 The Red Guard forced the publication of a special edition of the paper and then withdrew from the building. Franz Endler is one of those who doubt the truth of the story: Franz Endler, *Wien zwischen den Kriegen*, Vienna, 1983, pp. 2of.

64 Alice Urbach, "Old World", pp. 1, 5.

65 Leon Askin, *Quietude and Quest. Protagonists and Antagonists in the Theatre, on and off Stage as Seen Through the Eyes of Leon Askin*, Riverside, 1989, p. 41.

66 ibid.

67 Alice Urbach, "Old World", p. 15.

68 Alice Urbach's unofficial memoir. In her official memoir she romanticises the death for her children: "My husband was not of robust health. His work, day and night, among the poor, starved population, coupled with insufficient food – and with worry – killed him." Alice Urbach, "Old World", p. 1.

CHAPTER 3

1 *Wir Wunderkinder* from 1958 was an anti-Nazi film directed by Kurt Hoffmann. Alice's daughter-in-law Wera Frydtberg played the emigrant Vera.

2 Protocol, inventory 22/8/1920. The estate of Dr Maximilian Urbach, Wiener Stadt- und Landesarchiv. In her official memoir she downplays the financial situation in 1920, saying it did not worsen until later. Alice Urbach, "Old World", p. 1.

3 Döbling cemetery, Gate II, Group 2, Grave 17.

4 *Neue Freie Presse*, 30/10/1920.

5 See also Mayer/Samsinger, *1001 Nacht*, p. 111f, which assumes that the library with first editions had been already sold, but Felix Mayer appears to have kept large parts of it. WstLA, BG Döbling A 4/1 Verlassenschaften 827/1920 Sigmund Mayer and Verlassenschaften 259/1921 Pauline Mayer.

6 Sigmund Mayer's Will, p. 2. IIIA listed valuables worth 5,000 crowns, which were first to go to Pauline.

7 The family memoir "Some Members of the Mayer Family" does not give

an entirely accurate account of Arnold's life. Arnold was not baptised at birth, but appears – like all of Sigmund Mayer's other children – in the register of the Jewish Community. He converted later and lived for his work. Together with the historian Heinrich Rietsch (a pupil of Guido Adler) he published a book about the 15th-century Mondsee Manuscript of the Songs: F. Arnold Mayer/Heinrich Rietsch, *Die Mondsee-Wiener Liederhandschrift und der Mönch von Salzburg. Eine Untersuchung von Literatur- und Musikgeschichte nebst den zugehörigen Texten aus der Handschrift mit Anmerkungen*, 2 vols, Berlin, 1894–1896. The family memoir also gives the date of Arnold's death wrongly as 1910. He actually died in 1926 in Kassel.

8   Sigmund Mayer's Will, p. 4.

9   See Mayer/Samsinger, *1001 Nacht*, p. 112.

10 Alice Urbach, "Old World", p. 1.

11 ibid., p. 7.

12 Every year the whole family would go to Baden near Vienna to visit a spa. In the spa register the "businessman" Ignaz Urbach appears with eight family members "and servants". See die Badener Curliste, 29/5/1901, ANNO, Österreichische Nationalbibliothek.

13 The bank was at 2 Schauflergasse. Small private banks like Ignaz's one went by the far less ostentatious title of "bureaux de change". They were not just for exchanging money, however; they specialised in all sorts of stock market transactions. See Eran Laor, *Vergangen und ausgelöscht. Erinnerungen an das slowakisch-ungarische Judentum*, Stuttgart, 1972, p. 72.

14 "Der Tod des Bankiers Urbach", *Der Tag*, 6/7/1924, p. 5.

15 "Vom Interventionskomitee im Stich gelassen", *Illustrierte Kronenzeitung*, 5/7/1924, pp. 1f.

16 ibid.

17 "Der Tod des Bankiers Urbach", p. 5.

18 The *Kronenzeitung* offered a different scenario: "The investigation commission that established the facts of the case not only noted the peculiar position of the body right outside Dr Zeisl's door and parallel to the banisters, but also highlighted the strange type of injury, a fragmentation of the back of the head, which according to the doctor is not consistent with suicide. Hofrat Dr Rien believes that Urbach, who was diabetic, certainly intended to jump from the third floor, but then suddenly feeling unwell, abandoned his plan and went back down to the second floor to seek help from Dr Zeisl's office. Outside the door he was overcome by

dizziness, collapsed and shattered the back of his head on the stone tiles. Three cigars were also found beside the body, giving the impression that he had been holding them just before his death." The fact that Ignaz had intended to kill himself remained undisputed. But it also seems to be no coincidence that he ended up outside the doors of the two men who would not help his bank.

19 "Vom Interventionskomitee im Stich gelassen", p. 2. On Kux, Bloch & Co. see also Peter Eigner/Helmut Falschlehner/Andreas Resch (eds), *Geschichte der österreichischen Privatbanken. Von Rothschild bis Spängler*, Vienna, 2017.

20 Verlassenschaftsakte Dr Max Urbach. On 24/1/1925 Alice makes it known that the co-guardian of her sons, Ignaz Urbach, has died and a new co-guardian has been found: Leonhard Buchwahr, industrialist, 6th district, 95 Mariahilferstrasse, co-guardianship.

21 Alice Urbach, "Old World", p. 2.

22 Hirschfeld, *Wien*, p. 3.

23 ibid., p. 65.

24 ibid., p. 243.

25 Alice Urbach, "Old World", p. 21.

26 The Austrian architect Margarete Schütte-Lihotzky was a pioneer in revolutionising kitchens. See Mona Horncastle, *Margarete Schütte-Lihotzky. Architektin, Widerstandkämpferin, Aktivistin*, Vienna, 2019.

27 Alice's cousin Lily Bader wrote: "In the mid-1920s the currency seemed to stabilise and a period of relative prosperity followed [. . .] The housing construction programme undertaken by the city of Vienna was encouraging. Municipal housing was built on a scale never seen before [. . .] There was central heating, running hot water, laundry rooms with washing machines and dryers, beautiful courtyards, paddling pools and kindergartens." Bader, *Ein Leben*, pp. 190f.

28 In 1927 Hirschfeld estimated the number of bridge salons in Vienna to be about seventy. "They are always in one of the supposedly better establishments of the inner city [. . .] Usually two or three ladies set one up together, partly because of the need to have someone covering the day and night shifts, and partly because it increases the stock-in-trade of acquaintances." Hirschfeld, *Wien*, p. 248.

29 *Die Presse*, 17/2/2019, lifestyle supplement (print edition). Alice's recipe is given here under Rudolf Rösch's name. This was later amended online.

30 Alice Urbach, "Old World", pp. 7f.

31 ibid., p. 8.

32 ibid., pp. 8f.

33 ibid., p. 9.

34 On her pupils, see ibid, p. 19. Alice does not give the prince's first name, but it was probably Prinz Franz Joseph II, later Prince von Liechtenstein (1906–89). He did his final school exams in 1925 and then studied at the Viennese College for Soil Science. The American writer Amélie Louise Rives married the Russian Prince Pierre Troubetzkoy as her second husband. The ballerina Grete (actually Margarethe) Wiesenthal was discovered by Gustav Mahler in 1902 at the court opera. In addition to a successful solo career, she worked as a choreographer in Berlin with Max Reinhardt. In 1919 she founded a dance school in Döbling and in 1934 was appointed to teach at the Academy of Music and Performing Arts in Vienna. The "beautiful" daughter of the ambassador was Dorothy Vera Selby (1912–82), daughter of Sir Walford Selby.

35 Felix Mayer, "The Mayer Family".

36 See Alice Urbach, "Some Members of the Mayer Family".

37 In 1926 the same house published Sidonie's *Kochbuch des Junggesellen* (*The Bachelor's Cookbook*), co-written by Emma Schreiber, and in 1928 *Das Weekend-Kochbuch* (*The Weekend Cookbook*) with "practical recipes for the weekend house".

38 Several times a year Alice would announce new courses: "The afternoon modern cookery courses by Frau Alice Urbach, 7 Goldeggasse, 4th district (new, modern premises) for starters, confectionery and a variety of meat dishes will be held here in the company of an outstanding chef. A completely new programme (also suitable for former pupils to perfect their skills). Morning, afternoon and evening courses." *Neue Freie Presse*, 1/10/1933, p. 15.

39 Alice Urbach, "Old World", p. 10. *Der Wiener Tag*, for example, said, "To Frau Alice Urbach, the admirable and successful organiser of modern cookery courses, we owe this delightful exhibition of the most distinguished culinary pleasures, which have shown us yet again that 'The Viennese are winners!' [. . .] Unfortunately the exhibition had to be closed early because – understandably – it was sold out very quickly." *Der Wiener Tag*, 11/11/1931. Each exhibition had a different motto. On 1/12/1930 it was "Dinner's Ready!"

40 *Neues Wiener Journal*, 22/11/1928, p. 12.

41 The *Neue Freie Presse* cited Alice thus: "I'm reclaiming the honour of the girl at the stove [. . .] Experience shows that the girl – she may already be a young woman – wants to learn and does so with interest. Even girls who work and those still studying come to learn cookery." *Neue Freie Presse*, 27/11/1929, p. 7.

42 "It is all very democratic. Alongside the society ladies who come to listen to these practical cookery talks and who are now showing an interest in cookery – perhaps because of a career change or a late marriage – we find many a nice domestic help. They are all united by the same learning objective, which transcends any social differences." *Neues Wiener Journal*, 30/11/1930.

43 Alice announced in the *Neue Freie Presse* in January 1932: "Frau Alice Urbach's first Viennese 'Prepared Meals'. For only S 2 [two shillings] you can have your complete daily menu sent to your home or the office. Hot and ready to eat! Substantial and delicious!" Alice had to apply for an extra trade licence for this service. On 30/1/1932 the following was entered in the trade tax register: "Urbach, Alice commercial sale of ready meals off-premises with the exclusion of any activity linked to a concession, 1 Goldeggasse." WStLA, Steuerkataster, K2/1 – Zentralgewerberegister, URBACH Alice; Kochschule in 4. Goldeggasse 7.

44 Riz Remorf, "Neuzeitliche Küche für die moderne Frau", *Neues Wiener Journal*, 31/1/1932, p. 23.

45 In 1929 Alice's trade licence was extended to include Otto. Now he was permitted to offer courses in home cooking. Thanks to Sebastian Dallinger for finding the trade licence. Steuerkataster, K2/1 – Zentralgewerberegister, URBACH Alice; Kochschule in 4. Goldeggasse 7, WStLA.

46 On 16/11/1934 the Palestine Office in Vienna confirmed that "on 3rd August 1934 the above-named individual submitted an application, no. 1910, for an entry certificate for Palestine." Otto Urbach papers.

47 Alice Urbach, "My Sons". Four-page handwritten manuscript. Alice Urbach papers.

CHAPTER 4

1 Jobs's time as a student at Reed is portrayed in the 2013 film *Jobs* (with Ashton Kutcher in the title role).

2 There is another interesting aspect to Keezer which comes from his close

association with Morgenthau. It is probable that in the 1930s the Reed president was already part of the information network which Morgenthau built up in the treasury. It became an effective intelligence service that specialised in corruption cases and competed with Hoover's FBI. Morgenthau's "information network" was not only active in the US, but also gathered intelligence in Europe and Asia. In this way Morgenthau was more than just a treasury secretary for Roosevelt; he also acted as an important advisor on foreign policy issues.

3   "You don't live on intellect alone." See Dexter Keezer's obituary in *Reed Magazine*.

4   Richard Scholz, "Twice Refugee, Austrian Ski Expert Returns to US", *The Oregonian*, 17/9/1937.

5   Otto to Alice, 18/11/1935, Otto Urbach papers.

6   Otto to Alice, 23/9/1935, Otto Urbach papers. In another letter he attached an article about Mr Keezer from *Time* Magazine. "*Time* is the most-read intellectual magazine and it's excellent propaganda for Reed to be mentioned in this magazine. He [Mr Keezer] is really fantastic. I'm very worried about living conditions [in Vienna] and I know that you're seriously struggling. I will send you some money if you urgently need it [...] Greetings and warm kisses, Otto.".

7   Otto to Karl, 3/12/1935, Otto Urbach papers.

8   Otto to Alice, 25/11/1935, Otto Urbach papers.

9   Report for the college president from 28/1/1938 about the founding of the skiing team: "1934/35 No team [...] 1935/36: Class organized by Otto Urbach. 70 girls, 30 boys and 12 outsiders. Much advertising over ski slide. Team of 5 members entered the open competition sponsored by the Winter Sports Association. Team also went to the Intercollegiate meeting at Yosemite, winning fourth place." For finding this I would like to thank Caroline Reul from Special Collections and Archives, Reed College, Portland, Oregon. For skiing photos of Otto see Reed Digital Collections, Reed College Bulletin 1936, Vol. 15 (1), and of Cordelia Dodson: Reed College Bulletin 1937, Vol. 16 (1).

10 Another headline ran: "Ski school planned by Reed instructor: During the Christmas vacation, Otto Robert Urbach, student-instructor of skiing at Reed College, will conduct a ski school on the slopes of Mount Hood." In 1987 the Reed newspaper ran an article on Otto's founding of the ski school and the many accidents he and his pupils had during the first

competition in Yosemite. One of Otto's injuries was to his hip. See J. J. Haapala, "Origin of the Reed College Ski Team" in *Reed College Quest*, 23/2/1987, p. 7. The author thought that Otto was German.

11 The Vaterländische Front (Fatherland Front) was a state-sponsored Austrian patriotic movement, which was the face of the Austrofascist regime and devised as a counterweight to Nazi propaganda. Amongst other things the Front organised marches, youth movements and cultural activities, but ultimately failed to attract the same level of support as Nazism did in Germany.

12 Author's conversation with Clara Fontana about her great aunt Cordelia Dodson, London 2019.

13 Cited in McIntosh, *Sisterhood*, p. 176. McIntosh herself also worked for the OSS.

14 Undated letter written to Karl from China, 1936 or 1937. Otto Urbach papers.

15 For Pucci's time at Reed, see https://www.reed.edu/reed-magazine/articles/2014/emilio-pucci.html

16 Pucci's talk at Reed College: https://soundcloud.com/reedcollege/pucci-emilio-talk-on-design-at-reed-college-1962

17 Later, Reed collected memories of Pucci. Kathleen Cahill Dougall remembered him as "very handsome and known for dancing the tango." Elizabeth McCracken danced with him after he had taught her and a group of female students the Viennese waltz. See: https://www.reed.edu/reed_magazine/march2014/articles/features/pucci/pucci1.html

18 In 1935–36 he was still studying Agriculture at the University of Georgia. On this see the résumé of his life for the OSS. After the war Pucci wrote two reports. The first is from 24/5/1945. Cordelia Dodson typed the document which is full of mistakes (this remained a weakness of hers; in a 2003 letter to Karl she apologises for her typos). The second is dated 20/6/1945. The quotes reproduced here come from the second, more detailed report, RG 226, Entry 190C, Box 11, National Archives, Washington (hereafter referred to as Pucci Report).

19 File President Dexter Keezer, 28/1/1938, Reed Special Collections and Archives, Reed College, Portland, Oregon.

20 From 1921 to 1948 Ed's father was Professor of Comparative Literature at Reed College and also ran the theatre group. The Reed amphitheatre is named after him.

21 Otto to Alice, 1935, undated. Otto Urbach papers.

22 According to documents for the city of Vienna, Alice was registered at 22/16 Kirchstetterngasse in the 16th district from 3/5/1920 until 6/8/1935 (co-registered children: Otto, born 28/9/1913, and Karl, born 9/11/1917). From August 1935 at 7/4 Goldeggasse (co-registered child: Karl, born 9/11/1917).

23 For the list of foreign publishers represented by Perles, see Daniela Punkl, "Verlag Moritz Perles", Master's dissertation, University of Vienna, 2002, p. 161.

24 Hermann Jungck, *75 Jahre Ernst Reinhardt Verlag München Basel. Verlagsgeschichte*, Munich, 1974, p. 53.

25 Otto to Alice: "How is your second cookbook coming along?" Letter from Otto sent from China, undated, 1936, Otto Urbach papers. In 2020 Reinhardt Verlag disclosed that there were in fact two further manuscripts which Alice wrote for the publishing house. Shortly before her flight she gave up all rights to the books *Die fleischlose Kost* and *Wiener Mehlspeisen*. (See declaration from 5/9/1938 in Ernst Reinhardt Verlag archive, Munich.)

26 Alice Urbach, "Old World", p. 19. In her memoir Alice does not mention the cookbook she had already published with Sidonie. Alice tried to suppress everything about Sidonie after her sister was murdered.

27 ibid. Otto never told anyone apart from Alice what sort of a script it was. It might have had something to do with the film *The Incident*, about the Trinidad prisoner-of-war camp in Colorado, but this is pure speculation.

28 ZG represented several German publishing houses in Austria, including C.H. Beck and Kiepenheuer und Witsch. It later merged to become Mohr-ZG, and now is Mohr Morawa.

29 Jungck, *75 Jahre*, pp. 54f.

30 *Die Bühne*, December 1935, No. 414, p. 53. Even Otto got a copy of the magazine in America, albeit with some delay: "I've seen an article here in *Die Bühne* […] it was very complementary about your book." Otto to Alice, 17/3/1936, Otto Urbach papers.

31 *Die Reichspost*, 1/12/1935.

32 Toni Tipton-Martin, *The Jemima Code: Two Centuries of African American Cookbooks*, Austin 2015.

CHAPTER 5

1   Torberg, *Die Tante Jolesch*, p. 111.

2   Otto to Alice, September 1937, Otto Urbach papers.

3   The Cathay Hotel is today the Peace Hotel. Many roads too were renamed after 1945. Nanking Road is now Nanjing Road East. The Bund is Zhongshan No. 1 Road. Another important thoroughfare back in 1937, Avenue Edward VII, is called Yanan Road. And Bubbling Well Road, Otto's first address in Shanghai, is now Nanjing West Road.

4   Otto to Alice, undated letter, summer 1936, Otto Urbach papers.

5   Otto to Alice, 11/8/1936, Otto Urbach papers.

6   Otto to Alice, 18–20/6/1936, Otto Urbach papers.

7   Otto to Alice, 20–28/8/1936, Otto Urbach papers.

8   Otto to Alice, Otto Urbach papers.

9   Otto to Alice, 31/ 8/1936, Otto Urbach papers. The letters of introduction were addressed to a relative of Morgenthau who lived in China.

10 Otto to Alice, 31/8/1936, Otto Urbach papers.

11 Otto to Karl, 21/8/1936, Otto Urbach papers.

12 Otto to Alice, undated, Otto Urbach papers.

13 Joe Lederer, *Blatt im Wind*, Munich, 1951 (first edition Vienna, 1936), p. 25.

14 Otto to Alice, 11/10/1936, Otto Urbach papers.

15 Since 1934 a six-year plan had been in place to reduce opium addiction. Patriotic young people supported the "New Life Movement". They saw opium use as an "unpatriotic act" and suspected – quite rightly – the Japanese of supporting the heroin and morphine trade in China to "demoralize and stupefy" the Chinese. Frederic Wakeman, *Policing Shanghai, 1927–1937*, Berkeley, 1995, p. 268.

16 Otto to Karl, 4/3/1937, Otto Urbach papers.

17 Lederer, *Blatt im Wind*, pp. 24ff.

18 John R. Watt, *Saving Lives in Wartime China. How Medical Reformers Built Modern Healthcare Systems Amid War and Epidemics, 1928–1945* (China Studies), Leiden, 2014, p. 220.

19 Otto to Karl, 31/3–20/4/1937, Otto Urbach papers.

20 Otto to Alice, 21/10/1936, Otto Urbach papers.

21 Otto to Karl, 8/3/1937, Otto Urbach papers.

22 Otto to Karl, 30/1/1937, Otto Urbach papers.

23 Otto to Karl, 4/3/1937, Otto Urbach papers.

24 Otto to Karl, 30/1/1937, Otto Urbach papers.

25 I would like to thank Hiroaki Kuromiya for his generous help in analysing Otto's photographs and letters from China. See also Hiroaki Kuromiya, "Stalin's Great Terror and the Asian Nexus", *Europe-Asia Studies*, 2014, Vol. 66 (5) pp. 775–93.

26 In December 1936 Nazi Germany and Japan signed the Anti-Comintern Pact against the Soviet Union. Japan wanted to add an anti-Chinese component, but Nazi foreign policy had other priorities. Until 1938 Germany cooperated closely with China on a military level.

27 I would like to thank Nina Price for giving me the affidavit Otto wrote in 1939 for Renata Urbach and her parents Robert and Lola Urbach. Robert Urbach papers.

28 Otto to Karl, 30/1/1937, Otto Urbach papers. Japan was already a controversial host for the Games, and the war with China led to them being given back to the IOC in 1938.

29 Otto to Karl, 29/12/1936 and Otto to Alice, 18/1/1937, Otto Urbach papers. Otto announces that he will be travelling to Yokohama for Ford in March. What came of the trip can no longer be established.

30 Otto to Alice, 20/9/1936, Otto Urbach papers.

31 See the publishing contract from 25/1/1935, Verlagsarchiv Ernst Reinhardt, Munich.

32 See, for example, Otto to Alice, 11/8/1936, Otto Urbach papers: "Dear Mother, I just received your kind letter. I hope that in the meantime you've got more customers so that you at least break even. Don't worry so much."

33 See Jonathan Haslam, *The Spectre of War*, Princeton, 2021.

34 Cited in Elisabeth Young-Bruehl, *Anna Freud: a biography*, Vienna, 1995, p. 202.

35 Otto to Alice, 20/12/1936. On 18/1/1937 he wrote, "I bet you're very happy to be getting away from Vienna soon." Otto Urbach papers.

36 Alice Urbach's registration documents for Vienna, notice of change of address 10/2/1937 to Hove, England.

37 Otto to Karl, 8/3/1937. Inspired by reading *Blatt im Wind* he even considered writing about his experiences in China: "I've begun writing a novella, but I'm making very slow progress." Otto to Karl, 21/4/1937, Otto Urbach papers.

38 Otto to Karl, 21/4/1937, Otto Urbach papers.

39 Otto to Karl, 14/5/1937, Otto Urbach papers.

40 Otto to Alice, 25/7/1937, Otto Urbach papers.

41 It has been argued that the Japanese allowed themselves to be provoked in

August 1937, thereby playing into the hands of Chiang Kai-shek. It was in Chiang Kai-shek's interests for the conflict to spread from northern China to Shanghai, the international centre of finance. I would like to thank Hiroaki Kuromiya for the conversations we've had about this chapter.

42 Otto to Alice and Karl, 14–26/9/1937, Otto Urbach papers.

43 Andrew Meier, *The Lost Spy. An American in Stalin's Secret Service*, New York, 2008, p. 217.

44 "Then came the aerial attacks on the Settlement. The Japanese and Chinese carried out wild battles in the air [. . .] and it rained bombs and downed aircraft etc. The result: around 3,000 deaths in two hours. The Chinese performed very well in air combat, putting up surprising resistance." Otto to Alice and Karl, 14–26/9/1937, Otto Urbach papers.

45 Otto to Karl, 23/8–1/9/1937, Otto Urbach papers.

46 Paul French, *Bloody Saturday. Shanghai's Darkest Day*, London, 2017, p. 17.

47 ibid., p. 51.

48 Otto Urbach's photo album, Otto Urbach papers.

49 Otto to Alice and Karl, 14–26/9/1937, Otto Urbach papers.

50 "South Station Bombing at Shanghai described" article in Otto Urbach's photo album. It hasn't been possible to work out which newspaper the article appeared in. Otto Urbach papers.

51 Cordelia to Karl, 9/9/1937, Cordelia Dodson papers.

52 Scholz, "Twice Refugee".

53 Otto to Alice, 14–26/9/1937. Otto must have begun writing the letter on the ship, not finishing it until after arriving in America. His boat, the *President McKinley*, reached Seattle on 15/9/1937. Otto Urbach papers.

54 Cordelia to Karl, 1/10/1937, Cordelia Dodson papers.

55 Cordelia to Karl, 11/10/1937, Cordelia Dodson papers. Karl and Alice were very grateful to the Dodsons and Karl drafted a reply: "From Otto we have received a letter about his operation too. In the first moment it looked very hard to me [...] He also wrote that your mother was so kind to him [...] and this is so nice of her and because I don't know anybody of your family yet I have to thank you very much for all that kindness. I hope the boy will be all right again soon."

56 "Otto Robert Urbach, former ski instructor at Reed College, landed on 14th September in Seattle with photos that [...] show the suffering in China. Urbach's own tale of woe began two years ago [...] He was able to study in peace at Reed for one year and ski on Mount Hood. But then

his troubles began. His visa was only valid for one year. He tried extending it twice, once at the Mexican border and once at the Canadian border, but to no avail. While he was studying at Reed, much had happened in his home country. Dollfuss was killed in a bloody coup [...] Urbach was considered persona non grata und would have been enlisted in the army." Scholz, "Twice Refugee". Here it is clear that the journalist had a limited knowledge of Austrian politics. Dollfuss was murdered in 1934, the year before Otto's departure for the States. It seems as if Otto had no interest in correcting this mistake. In truth, of course, he had several reasons not to return to Vienna.

57 Richard Scholz, "Shanghai Battle declared screen. Ex-Reed Instructor asserts Japan Fooling World", *Oregonian*, 20/9/1937.

58 To date the figure has not been verified. Some historians think it was "only" 50,000, others reckon the number to be 300,000.

59 Otto to Karl, undated, late 1937, Otto Urbach papers. Victor Pollitzer (b. 1892) was the brother of Dr Robert Pollitzer and Otto's second cousin.

60 A newspaper article amongst Otto Urbach's papers talks incorrectly of a Chinese medal. Judging by the red-and-white ribbon it was a medal presented by the Jewish section of the SVC.

CHAPTER 6

1 Their address was "Karl Urbach and Willy Schultes, 48/12 Wiedner Gürtel, 4th district". See also postcards and letters sent to them, in the Cordelia Dodson papers.

2 The Palastkino was at 43–45 Josefstädterstrasse. Officially the owner was Paula's father, Alfred Ticho, but the cinema was run by his daughters Bertha Ticho, Selma Haas und Paula Sieber.

3 In 1914 there were already 150 cinemas in Vienna, and even though foreign films were banned in the First World War, Austrian productions quickly filled the gap.

4 Paula's son from her first marriage was Erich, later Eric Stoessler, who fled to England in 1938 and got Paula to join him later.

5 Otto to Karl, 29/12/1936 and 18/1/1937, Otto Urbach papers.

6 Cordelia to Karl, 4/4/1937, Cordelia Dodson papers.

7 Karl Urbach's memoir, written in English in 1937 as an exercise. Karl Urbach papers.

8   Cordelia to Karl, October 2003, Cordelia Dodson papers.

9   The Ständestaat, or corporate state, was the regime that governed Austria following the end of parliamentary democracy in 1933. In reality, the "corporate" nature of the system was only partially implemented by the time of Anschluss in March 1938 and Austria remained an authoritarian state during this period.

10 Karl Urbach's memoir.

11 Cordelia to Karl, 2003, Cordelia Dodson papers. Cordelia was the friend of Ed's sister Barbara Cerf.

12 Built 1932, it was home to four famous artists. The dance hall on the 16th floor has gone, and has been replaced by penthouse apartments.

13 Karl Urbach's memoir.

14 ibid.

15 ibid.

16 Poldi Schück was the son of Max Urbach's sister Rosa. Rosa had married Emil Schück, who owned a schnapps distillery in Janowice. Poldi Schück was born in 1897, and he and his wife Olga had three children: Hanka, Milena and Jenda Schück.

17 Karl Urbach's memoir, Karl Urbach papers. On 14/5/1937 Otto wrote to Karl: "I'm very grateful to you for having looked after Cordelia so well. It seems as if she really liked Vienna and I'm sure you had fun together." Otto Urbach papers.

18 Today this building belongs to Speising orthopaedic hospital. It is not known whether it was Aryanised after the Anschluss. https://www.oss.at/ueber-uns/

19 *Neue Freie Presse*, 26/9/1937, p. 38.

20 Tamara Ehs, "Hochschullager im Austrofaschismus 1935–1937", https://geschichte.univie.ac.at/de/artikel/hochschullager-im-austrofaschismus

21 Karl does not give the name of the camp. It could either be Ossiach (because there was a monastery and lake there) or the camp at Kreuzberg on the Weissensee.

22 The training was not quite so much of a game, however, as a daily schedule shows:

    06.00: Wake up
    06.15–06.45: Morning exercises, maybe swim in the lake
    07.00: Breakfast
    07.10–07.40: Room tidying

07.45–08.00: Raising the flag, announcement of daily programme, presentation of the sick, camp report

08.05–10.00: Exercises, classes, possible second breakfast at 10.00

10.30–12.30: Shooting practice, physical exercises

13.00–13.30: Lunch

13.30–14.30: Rest

14.30–15.00: Lecture by camp leader

15.00–16.00: Physical exercises at shore of lake; possible snack at 16.00

16.30–18.30: Exercises or lecture by camp leader, issue of orders, roll call

19.00–19.20: Evening meal

20.00–21.15: Recreational activities

22.00: Bedtime

after 22.30: No talking, absolute silence in the building

In Ehs, "Hochschullager im Austrofaschismus".

23 The standard "uniform" consisted of camp trousers and a grey-green windcheater, ibid.

24 Karl Urbach's memoir.

25 ibid.

26 Cordelia to Karl, 8/6/1937, Cordelia Dodson papers.

27 Cordelia to Karl, 9/9/1937, Cordelia Dodson papers.

28 Otto to Karl, undated, autumn 1937. At the same time his prospects of obtaining American citizenship had improved: "I got my 'first papers' a few days ago, which means I'm on my way to becoming an American citizen. It's a really good feeling. Is there a sense in Austria that a European war is inevitable? Here the newspapers are full of war rumours." Otto to Karl, 24/10/1937, Otto Urbach papers.

29 Cordelia to Karl, 2003, Cordelia Dodson papers.

CHAPTER 7

1 Alice Urbach's application to the assistance fund is in the Österreichisches Staatsarchiv: VA. 13 480, AHF. 5529 NHF. 5003 and NHF 16 759. The apartment in Ebendorferstrasse later became a "Sammelwohnung" (collective apartment) for Jews, with 23 people staying there. Thanks to Daliah Hindler for this piece of information. See: Datenbank des

Dokumentationsarchivs des Österreichischen Widerstandes and https://www.memento.wien/address/74/

2   According to the files in the Vienna registry office Alice lived at 111 Speisingergasse until 22/2/1938. Then the Jewish owner of the sanatorium must have fled. From 22/2/1938 until 10/4/1938 Alice stayed with Paula Sieber again at 3 Schreyvogelgasse. From 11/4 to 29/4/1938 she was at Pension Cosmopolite 8 in Alser Strasse. The following six months were back with Paula Sieber in Schreyvogelgasse und then she stayed the last few days before her departure (24–28/10) with her sister Helene at 10–12 Ebendorferstrasse. Alice would never fill out another registration card in Vienna.

3   Alice Urbach's unofficial memoir, Alice Urbach papers.

4   Otto to Karl, 10/2/1938, Otto Urbach papers.

5   See Karl Urbach's memoir.

6   Otto to Karl, undated, turn of the year 1937–38, Otto Urbach papers.

7   For the full text of the speech see https://www.diepresse.com/1348149/kurt-schuschnigg-warnt-die-osterreichischen-nationalsozialisten

8   Cordelia to Karl, 2003, Cordelia Dodson papers.

9   Audio recording to be found at https://www.mediathek.at/atom/015C6FC2-2C9-0036F-00000D00-015B7F64

10 Cordelia to Karl, 22/6/1938, Cordelia Dodson papers.

11 Private letter written by a Viennese woman from 13/3/1938, see https://www.derstandard.at/2000075776312/Ein-Brief-ueber-den-Anschluss-1938-Und-dann-kam-ER

12 In real life Moser was married to a Jewish woman whom he did not abandon in 1938.

13 Ernst Haeusserman, *Mein Freund Henry*, Vienna, 1983, p. 46.

14 The authors were Helmut Qualtinger and Carl Merz. Qualtinger played Herr Karl.

15 https://www.youtube.com/watch?v=2G4uj7Mcyro

16 Otto to Karl, 13/3/1938, Otto Urbach papers.

17 Otto to Alice, 28/3/1938, Otto Urbach papers.

18 Otto to Karl, 10/4/1938, Otto Urbach papers.

19 Torberg, *Tante Jolesch*, p. 524.

20 ibid., pp. 524f.

21 See Chapter 11. In his draft novel "The Mission", Felix describes an emigrant who can't decipher a message from his wife still in Vienna. The

story is based on Felix's own experiences. Felix Mayer, "The Mission", Leo Baeck Institute Archives, Manuscript Collection MS 102c, New York/Berlin.

22 Cordelia to Karl, 2003, Cordelia Dodson papers.

23 ibid.

24 Cordelia to Karl, April 1938, Cordelia Dodson papers.

25 Cordelia to Karl, 6/5/1938, Cordelia Dodson papers.

26 Georg Kreisler on 28/2/2003, BR programme "Forum", https://www. br.de/fernsehen/ard-alpha/sendungen/alpha-forum/georg-kreisler-gespraech100.html

27 Afterword by Dorit Whiteman, in *Bader, Ein Leben*, pp. 228 ff.

28 ibid., p. 229. "With persistence, reticence and even bribery" Dorit's mother succeeded in getting the necessary documents.

29 See the entry for Julius Rosenberg in the register of the Jewish Community of Vienna.

30 After Anschluss "Austria" was erased from the map of Europe, becoming known merely as the "Ostmark" or "Eastern March" of the German Reich.

31 Otto to Alice, 24/4/1938, Otto Urbach papers.

32 See Karina Urbach, "England is pro-Hitler. German opinion during the Czechoslovakian Crisis 1938", in Julie Gottlieb/Daniel Hucker/Richard Toye (eds), *The Munich Crisis, Politics and the People*, Manchester, 2021.

33 Otto to Karl, 8/5/1937 (in a fluster, Otto had put the wrong date on the letter; the contents make it clear that it was written in 1938). Otto Urbach papers.

34 Otto to Karl, 5/6/1938, Otto Urbach papers.

35 Affidavit from Otto Urbach, 16/6/1938, Otto Urbach papers. Despite this the tone in the brothers' letters became pricklier over the course of the next few weeks. Out of nervousness Karl began to make mistakes. He had now found out that he needed a form 575 from Washington for his application, and Otto wrote to him at the end of June: "This will mean quite a delay and I can't imagine why you haven't written to me about it earlier. In the meantime you will have heard from the Dodsons, and Mr Dodson has written to tell me he will give you an affidavit. So it's fairly likely that you'll get a visa." Otto to Karl, 25/6/1938, Otto Urbach papers.

36 Besse Ellen Krumm Dodson (1875–1940) was an unusual woman who opened one of the first photographic studios in America. She had three children with William Dodson: Cordelia Besse Dodson (1913–2011, later

Hood), Elizabeth Leila Dodson (1916–2013, later Fisher) and Daniel Dodson (1918–91).

37 Cordelia to Karl, 22/6/1938, Cordelia Dodson papers.

38 Barnet Litvinov (ed.), *The Letters and Papers of Chaim Weizmann: Series B, Papers 1898 – 1931*, London, 1983, p. 102.

39 Heinz Boberach (ed.), *Meldungen aus dem Reich. Die geheimen Lageberichte des Sicherheitsdienstes der SS 1938–1945*, Bd. 2, Herrsching, 1984, p. 23.

40 "I can imagine that it must be dreadful to be stuck in Vienna, but you have to be patient. Mother will not be able to get a job here. All domestic staff are in a union and it's totally out of the question. There is no way I can look after you both financially here. On the other hand, I can provide for Mother in Europe, even if you're here. I can tighten my belt so we don't spend any more [...] Focus now on getting entry to the US and when you're here we will see [...] What's happening there to make Mother suddenly want to come here?" Otto to Karl, 23/7/1938, Otto Urbach papers.

41 Karl to Otto, 3/8/1938, Otto Urbach papers. Arthur Horowitz later provided an affidavit for Otto and Karl's cousin Robert Urbach. Despite this nobody in the family can remember meeting Horowitz. There was an Arthur Horowitz who was born in Poland in 1914 and died in 1990 in Queens, New York. It cannot be established, however, whether this man was Karl's friend.

42 Cordelia to Karl, 8/8/1939, Cordelia Dodson papers.

43 Otto to Karl, 8–16/8/1938, Otto Urbach papers.

44 Otto to Karl, undated, around September 1938, Otto Urbach papers. Otto was not the only emigrant who dreamed of bringing the charm of Austrian ski resorts to America. The stunning actress and emigrant Hedy Lamarr pursued the same idea. In the 1950s she managed to turn the small town of Aspen, Colorado, into an exclusive winter sports region. Just as in Davos, politicians and business chiefs still meet here for après-ski discussions.

45 The first to emigrate was Alice's nephew, eleven-year-old Thomas Mayer. Rose found a place for him at an English school in September 1938.

46 Charles Landstone, *I Gate-Crashed* (London 1976), p. 157. See also Laor, *Vergangen*, pp. 60f.

47 Charles Landstone, a theatre producer who wrote books and plays, was born in 1891 in Vienna, grew up in England, and was awarded an OBE.

48 Otto to Karl, 17/9/1938, Otto Urbach papers.

49 Otto to Karl, 26/9/1938, Otto Urbach papers.

50 Lisbeth Dodson was as thrilled as Karl and Willy: "It's wonderful what Chamberlain, Mussolini and Daladier have achieved. One can really be proud of being a contemporary of theirs." Lisbeth also wanted to help out with the affidavit: "I got your letter this morning and you can imagine how sorry Cordelia and I am. I've no idea what's happened with the affidavit that Daddy sent you, but we'll write to him straightaway and find out. As soon as we're home we'll do everything in our power to help you. Until then, Karli, be brave." Lisbeth to Karl, 30/9/1938, Cordelia Dodson papers.

51 Poldi had three children; nothing is known about their deaths. His wife Olga died later in a camp, either alone or with them.

52 Cordelia and Lisbeth to Karl, undated, October 1938, Cordelia Dodson papers. At the same time Otto wrote to Karl: "If it doesn't work out in Vienna with the affidavit and US visa, you must leave anyway. I've been expecting news from you regarding an [application] for New Zealand. I can muster up to 500 dollars for you. I think you would have to show a certain amount in pounds [...] At any rate I want you to get out of Europe as soon as possible, before the next crisis [...] How are you for money? What about Mother? I hope to hear from her soon from England." Otto Urbach papers.

53 Otto to Karl, 16/11/1938, Otto Urbach papers.

CHAPTER 8

1 Egon Erwin Kisch, "Magdalenenheim", in *Marktplatz der Sensationen*, Berlin, 1947 (2019 edition), p. 331. See also Karina Urbach, "Geraubte Bücher", *Die Zeit*, Nr. 52, 10/12/2020, p. 21.

2 See Thomas Jahn, "Suche nach 'arisierten' Büchern in den Beständen der Bayerischen Staatsbibliothek. Forschungsstand – Methoden – Ergebnisse", http://archiv.ub.uni-heidelberg.de/artdok/volltexte/2007/398

3 See Volker Dahm, *Das jüdische Buch im Dritten Reich*, Munich, 1993, p. 17. "From April to July 1935 another 10% of 'non-Aryan' authors were 'retired', and so in summer 1935 the 'de-Jewification' of the Reich association of German writers was almost complete, with an exclusion/rejection quota of 96 per cent." Dahm, p. 50.

4 Angelika Königseder, *Walter de Gruyter. Ein Wissenschaftsverlag im Nationalsozialismus*, Tübingen, 2016, p. 71.

5   These were: 1. Goebbels' Reich ministry of public enlightenment and propaganda, 2. the Reich chamber of literature, 3. the Reich ministry of science, education and culture, 4. the foreign office, 5. the literature department of the Rosenberg office, 6. the official Party commission for the protection of National Socialist literature, 7. the staff of the deputy Führer, quite apart from the Gestapo, the security service and even the Wehrmacht. See Königseder, *Walter de Gruyter*, p. 18.

6   According to Jungck even this wasn't much of an obstacle: "Although we could continue to consider and propose what we wanted, we might not get any paper for the book in question. Most presses, however, bought paper in so-called preparations, i.e. they ordered 2,000 kg or more in a certain format from the paper factory [...] Until the last days of the war almost no application was rejected if the publishing house could provide their own paper.' Jungck, *75 Jahre*, p. 68.

7   See Reinhard Wittmann, "Ein konservativer Verlag im Dritten Reich. Das Beispiel Oldenbourg", in Klaus G. Saur (ed.), *Verlage im Dritten Reich*, Frankfurt am Main, 2013, p. 39.

8   Dahm, p. 29.

9   ibid., p. 43.

10 "In 1933 alone, around 100 publishing houses were banned or closed, or Aryanised." See Saur, *Verlage im Dritten Reich*, p. 7.

11 ibid., p. 9.

12 Christian Adam, *Lesen unter Hitler. Autoren, Bestseller, Leser im Dritten Reich*, Berlin, 2010, p. 109.

13 Klaus-Peter Horn, *Pädagogische Zeitschriften im Nationalsozialismus. Selbstbehauptung, Anpassung, Funktionalisierung*, n.p., 1995, Vol. 3, p. 16, note 19. In 1999 C.H. Beck Verlag, as well as Carl Heymann (Cologne) and W. Kohlhammer (Stuttgart), were still claiming that their archives had been destroyed during the Second World War. Since then, however, Beck Verlag has found its holdings. See Lothar Becker, *Schritte auf einer abschüssigen Bahn. Das Archiv des öffentlichen Rechts (AöR) im Dritten Reich*, Tübingen, 1999, pp. 7f.

14 E-mail from Ernst Reinhardt Verlag to the author on 26/7/2018. Another dismissive e-mail worded almost identically was sent a few weeks later to Eva Holpfer at the restitution department of the Jewish Community of Vienna.

15 "In this regard the management responded positively to offers from

Jewish and politically undesirable authors to withdraw from their contracts." Cited in Königseder, *Walter de Gruyter*, p. 177.

16 ibid., pp. 59, 300. I would like to thank Angelika Königseder for her suggestions and detailed answers to my questions. See also her comments in a Deutschlandfunk Kultur programme: https://www.deutschlandfunk-kultur.de/der-milde-blick-wie-deutsche-verlage-mit-ihrer-ns.976.de.html?dram:article_id=386423

17 Königseder, *Walter de Gruyter*, p. 71.

18 Kern would survive the war and later published again with Reinhardt Verlag. Other authors were less lucky.

19 Dahm, p. 44, footnote 52.

20 See, for example, Jungck, *75 Jahre*, p. 48.

21 The *Wandervogelbewegung* was a youth movement that began as a reaction against industrialisation and looked back to the ideals of the Romantic era. It had an emphasis on the natural world and outdoor activity such as hiking.

22 See Junck, *75 Jahre*, p. 49.

23 David Mamet, "Missbraucht sie, beutet sie aus" in *Die Zeit*, 29/6/2019.

24 Cited in Max Friedlaender, *Die Lebenserinnerungen des Rechtsanwalts Max Friedlaender*, https://brak.de/w/files/01_ueber_die_brak/friedlaender.pdf, p. 1521.

25 Around 1,750 lawyers were affected by this, see Michael Löffelsender, *Kölner Rechtsanwälte im Nationalsozialismus*, Tübingen, 2015, p. 43.

26 Friedlaender, *Lebenserinnerungen*, pp. 152f.

27 ibid., p. 152.

28 Martin Doerry, "Kräftig arisiert", *Der Spiegel*, No. 17, 20/4/2019, pp. 114f.

29 Peter Voswinckel, *Dr. Josef Löbel. Botschafter eines heiteren deutschen Medizin-Feuilletons in Wien-Berlin-Prag*, Berlin, 2018. The Aryanisation of the medical dictionary only became public in 2017. See Günther Fetzer, *Droemer Knaur. Die Verlagsgeschichte 1846–2017*, Munich 2017, pp. 230f.

30 Peter Voswinckel, "Um das Lebenswerk betrogen: Walter Guttmann (1873–1941) und seine Medizinische Terminologie" in *Medizinhistorisches Journal* 32 (1997), pp. 321–54.

31 In her obituary it reads: "From the summer semester of 1930 until the summer semester of 1935 she attended Ludwig-Maximilian University of Munich, and in 1936 was awarded her doctorate for her thesis on 'Rickets in Munich in 1935' [...] In 1992 she moved into St Nikolaus old people's home in Eggenfelden, where she died on 9 April 1996." See Hubert Kolling,

"Riederer von Paar, Viola" in *Journal für Pflegewissenschaft und Pflegepraxis*, 2004, Vol. 3, pp. 237f.

32 Viola Riederer von Paar, *Vererbungslehre für Studierende und zum Selbstunterricht. Grundriß, Kurzes Repetitorium, Prüfungsfragen und Antworten, Reinhardts naturwissenschaftliche Kompendien*, Vol. 9, Munich, 1937 (5th edition 1945).

33 Jungck, *75 Jahre*, p. 94.

34 ibid., p. 78.

35 Christoph Jungck, *100 Jahre Ernst Reinhardt Verlag*, Munich 1999, p. 32.

36 ibid., p. 33.

37 ibid., p. 37.

38 Jungck, *75 Jahre*, p. 55.

39 ibid., p. 56.

40 Alice Urbach, *Old World*, p. 19.

41 On 15/9/1938 the clarification of 5/9 was affixed with a seal from the Munich tax office. The document was found in the Ernst Reinhardt Verlag archive in 2020 after the publication of Alice's story.

42 Paul Perles cited in Murray G. Hall, "Epitaph auf den Verlag Moritz Perles in Wien, 1869–1938", online publication at: http://www.murrayhall.com

43 Jungck, *75 Jahre*, p. 56. The foreword of the 1939 Rösch edition is signed "autumn 1938". In his 1974 history Jungck mentions that in the 1930s Rudolf Rösch took over the highly successful illustrated cookery calendar. In fact Rösch isn't yet mentioned as an author in the advertisement for the 1938 calendar.

44 I would like to thank Walter Schübler for his valuable suggestions. See also Walter Schübler, "Eine Jaffa-Torte passte nicht ins deutsche Kochbuch" in *Frankfurter Allgemeine Zeitung*, 24/10/2020.

45 Alice Urbach, *So kocht man in Wien!*, Munich, 1935, p. 6.

46 Rudolf Rösch, *So kocht man in Wien!*, Munich, 1939, p. 6.

47 Alice Urbach, *So kocht man in Wien!*, p. 458.

48 ibid., pp. 450f.

49 From the German National Archives in Lichterfelde (Berlin): "In the documents you specified relating to persons by the name of Rudolf Rösch no references could be found to the city of Vienna nor to any activity as a writer." In particular I would like to thank Robert Luther from the German National Archives in Lichterfelde for his help in the search for Rudolf Rösch.

50 From the director of Salzburg City Archive, Peter Kramml, 2019: "I assume he merely had the same name. The Rudolf Rösch you identified was born in Salzburg and lived there all his life [...] He died in Salzburg on 21/10/1977. He is constantly referred to as a businessman and served in the Wehrmacht from 1939 to 1945."

51 Telephone conversation between the author and the CEO of Reinhardt Verlag after the publication of the first edition of this book in German, on 13/10/2020.

52 See BR, Historisches Archiv, PER.BR.96. I would like to thank Sabine Rittner from the Bayerischer Rundfunk archive for the information about Rudolf Rösch's Munich programmes.

CHAPTER 9

1 The German Jewish Aid Committee, Woburn House, Upper Woburn Place, London, WC1. Woburn House was also home to the Board of Deputies of British Jews. The aid organisations moved in March 1939 from Woburn House to Bloomsbury House.

2 Clip from 1939 at https://www.youtube.com/watch?v=gYJXdW7PHFM

3 *While You Are in England. Helpful Information and Guidance for Every Refugee*, published by the German Jewish Aid Committee, Jewish Board of Deputies, London, c.1938. *Für die Zeit ihres Aufenthalts in England: Hilfreiche Informationen und Anleitungen für jeden Flüchtling*. Refugee Pamphlets, S3b 081, Wiener Holocaust Library. I should like to thank the archivist Howard Falksohn for his help.

4 Alice Urbach, "Old World", pp. 20f.

5 ibid., p. 21.

6 Torberg, *Tante Jolesch*, p. 71.

7 Charles Neilson Gattey, *The Incredible Mrs. Van der Elst*, London, 1972.

8 ibid., p 159. I would like to thank Linda Dawes from the Harlaxton Manor archive for the information she provided about the house and its employees in the 1930s.

9 Mrs Van der Elst, her estate and her secretary can be seen in a film clip from 1939: British Pathé, https://www.youtube.com/watch?v=8sqtef_StsE

10 Torberg, *Tante Jolesch*, p. 264.

11 Gattey, *The Incredible*, p. 99.

12 Tony Kushner, "Politics and Race, Gender and Class. Refugees, Fascists and Domestic Service in Britain, 1933–40", in Tony Kushner/Kenneth Lunn, *The Politics of Marginality. Race, the Radical Right and Minorities in Twentieth Century Britain*, Oxford, 1990, pp. 49ff.

13 The chauffeur was a Mr Winston, a Jewish jeweller from London. On him and Ray, see the recording made by Mr Crane on 5/6/2003, visit to Harlaxton College by Mr and Mrs Crane and their son Stephen Crane, Harlaxton archive.

14 "The Nazis sent me to a Concentration Camp", *Sunday Oregonian*, 21/5/1939, article by Francis Murphy, based on an anonymised interview with Karl Urbach.

15 ibid.

16 It must have been either the school at 2 Kenyongasse or the one at 14 Karajangasse.

17 See the assistance fund documents on Felix Mayer, 17/7/1956, Archivbestände der Vermögensverkehrsstelle und Hilfsfonds für politisch Verfolgte, VA 39 035 and VA 39 036, Österreichisches Staatsarchiv. All Alice heard later was that the extensive library belonging to her father Sigmund and all the books of riddles written by Felix himself had been plundered. It is not known whether this happened at the time of the arrest in November 1938, nor is it known when Felix's apartment was Aryanised.

18 Kreisky was lucky: he was released on condition that he emigrate. He went to Sweden.

19 Franziska Tausig, *Shanghai Passage. Emigration ins Ghetto*, Vienna, 2007, p. 57.

20 Felix Mayer assistance fund documents.

21 "The Nazis sent me to a Concentration Camp".

22 It is not known whether Willy also informed the Dodsons in America. In 2003 Cordelia wrote to Karl: "How did we find out? Did Willy write or, as I recall, Otto was involved." Cordelia Dodson papers.

23 Marie Urbach was the widow of the banker Ignaz Urbach, who committed suicide in 1924. She was an "Aryan" and thus her children were "half-Jews". Her son Robert Urbach emigrated to America with his family; her daughter Anni stayed in Vienna. Robert was married to Lola Finkelstein, who became one of Alice's best friends.

24 Otto to his aunt Marie, 27/11/1938, Otto Urbach papers. On 28/11/1938 Otto wrote a similar letter to Marie's son Robert Urbach: "Second, I've

indirectly let Karli's friend know that there is money available for Karli. At any rate I meant to transfer the money to someone in our family. I do not know Karli's friend Willy personally and I do not even know his surname. I hope that he has got in touch with you." Otto Urbach papers.

25 "The Nazis sent me to a Concentration Camp".

26 See *Wien wehrt sich mit Witz! Flüsterwitze aus den Jahren 1938–1945*, Gmunden, 1946, p. 11.

27 On 1 April the first 151 people, high-ranking politicians, officials and functionaries, were sent to Dachau concentration camp.

28 Part of her campaign was the publication of a book against the death penalty. Violet Van der Elst, *On the Gallows*, London, 1937.

29 Alice Urbach, "Old World", p. 21f.

30 Interned 15/11/1938, prisoner number 28194, released 18/1/1939, prisoner category: Jew, protective custody. See KZ-Gedenkstätte Dachau, Stiftung Bayerische Gedenkstätten, Karl Urbach, NARA Zugangsbuch No. 105/28186.

31 "The Nazis sent me to a Concentration Camp".

32 ibid.

33 ibid.

34 See Eva Holpfer, "Der Fall Novak. Eichmanns Transportoffizier – der letzte Schuldspruch". Lecture on 1/12/2005 at the Vienna criminal court: http://www.kreuzstadl.net/downloads/novak_referat_dezember05_holpfer.pdf

35 Marischka, *Immer nur lächeln*, p. 134.

36 "The Nazis sent me to a Concentration Camp".

37 Letter of 5/6/1938, cited in Friedrich Torberg, *Eine tolle, tolle Zeit. Briefe und Dokumente aus den Jahren der Flucht 1938 bis 1941*, Munich, 1989, pp. 24f.

38 The two men's quarrels were partly down to the fact that, in the 1950s, the woman they were fighting over, Otto's wife Wera, kept lending Torberg money for gambling (and never asked for it back).

39 Grünbaum died 1941 in Dachau; his wife was deported. His Schiele collection was thought missing for many years, but some pictures were later returned to the heirs.

40 "The Nazis sent me to a Concentration Camp".

41 Karl to Alice, undated, January 1939, Alice Urbach papers.

42 Charles Linza McNary (1874–1944) was the Repubican senator for Oregon.

43 Otto to Karl, undated, January or February 1939, Otto Urbach papers.

44 Email from Albert Knoll, archivist at Dachau concentration camp memorial: "We don't know how your uncle was freed from the camp. The relevant documents were in the prisoner files, which were destroyed. What is certain is that they had to be able to show an emigration certificate or permission to emigrate."

45 Date of release was 18/1/1939.

46 In her memoir Alice wrote: "[He was] imprisoned in the hell of Dachau for no other crime than that of not being 'Aryan Blood'. Due to the frantic efforts of my older son [...] he came out alive!" Alice Urbach, "Old World", p. 20.

47 Otto to Karl, undated, early February 1939, Otto Urbach papers.

48 Message from senior official Emil Engel, grant for USA ticket: 250 MK. Jewish Community of Vienna.

49 "The Nazis sent me to a Concentration Camp".

50 Karl to Alice, 25/2/1939, Karl Urbach papers.

51 Karl to Alice, 6/3/1939, Karl Urbach papers.

52 The island in the Hudson River was the headquarters of the American immigration authorities until 1954.

53 Askin, Quietude and Quest, p. 212. What Askin couldn't have known at the time was that years later he would become famous for playing a Nazi in the television series Hogan's Heroes. That role would give him his longed-for financial security.

54 Karl later wrote to his granddaughter Erin: "My friends in Oregon had offered me their family's hospitality and I went there by bus – across all of the USA. A great adventure [. . .] I could speak some and understand English but could not read or write it too well. Psychologically I was not in a very good shape after Dachau." 2002, Karl Urbach papers.

55 See Deborah E. Lipstadt, Beyond Belief. The American Press and the Coming of the Holocaust 1933–1945, New York, 1986.

56 "Crown Prince denies Germany is abusing Jews" in Chicago Tribune, 28/3/1933; "Ex-Crown Prince denies Atrocities", New York Times, 28/3/1933; "Former Crown Prince calls stories 'Propaganda of Lies'", Baltimore Sun, 28/3/ 1933; New York Herald Tribune, 27. 8. 1933. For the Hohenzollern debate see Stephan Malinowski, Die Hohenzollern und die Nazis. Geschichte einer Kollaboration, Berlin, 2021.

CHAPTER 10

1   George Mikes, *How to Be a Brit*, London 1984.

2   Veronika Zwerger, Ursula Seeber, *Küche der Erinnerung. Essen und Exil*, Vienna, 2018, p. 163.

3   Alice's address in London at the time was 38 Guilford Street, WC1. Her employer may have worked at nearby Great Ormond Street Hospital.

4   Zwerger/Seeber, *Küche der Erinnerung*, p. 152.

5   Her two other half-brothers, Arnold and Siegfried Mayer, had both died in the 1920s.

6   *While You Are in England*.

7   From the Leo Baeck Institute collection, New York, Kindertransport exhibition 2019. On the Kindertransport see also Eva Haas, "Ein Schild mit Namen und Nummer um den Hals" in Martin Doerry, *"Nirgendwo und überall zu Haus". Gespräche mit Überlebenden des Holocaust*, Munich 2006, p. 68.

8   See Rebekka Göpfert, *Der jüdische Kindertransport von Deutschland nach England 1938/39. Geschichte und Erinnerung*, Frankfurt am Main, 1999; Anja Salewsky, *Der olle Hitler soll sterben*; and Ela Kaczmarska, "Kindertransport. Britain's rescue plan", https://media.nationalarchives.gov.uk/index.php/kindertransport-britains-rescue-plan/

9   Peter Sieber, "The Newcastle-upon-Tyne Hostel for Jewish Refugee Girls. In recognition of the Hostel Committee who initiated the Hostel and managed it, and of the Newcastle Jewish Community who supported it", unpublished manuscript 4184, March 2000, Wiener Holocaust Library.

10 ibid.

11 http://www.kinthetop.at/forschung/kinthetop_chronik.html

12 Still alive at the start of 2020 were Lisl Scherzer (later Alisa Tennenbaum), Ilse Gross (later Camis, died August 2020) and Elfi Reinert (who died in spring 2021). The rest of the group have been anonymised. They were: Inge A. and her sister Ruth from Breslau (now Wrocław), Dasha from Prague, Annie from Augsburg, Lore from Königsberg (now Kaliningrad), Sophie from Langenselbold, Edith G. from Düsseldorf, Margot H. from Frankfurt/Main, Paula K., Eva L. and Marion M. from Berlin, Ruth O. from Frankfurt, the sisters Vera and Lisl R. from Czechoslovakia, and Hilde, Freda and Lea R. from Köln.

13 Interview with Lisl Scherzer.

14 Correspondence between the author and Lisl Scherzer in December 2018. I would like to thank Dina Kraft for recording the first interview with Lisl.

15 Sieber, "The Newcastle-upon-Tyne Hostel".

16 ibid.

17 ibid.

18 Alice Urbach, *So kocht man in Wien!*, pp. 467f.

19 Interview with Lisl Scherzer.

20 Sieber, "The Newcastle-upon-Tyne Hostel".

21 "Alice Urbach, Female Enemy Alien – Exemption from Internment-Refugee

   Normal occupation: Cookery Expert

   Present occupation: Cook

   Decision of Tribunal: Exempt from internment, Date: 6/11/1939

   Reasons for Decision: Refugee, Anti-Nazi, two sons in the USA. Widow."

   National Archives, Kew, HO 396/94.

22 Interview with Lisl Scherzer.

23 Cited in Zwerger/Seeber, *Küche der Erinnerung*, p. 167.

24 Interview with Lisl Scherzer.

25 *While You Are in England*, pp. 12, 14. Another booklet reiterated the advice
   for emigrants: "Do's and Don't's for Refugees: Do be as quiet and modest
   as possible. If you do not make yourself noticeable other people will not
   bother about you." Cited in Anne Joseph (ed.), *From the Edge of the World:
   The Jewish Refugee Experience through Letters and Stories*, London, 2003, p. 155.

26 I would like to thank in particular Deborah Cantor from Jewish Relief
   for being able to view these files. In agreement with her, all the children's
   details have been anonymised.

27 Ruth David, *Child of Our Time: A Young Girl's Flight from the Holocaust*,
   London, 2003, pp. 78f. Ruth David was unable to consult the files of the
   Jewish Refugees Committee, which were not made accessible until long
   after the publication of her book.

28 Alice Urbach, *So kocht man in Wien!*, p. 474.

29 Author's interview with Ilse Camis, 2019.

30 Alice Urbach, cassette interview. Alice Urbach papers.

31 In 1944 she published together with Dorothy Burlingham her study, *Infants
   Without Families. The Case For and Against Residential Nurseries*, New York,
   1944.

32 "In the evacuation of children it has been found advisable to make a
   division into two wide groups, the larger group being for over 5 years
   of age and up to 15 or 16, the other group being under 5 years of age to 2 or

3 years of age. To sum up, evacuation of children is best accomplished on a boarding school or school camp plan consisting of rural displacement of their own school organization." Anna Freud papers, Library of Congress, Box 114 on evacuations, as well as Freud/Burlingham, *Infants Without Families*.

33 On food, see David, *Child of Our Time*, p. 57.

34 Alice Urbach, *So kocht man in Wien!*, p. 460.

35 See David, *Child of Our Time*, p. 58.

36 Alice Urbach, *So kocht man in Wien!*, pp. 453, 455.

37 Young-Bruehl, *Anna Freud*, p. 252.

38 Interview with Lisl Scherzer.

39 David, *Child of Our Time*, p. 74.

40 I would like to thank Ilse Camis for her many memories of Alice (and for the interesting anecdotes about the Shand Kydds).

41 Interview with Lisl Scherzer.

42 ibid.

43 *While You Are in England*, p. 22.

44 Scotland has always had its own education system.

45 Alice Urbach, "Old World", pp. 23f, Alice Urbach papers.

46 See also ibid., p. 24.

47 Child development under the impact of war conditions, Box 127, Anna Freud papers, Library of Congress.

48 "I have clear recollections of having frequent temper tantrums and being sent to bed where I would cry myself to sleep. I used to cry at the slightest provocation. At times I would find solace by withdrawing into my private play world with my favourite doll." Lore F.'s memoir in her family's possession. See also Alice Urbach, "Old World", p. 24 and the interview with Lisl Scherzer.

49 Alice Urbach, cassette interview, Alice Urbach papers.

50 Alice Urbach, "Old World", p. 24.

51 A copy of this is also in Elfi Reinert's photograph collection (Birmingham).

52 ibid.

53 Peter Sieber, "The Newcastle-upon-Tyne Hostel for Jewish Refugee Girls". In her innovative book *Survivors*, Rebecca Clifford shows how the memory and treatment of rescued children changed over the last 70 years. Rebecca Clifford, *Survivors. Children's Lives after the Holocaust*, Yale, 2020.

54 Dorit Bader-Whiteman, *The Uprooted. A Hitler Legacy. Voices of Those Who*

Escaped before the "Final Solution", New York, 1993, pp. 233f. Unlike the critical child cited here, Elfi Reinert thought that Alice was stricter than Paula. Alice did try, however, to explain to her the facts of life. Elfi said that after this she had even less of a clue.

CHAPTER 11

1 Cited in Torberg, *Tante Jolesch*, p. 269.

2 According to his internment file, Felix lived at 78 Oakwood, Blackhill. The house is no longer standing. Felix's internment card still has "Israel" as part of his name, which had been a compulsory addition for Jewish men in the Third Reich: Felix Israel Mayer. HO 396/113, National Archives, Kew.

3 Felix Mayer, "The Mission", Leo Baeck Institute Archives, Manuscript Collection MS 102c, New York/Berlin. Felix's manuscript was a combination of fact and fiction. The chapter about his internment on the Isle of Man, however, is based on his real experiences, which he was able to recount only in the third person.

4 His son described him as a shy and modest man who loved languages and had no aptitude for commerce. See "Thomas Mayer" in Roger Backhouse and Roger Middleton (eds), *Exemplary Economists. North America*, Vol. 1, Aldershot, 2000, p. 101.

5 Felix was chief clerk at A. Mayer und Co. in Vienna until 1927, after which he worked as a freelance commercial agent.

6 Alice Urbach, cassette interview, Alice Urbach papers.

7 I would like to thank Regina Zodl from the archive/provenance research at Vienna University of Economics and Business (WU) for finding the book. It was reinstated in a ceremony on 22nd July 2021. See: https://www.wu.ac.at/en/the-university/news-and-events/news/details-news/detail/books-stolen-by-the-nazis

8 Thomas describes how his father found an excellent school for him. Bunce Court, which was relocated from Kent to Shropshire during the Battle of Britain. It was run by emigrants. See "Mayer", in Backhouse/Middleton, *Exemplary Economists*, p. 101.

9 Although the manuscript is in German, Felix has the English characters speak English.

10 Felix Mayer, *The Mission* (the following quotations are all from this

manuscript too). The painter Fred Uhlman, another internee, also described how he had to surrender his razorblade at the police station. On Uhlman's recollections of internment see Fred Uhlman, *The Making of an Englishman. Erinnerungen eines deutschen Juden*, Zürich, 1998, p. 281.

11   Peter was deported to Canada for two years. In 1942 he was able to return to Britain and volunteered for one of the most dangerous jobs in the British army, as a mine clearer I would like to thank Vivien Sieber for her memories of her father.

12   Franz Marischka, *Immer nur lächeln*, p. 101.

13   Fred Uhlman describes something similar: "But there were two things that made internment particularly unbearable. The first was the feeling of injustice and a total waste of energy that could have been put to far better use. (Think of how successfully Hitler could have used thousands of British refugees!) The second was a particular form of torture, known as 'redundancy' [. . .] Were you 'important for the war effort' or not? Some government official had to make that decision. As you might expect of an Englishman, he of course deemed businesspeople, engineers etc. important, but not artists, musicians, university professors, leading anti-Nazis and so on." Uhlman, *Englishman*, p. 284.

14   On the *Daily Mail* campaign "Intern the lot!" see Robert Mackay, *The Test of War. Inside Britain*, London, 1998, p. 104.

15   Not all British surrendered to the mass hysteria: "Bauer was deeply touched when one day the ladies from the Quaker committee came to visit their charges." Felix Mayer, *The Mission*.

16   "The building was described to me as worse than any concentration camp, derelict, filthy, almost all windows broken and the floors covered in rubbish. The commander stole like a magpie: money, typewriters, whatever he could get his hands on [Felix mentions this too]." Uhlman also heard of the seriously ill patients in the camp, suffering from cancer and diabetes. "The German doctors did not have any hypodermic needles or medicine. Three hundred and eighty men slept in one room and the excrement flowed across the floor. Cooking pots, thermos flasks and hats had to be used for urinating in. Nervous breakdowns, followed by acts of violence were the order of the day." Uhlman, *Englishman*, p. 286.

17   See Connery Chappell, *Island of Barbed Wire. The Remarkable Story of World War Two Internment on the Isle of Man*, London, 1984, p. 37.

18   This might be Felix Perger from Vienna (b. 20/7/1887).

19 "The trip across the sea was a pleasant interruption to the endless monotony, it was refreshing to see something different from the barbed wire, to learn that the world, the sea, nature still existed – peaceful, sure, permanent. They arrived in Douglas, disembarked and marched along the quai – a very long procession. To the right was the sea, to the left the promenade, one hotel after another. Soon they stopped again by a gate with barbed wire." Felix Mayer, *The Mission*. I would like to thank the archivist Kim Holden from the Manx Museum on the Isle of Man for her help. See also Chappell, *Island of Barbed Wire*, p. 36.

20 ibid., p. 30.

21 Felix wrote about the internal organisation: "Each house elected a warden and all the internees elected a camp leader. The vote went to a likeable Protestant pastor who had been in the group around Niemöller. A hospital was set up too, where the many imprisoned doctors performed their duties. It [...] was always full."

22 Uhlman, *Englishman*, p. 287.

23 Marischka, *Immer nur lächeln*, p. 102.

24 The faith of the eastern Jews was unfamiliar to Felix and Fred Uhlman. Uhlman describes how there was an air-raid warning on the Sabbath and all the houses were immediately blacked out apart from the one housing the Orthodox Jews: "They said the commander tried ringing, but without success, as no Orthodox Jew answers the telephone on the Sabbath. The commander then sent a messenger with the order to turn off the bloody light. The messenger came back saying he had tried to turn the light off, but was stopped. As he himself was a Jew the others had prevented him from committing such a sin. Now irate, the commander tried to find a non-Jew in the camp, which consisted of 90 per cent Jewish internees. But by the time he found one the alert was over." Uhlman, *Englishman*, p. 299f.

25 To counter the rumours spread by the interned Nazis, newspapers were soon allowed inside the camp. See Chappell, *Barbed Wire*, p. 61. Fred Uhlman, however, does not share Felix's opinion that the British had no idea who the Nazis were in the camp. He wrote: "I'm absolutely certain that our secret service officers knew what was going on in the camp. There were informants and camp spies that kept them up to date." Uhlman, *Englishman*, p. 301.

26 Chappell writes that the outgoing post was read relatively quickly by the censors in Douglas, but the post coming into the camp was checked in

Liverpool, where postal sacks piled up and there were long waiting times. Chappell, *Barbed Wire*, p. 61.

27 Uhlman, *Englishman*, p. 290.

28 ibid., p. 295.

29 In fact the American consulate in Vienna closed a few months after Felix's attempt in July 1941.

30 Alice later said that the family suffered from the separation and desperately tried to get back together in America. Apparently, Helene managed to get through to Eleanor Roosevelt, and in a public hearing read out the letters from her son Thomas, breaking down in tears as she did so. But her efforts were successful. In 1944 Felix und Thomas were able to emigrate and the family were reunited in New York.

31 Felix did not have a high opinion of his poems. He writes about his alter ego Georg Bauer: "He'd often written poetry, good, bad, and all of it more or less amateurish."

32 Written in London in 1942. Felix Mayer, "Gedichte", LBI MS 102a, Leo Baeck Institute Archives, New York/Berlin. Alice also recites it in her cassette interview from the 1970s.

CHAPTER 12

1 Alice Urbach, "My Sons".

2 Interview in Steve Karras's documentary *About Face. Jewish Refugees in the Allied Forces*, USA, 2005.

3 During the crossing Brombert was very bellicose, and a comrade said to him. "You've got the bug." Victor Brombert, *Trains of Thought. Paris to Omaha Beach, Memories of a Stateless Youth*, New York, 2002, p. 265.

4 Brombert wrote: "I was not in the least religious; I was indeed hostile to any form of dogma. The [letter] bothered me, and not only because of what it might mean if I should fall into the hands of the Germans." ibid., p. 254.

5 Marischka, *Immer nur lächeln*, p. 103.

6 It also says "Catholic" on his marriage certificate from November 1947. Otto Urbach papers.

7 Hermann Bondi's parents were friends of Alice, and Hermann himself had been interned on the Isle of Man with Felix.

8 Alice was very fond of Bondi and in her cassette interview said, "During

the Second World War Thomas Gold and Hermann Bondi lived in a hut in a very remote location, where they didn't even allow a woman in to clean, as their work was so discreet." (By "discreet" Alice meant secret government work.) She was delighted that Bondi still wrote to her in the 1970s. I would like also to thank Peter Goddard for his memories of Hermann Bondi.

9   Rudolf Moritz Theodor Urbach, b. 16/2/1908 in Duisburg, see birth registrations of the city of Duisburg. He arrived in New York on 10/12/1928. In Camp Ritchie he was in training class 20. There is a time overlap here, however. Camp Trinidad was opened in May 1943, but Rudolf Urbach didn't pass his secret service training until August 1944. Was he already head of Camp Trinidad before this training or was it Otto? I would like to thank Daniel Gross and Heather Steele for their help in researching Rudolf Urbach and his training at Camp Ritchie.

10 Rüdiger von Wechmar, *Akteur in der Loge. Weltläufige Erinnerungen*, Munich, 2000, p. 77. Otto's wife Wera Frydtberg recalled the conversations Otto had with Wechmar.

11 In his memoir the emigrant Kurt Landsberger only mentions Rudolf Urbach. See Kurt Landsberger, *Prisoners of War at Camp Trinidad, Colorado 1943–1946. Internment, Intimidation, Incompetence and Country Club Living*, Wisconsin, 2007.

12 Georg Kreisler on 28/2/2003 in the Bayerischer Rundfunk programme "Forum". Some Viennese emigrants later turned out to be as creative as Kreisler: Marcel Prawy, Hans Habe, Peter Beauvais or the Viennese theatre director Ernst Haeusserman. But not all of them wanted or were able to talk about this episode in their lives in post-war Austria. Otto had every reason to keep quiet about it. All he told his wife Wera was that he had been on the same boat as Peter Lert, the son of the writer Vicky Baum. Lert also trained at Camp Ritchie in Maryland: Lt Peter J. Lert, Class 13. He was in the IPW Team 44 of VII Corps.

13 Hans Habe, *Im Jahre Null*, Munich, 1977, p. 8f. See also Brombert, *Trains of Thought*, p. 259. On Camp Ritchie see the excellent documentary and book by Christian Bauer and Rebekka Göpfert, *Die Ritchie Boys: Deutsche Emigranten beim US-Geheimdienst*, Hamburg, 2005.

14 Even the emigrant Landsberger was impressed by Urbach's 'good' German. Landsberger, *Prisoners of War*, p. 18.

15 Cited in Felix Römer, *Kameraden. Die Wehrmacht von innen*, Munich, 2014, p. 47.

16 The power struggles that played out between the inmates here would later form the basis for a TV film with Walter Matthau. *The Incident* (1990) takes place in a fictitious camp in Colorado, which in many ways is reminiscent of Camp Trinidad. The screenwriters were obviously given plenty of information by insiders.

17 Anna Freud only found out in 1946 that her aunts, Sigmund Freud's sisters, had been murdered in 1942. See Young-Bruehl, *Anna Freud*, pp. 280f.

18 See information from the International Tracing Service, Bad Arolsen. I would like to thank Sabine van der Horst of ITS for all the information about Alice's relatives.

19 Emma Middleton von Schirach (1872–1944) was a descendant of Arthur Middleton, a signatory of the American Declaration of Independence. Letter from Emma Schirach to Poultney Bigelow, 27/4/1941, Bigelow Papers, New York Public Library, Box 9.

20 It is possible that they tried too late to emigrate. Maybe Georg Eissler thought he was safe because he'd converted at the age of twenty-five and had fought in the First World War. His biographical data: Georg Alexander Eissler, b. 22/4/1885, Schottenbastei 11, Vienna 1, baptised into the Roman-Catholic faith on 23/10/1910. Son of Hermann Eissler and Auguste Abeles. See Gaugusch, *Wer einmal war*, p. 2256.

21 *Wolfgang Trepper – live!* ARD programme from 1/2/2019.

22 The episode is reconstructed in detail in Günther Schwarberg's biography of Beda. The criminal inmate Josef Windeck understood the director's words as an invitation and he beat Beda to death. See Günther Schwarberg, *Dein ist mein ganzes Herz. Die Geschichte von Fritz Löhner-Beda, der die schönsten Lieder der Welt schrieb, und warum Hitler ihn ermorden ließ*, Göttingen, 2000, p. 167. Alice's favourite poem by Beda was "Juden, Christen und andere Antisemiten" (Jews, Christians and other anti-Semites). She recites it on her cassette interview from the 1970s.

23 In her memoir Alice writes: "I want to set a memorial to them, also noble-minded women, whose graves I cannot visit, who clinging to each other in their last terrible hours perished in the gas chamber of one of the Nazi concentration camps." Alice Urbach, "Old World", p. 2.

CHAPTER 13

1 Cited in Reed College's obituary of Cordelia Dodson, 2011 (https://www.
   reed.edu/reed-magazine/in-memoriam/obituaries/december2011/corde-
   lia-dodson-hood-1936.html)

2 McIntosh, *Sisterhood of Spies*, p. 176.

3 Daniel Dodson studied French literature and flew a B-24 over China
   during the war. After the war he became a professor at Columbia
   University. He wrote a number of novels. See also his obituary in the
   New York Times of 12/1/1991.

4 OSS file Cordelia Dodson, RG 226, Entry A1224, Box 191, National Archives
   Washington.

5 Anybody who worked there saw the precious "Ultra" material, which
   included Wehrmacht radio messages that had been decrypted by the
   British, providing a big strategic advantage. Nowadays it is accepted that
   this decryption shortened the war by two years.

6 OSS file Cordelia Dodson, which also contains her CV: Reed College,
   1932–36 BA in 1936, University of Grenoble, France 1936–37, University of
   Vienna, Vienna 1937–38, American Institute Vienna, 1937–38, Reed College
   1939–41 MA (studied German, French, Literature, Psychology). References
   from Dr E.N. Barnhart, OSS Washington, Psychologist; Dr Dexter Keezer,
   War Labor Board, Economist; Dr H.F. Peters, Reed College, Portland,
   Head of German Department; E.R. LeRoy, G-2 MIS Army, Pentagon
   Building, Washington DC. (E.R. LeRoy worked for military intelligence.)

7 ibid.

8 ibid.

9 His harshest critic is Stephen Kinzer, *The Brothers. John Foster Dulles, Allen
   Dulles and their Secret World War*, New York, 2013.

10 His worst OSS agents were the opposite of this. The gossip columnist
   Drew Pearson described them as "one of the fanciest groups of dilettante
   diplomats, Wall Street bankers, and amateur detectives ever seen in
   Washington." ibid., p. 66.

11 The British had used these methods before the Americans. See also the
   OSS file on Peter Viertel, Theatre Service Record, Principal Civilian
   Experience, Scenario Writer, August 1945: "At a time when intelligence
   penetration of Germany was an unexplored field, Lieutenant Viertel
   tackled the problem with dogged determination. With unfailing energy
   and sound judgement he screened, recruited and trained many agents

who were put in the field by his organization." OSS file Peter Viertel, Box 802 National Archives, Washington.

12 *Decision before Dawn* was based on George Howe's novel *Call It Treason*. Howe and Viertel worked in the same unit. Viertel wrote about Howe's novel: "It was a fictionalised account of an intelligence mission behind the enemy lines that had been undertaken by a young German soldier I had, in fact, recruited, a mission that failed and had ended tragically, with the death of the young German. These small tactical operations had been called "tourist missions" and had been launched by us at the request of 7th Army intelligence." Peter Viertel, *Dangerous Friends. At Large with Huston and Hemingway in the Fifties*, London, 1992, p. 68.

13 In the 1990s Cordelia said, "It was a pretty hairy trip. They were taking engine parts and also what were called 'border crossers': German prisoners of war who had agreed to go back across the border and transmit information [...] We landed in Lyons in a blizzard." Cited in Robert S. Greene, *Blum-San! Scholar, Soldier, Gentleman, Spy. The many lives of Paul Blum*, New York, 1998, p. 107.

14 McIntosh, *Sisterhood of Spies*, p. 174.

15 Greene, *Blum-San!*, p. 198. Cordelia was particularly fascinated by Paul Blum's tales about Japan and China, places that Otto had already interested her in. There was a rumour that Cordelia and Blum, who was twenty years older, were in love, but in 1950, after much humming and hawing, Cordelia married the younger William Hood.

16 ibid., p. 102.

17 Her name was Diane and she trusted Cordelia more than she did Blum, ibid., p. 204.

18 McIntosh, *Sisterhood*, p. 176.

19 Greene, *Blum-San!*, p. 238.

20 Hood would later highlight only Blum's role in the operation. See ibid., pp. 237f. On the promotion see OSS file Cordelia Dodson.

21 Pucci report (see Chapter 4, note 17).

22 Cited in McIntosh, *Sisterhood*, p. 177.

23 See student memories of Pucci at: https://www.reed.edu/reed-magazine/articles/2014/emilio-pucci.html

24 Emilio Pucci's "Fascism: An Explanation and Justification" has been on loan from Reed since 2018, and by May 2020 the author had still not been able to read it.

25 Pucci report.

26 In his second OSS report (Pucci report), he does not give a date to the audience. It must have taken place before the British and Americans landed in Sicily on 9–10 July 1943.

27 Pervitin was known as the "pilots' drug", but it was taken by other soldiers too. See Pucci report, p. 9. On Pervitin, see Norman Ohler, *Blitzed: Drugs in Nazi Germany*, London, 2016.

28 McIntosh, *Sisterhood*, p. 177.

29 Her son Fabrizio later used this phrase as the title of his autobiography. Fabrizio Ciano, *Quando Il Nonno Fece Fucilare Papà*, Milan, 1991.

30 Pucci report.

31 McIntosh, *Sisterhood*, p. 177.

32 Lorie Charlesworth and Michael Salter, "Ensuring the after-life of the Ciano diaries: Allen Dulles' provision of Nuremberg trial evidence", *Intelligence and National Security*, Vol. 21, No. 4, August 2006, p. 570. The "ratlines", via which Nazi criminals were smuggled to South America, were the flipside of these compromises. Because Pucci had betrayed the Fascist cause, but didn't get any sympathy from the Italian opposition either, OSS agreed to help him try to get a foreign passport. See his OSS file, 22/11/1945, Subject: Marchese Emilio Pucci di Barsento, Conversation in Rome about Pucci, RG 226, Entry 211, BOX 38. National Archives, Washington.

CHAPTER 14

1 Lisl forgot that Helga's father worked in England too. Lisl Scherzer interview.

2 ibid.

3 Sieber, "The Newcastle-upon-Tyne Hostel".

4 Later it was established that Margot's parents, Alfred and Bella H., were murdered in the Łódź Ghetto in 1941.

5 Historical records for the children who came on the Kindertransport, World Jewish Relief Archives (files have been anonymised).

6 Sieber, "The Newcastle-upon-Tyne Hostel".

7 Interview with Lisl (Alisa Tennenbaum) for the arte/ZDF TV documentary in 2021. The story of the concentration camp children was turned into a 2020 film entitled *The Windermere Children*. Today Trevor Avery is

head of the Lake District Holocaust Project in Windermere.

8 These warehouses are also mentioned in the BBC Radio 4 programme, "Poisoned Angel. The Story of Alma Rose", broadcast in 2004.

9 In the post-war context this word was seen as positive.

10 Affidavit from W. Dodson, undated. Karl Urbach papers.

11 He was part of the crew of the *Carpathia*, which came to the scene of the accident.

12 Alice Urbach, cassette interview. Alice Urbach papers.

13 She worked for the Albert Pick hotel chain founded by a Jewish immigrant in the nineteenth century. See https://matchpro.org/Archives/2004/alpick.pdf

14 Habe, *Im Jahre Null*, p. 21.

15 There is a yawning gap between Otto's work in Teddington in 1944 and when he turned up in Germany. In 1946 he worked in Stuttgart, CIC region 1. His first extant report is from April 1946.

16 According to this information Odessa was renamed "Skorzeny" in Dachau. The CIC suspected, however, that Otto Skorzeny's name was only used for reasons of prestige and that he never headed the organisation himself. See Operation Brandy, Skorzeny Group, RG 319, Entry A1134 A, National Archives, Washington.

17 ibid. See also Walters, *Hunting Evil*, p. 141.

18 The organisation "Stille Hilfe für Kriegsgefangene und Internierte" (Silent Aid for Prisoners-of-War and Interneees) was supported by Himmler's daughter Gudrun for decades. Even as a child she had been taken by her father to see his work. In 1941, for example, the two of them visited Dachau together. Gudrun liked it.

19 E-mail from Frederick Forsyth to the author on 30/8/2018 about the genesis of his Odessa novel. In 1963, working as a Reuters journalist in East Berlin, Forsyth contacted the defector John Peet who told him about Odessa. Forsyth later discussed it with Simon Wiesenthal, who confirmed parts of the account.

20 Tom Segev, *Simon Wiesenthal. Die Biographie*, Munich, 2010, p. 135.

21 "We were instructed to arrest – if we could find them – *Kreisleiter* (heads of a region) and lesser Nazi officials. It was an endeavor into which I threw myself with some zeal [. . .] After considerable detective work [. . .] we did manage to make a few arrests. The only trouble was that within at most 48 hours, not only were they set free again, they were put in

charge of various town and city administrations. The U.S. military government insisted that the former Nazi officials were indispensable to run things. It was a comedy. We made arrests, while our commanders, more concerned with maintaining law and order and nightly curfews than with the misdeeds of Nazi ideologues, reinstated these "able Germans," and indeed thanked us for having found them in their hiding places." Brombert, *Trains of Thought*, pp. 312f.

22 This also included the rat line. See James V. Milano and Patrick Brogan, *Soldiers, Spies, and the Rat Line. America's Undeclared War Against the Soviets*, Washington DC, 2000 and Philippe Sands, *The Ratline: Love, Lies and Justice on the Trail of a Nazi Fugitive*, London 2021.

23 Rudolf Diels, *Der Fall Otto John. Hintergründe und Lehren*, Göttingen, 1954, p. 18.

24 The fiancé Mr Stone is also mentioned in Wera's personal file. See Württembergisches Staatstheater Stuttgart, Personalakte Wera Friedberg, Staatsarchiv Ludwigsburg, EL221/6, Bü 467.

25 On the Stuttgart black market and CIC, see 14 – Hauptkartei Gruppe o, Nr. 49, November 1945–Dezember 1946, Stadtarchiv Stuttgart.

26 Wera Frydtberg in conversation with the author in the 1990s.

27 Israel Friedberg (1780–1822), Eduard Friedberg (1811–1891), Heinrich Friedberg (1813–95).

28 Herbert Friedberg was supposed to be awarded his licence to practise medicine, but he was not permitted to take receipt of it. According to the Nuremberg Race Laws he was prohibited from working as a doctor. He then practised "illegally" at a hospital in Überlingen. Only during the war, when there was a shortage of doctors, was he entrusted with running a field hospital in Warsaw. See also Wiedergutmachungsakte F 196/2 Nr. 1957, Dr Herbert Friedberg, Staatsarchiv Freiburg. I would like to thank Cornelia Matz for her help with my research in Baden-Württemberg.

29 *Stuttgarter Zeitung*, 17/ 7/1946.

CHAPTER 15

1 After the war Polgar lived in Zürich and occasionally visited Friedrich Torberg in Vienna. "When it was time for him to leave again I accompanied him to the station and asked him what he'd liked about Vienna. 'I have to pass withering judgment on this city,' Polgar said. 'Vienna is

still Vienna.'" Cited in Torberg, *Tante Jolesch*, p. 265. On a similar atmosphere in Germany see Christian Bommarius, *1949. Das lange deutsche Jahr*, Munich, 2018.

2 According to the passenger data in the Ellis Island Archive, Alice left from Southampton for New York on 27/8/1949. As there is no information on her arrival, we cannot say how long she was in Europe.

3 Ernst Lothar, *Die Rückkehr*, Vienna 2018 (first published 1949), p. 100.

4 ibid., pp. 101f.

5 It was still a relatively minor problem in comparison to abductions. Scientists and engineers were kidnapped, but also ordinary Austrians who had been denounced by their neighbours to the Soviet authorities as spies. One female British student was abducted because a spurned lover persuaded some Soviet soldiers that the girl was running a British spy ring. Such denunciations were seldom checked; the authorities preferred to act straightaway. But for Alice it was nothing new to hear that people in Vienna were simply carried off. See Gordon Corera, *The Art of Betrayal. Life and Death in the British Secret Service*, London 2011.

6 Otto had probably been transferred to Vienna because he knew Czechoslovakia well. See entry in Rear Admiral Hillenkoetter's diary: "26 February 1948: Lt. Otto R. Urbach, CIC, Baltimore, Md. – Now instructor at CIC school. He has recently returned from Eastern Europe where he served with 970th CIC Detach. and has some positive intelligence which he desires to pass on to proper people." Diary of Rear Admiral R.H. Hillenkoetter, NARA, und online: https://www.cia.gov/library/reading-room/document/cia-rdp80r01731r002600430001-0

7 The Viennese registry office has Otto and Wera's arrival recorded in May 1949.

8 Cited in Torberg, *Tante Jolesch*, p. 264.

9 Otto was working undercover in Vienna as a businessman: Mr. Otto R. Urbach & Foreign Distribution Associates. For emergencies he gave the family a postal address that had nothing to do with this business: Mr. Otto R. Urbach, c/o American Legation Wien IX, Boltzmanngasse. As a "businessman" Otto came to the attention of other American firms who could not understand what he was doing in Vienna. In 1952, USCOA (United States Command, Austria) received an enquiry from the Federal Supply Co., asking what Otto R. Urbach's firm actually did. See USCOA Economics Division, February 1951, Classification: Secret. Otto wound up

the firm soon afterwards. From 1952 he was listed as an employee of the State Department, resident in Berlin.

10 Alice Urbach, cassette interview, Alice Urbach papers.

11 https://www.literaturhaus-muenchen.de/ausstellung/100-jahre-ernst-reinhardt-verlag/

12 Memorandum in the archives of the IHK for Munich and Upper Bavaria (BWA K1, XXI 16, 91. Akt, Fall 20), Bayerisches Wirtschaftsarchiv, München. I would like to thank Richard Winkler for finding this note.

13 Christian Adam in a piece for Deutschlandfunk Kultur: https://www. deutschlandfunkkultur.de/der-milde-blick-wie-deutsche-verlage-mit-ihrer-ns.976.de.html?dram:article_id=386423 See also Christian Adam, *Der Traum vom Jahre Null. Autoren, Bestseller, Leser. Die Neuordnung der Bücherwelt in Ost und West nach 1945*, Berlin, 2016.

14 By then Jungck knew how Wessel and his parents had suffered: they lived in "miserable circumstances". Jungck, *75 Jahre*, p. 79.

15 ibid., pp. 78f.

16 Apparently his chief clerk had – against Jungck's will – signed another contract with Wessel for the series and the physics book. ibid., p. 80.

17 ibid.

18 ibid., p. 56 (fn. 1)

19 ibid.

20 Letter from Alice Urbach to Hermann Jungck on 26/4/1953. Ernst Reinhardt Verlagsarchiv, Munich.

21 Jungck, *75 Jahre*, p. 56.

22 Ernst Reinhardt Verlag archive.

23 See Jungck, *75 Jahre*, p. 56. Jungck probably just brought the date forward here.

24 ibid., pp. 56f.

25 Alice to Hermann Jungck, 10/7/50, Hotel Missouri, Jefferson City, MO. Ernst Reinhardt Verlag archive, Munich.

26 Alice to Jungck, 7/9/50, Ernst Reinhardt Verlag archive.

27 Alice to Jungck, 29/7/52.

28 Alice to Jungck, 31/8/52.

29 Alice to Jungck, 21/3/54.

30 Alice to Jungck, 6/8/53.

31 Alice to Jungck, 15/5/54.

32 Alice was mistaken here. She probably submitted the manuscript in

1934 but it didn't appear until 1935. Below she accidentally wrote "Rudolf Rauh" instead of "Rudolf Rösch", but this was corrected in the copy.

33   https://www.geschichtewiki.wien.gv.at/Gerlach_%26_Wiedling After Alice asked her daughter-in-law to help out in the fight for her cookbook, Wera contacted Reinhardt Verlag too. She lived in Munich and the publishing house's offices were not far away. We have no record of what she was told. But in another letter Alice thanked Wera for at least trying.

34   One reason for this was the availability of sources. Michael Verhoeven's 2008 documentary *Menschliches Versagen* (Human failure) illustrates the problems historians and those affected had when trying to access files on Aryanisation.

35   Christoph Jungck, *100 Jahre*, p. 126.

36   ibid., p. 43.

37   Blurb for Rudolf Rösch, *So kocht man in Wien!*, Forum Verlag, Vienna, 1966.

38   Christian Enzensberger, "Der Aufruhr der Regeln". Afterword to his translation of Lewis Carroll, *Alice im Wunderland*, Frankfurt am Main, 1963.

39   Alice's last letter to Jungck, 15/5/54.

40   Königseder, *de Gruyter*, p. 129.

41   ibid., pp. 130f.

42   ibid., p. 132.

43   Only in 1990 did the legal basis change for compulsory sales that took place in the Nazi era. Sales that occurred after the Nuremberg Laws came into force on 15/9/1935 now came under the Federal Act for the Compensation of the Victims of National Socialist Persecution (See Chapter 8: "Book thieves"). For works of art the 1998 Washington Declaration also applies. For transactions made with Jewish partners after 1935, the reverse onus principle applies. There must be proof, therefore, that these transactions were regular.

CHAPTER 16

1   These are "average prices" for Manhattan. Like many New York apartment blocks, the Riviera is now a co-op in which cooperative shares are purchased.

2   To commemorate the building's centenary in 2010 a website was set up: http://www.790rsd100.org/people.html. It includes memories of tenants from the 1950s and 1960s.

3   Alice Urbach, "Old World", pp. 19f.

4   I would like to thank Dorit Whiteman for her memories of these
    encounters.

5   Alice Urbach, "Old World", p. 20.

6   Another reason for Horch's interest may have been that his wife (like
    Alice's mother) was a Gutmann.

7   Jungck's letters have not survived, but he will doubtless have referred
    once more to the 1938 contract that also dealt with translation rights.
    Alice fought her corner for a long time, writing to Jungck: "Your uncle
    Reinhardt gave me the translation rights. Later, after he died and I went to
    England, you asked me to find an English translation firm in London,
    to whom you sent a *So kocht man in Wien!* and who were going to do
    a translation. (The political situation meant nothing came of this). In
    connection with this I had (and I still do have) a letter from you in which
    you say: I know that Uncle gave you the translation rights for the book
    So kocht man in Wien! and so I won't stand in your way, even though the
    suggestion came from me. Perhaps, Herr Jungck, you now have a slightly
    clearer view of the situation. I hope you've had a very pleasant holiday."
    Alice to Jungck, 22/2/53. And a few weeks later: "Of course it is premature
    to claim rights before the issue of translation becomes a reality. In my
    hands I have your letter of 7th September 1938, from which it is clear
    that I have sole rights for the translation of the cookbook in its entirety,
    and I can send you a photocopy at any time." Alice to Jungck, 12/3/53.
    Jungck seems to have argued that there were no sales prospects for such a
    book. Alice wrote in this regard: "But once more I would like to emphasise
    that if my book had been on sale in English and American bookshops
    it would have done well. I am an established cook, whereas 'Rösch' is
    unknown. I would be very interested to find out what you think of my
    plan for a new, much smaller cookbook in English, and whether you
    might want to publish such an English cookbook by me. I feel wholly
    competent to write such a book. My English is good, as is my knowledge
    of the circumstances in England and America. But if the large book is
    to be translated, then why not the original 'Urbach'? The [unreadable]
    are not to be used! And do you not think, Herr Jungck, that I am entitled
    to compensation for all the injustice you could, of course, do nothing
    about? And if you translate the Rösch book, which contains so few
    changes, you will be infringing my translation rights – and I know you
    have no wish to do wrong by me." 12/3/53. In May 1954 Jungck seems

finally to have confirmed that he received the photocopy (15/5/1954, letters in Ernst Reinhardt Verlag archive).

8 The book by Olga Hess (1881–1965) was translated into English by Clara Schlesinger. Hess had published several books by 1916: Olga Hess: *Die moderne Kochkunst. Kochbuch zusammengestellt aus den vorzüglichsten Rezepten der Großen Ceres-Preiskonkurrenz ergänzt durch Rezepte des Wiener Seminars zur Ausbildung von Kochlehrerinnen*, Vienna, 1908; Olga and Adolf Hess: *Wiener Küche. Sammlung von Kochrezepten der Bildungsanstalt für Koch- und Haushaltungsschullehrerinnen*, Vienna, 1913; Olga and Adolf Hess: *Die Aufschreibungen der Hausfrau. Ein Beitrag zum Unterrichte in der hauswirtschaftlichen Buchführung*, Vienna, 1916.

9 Margarete Klemperer (b. Vienna 1890, d. New York 1966), married to Dr Hugo Klemperer. The couple had a son, Hans Klemperer.

10 Hilfsfonds und Vermögensverkehrsstelle, VA 13 480, AHF 5529, Österreichisches Staatsarchiv, Wien. Without the help of her sons Alice would not have been able to afford her trips to Europe. According to passenger lists she left from Southampton by boat in 1949, 1954 and 1956. Later she flew to Europe.

11 Perhaps she would have been more impressed if she had known that Julia Child, like Cordelia Dodson, had worked for the OSS during the war and thus had made a contribution to the fight against National Socialism.

12 When Ilse Camis's daughter Susan asked Alice in the 1970s what she thought of the famous TV cook Julia Child, she replied firmly, "completely overrated." Susan was speechless, because in America Julia Child was seen as the great cook. Author's conversation with Susan Camis, 2019.

13 Letter from Pat Tovey to the programme *Over Easy*, 30/12/1980, Alice Urbach papers. I would like to thank Patricia and Siska Tovey, San Francisco, for their memories of Alice and for letters from this time.

14 See, for example, Harvey Steiman, "In the kitchen at 92", *San Francisco Examiner*, 1. 11. 1978; Jinx Morgan, "Viennese Table", *American Way*, April 1981, p. 22; Lana Severn, "Alice Urbach: teaching again at 94", *Marin Independent Journal*, 1980; "Nachruf Alice Urbach", *Aufbau* Bd. XLIX, Nr. 31, August 1983.

15 According to the school prospectus she started teaching there in 1977. In 1981 she was offering a course on Fridays at 10 am and one on Mondays at 6.30 pm.

16 I would like to thank Ilse Camis for access to her correspondence with

Alice. See also a letter from Karl Urbach to Ilse Camis, 15/9/1983: "[Alice] left her body to the medical faculty. We bought a commemorative plaque for her in Golden Gate Park, where she used to like going. I could tell her that she'd become a great grandmother."

17 The programmes broadcast by the PBS are culturally more sophisticated than those put out by their commercial rivals. The presenter was Mary Martin, who is known to the American public for two reasons: as a former musical star and as the mother of Larry Hagman, JR from *Dallas*.

18 Death certificate, Alice Urbach papers.

19 Alice cited in Lana Severn's article "Alice Urbach: teaching again at 94", *Marin Independent Journal*, 1980.

20 Eva-Maria Schnurr, "Aber meine jüdischen Hände auf den Fotos blieben drin", *Spiegel online*, 8/10/2020, https://www.spiegel.de/geschichte/alice-urbach-wie-nazis-einer-juedin-ihren-kochbuch-bestseller-raubten-a-3c9d3c5f-443f-4a9e-97f2-0832c8d8ba8d. See also Andreas Fanizadeh, "Der geraubte Bestseller", *taz*, 10/10/2020. On giving back the rights see Martin Docrry, "Arisierter Topfenstrudel", *Spiegel*, 24/10/2020; Leonie Feuerbach, "Wie die Nazis ein Kochbuch stahlen", *FAZ Magazin*, November 2020, pp. 60–61; Susanne Kippenberger, "Wiener Strudel", *Tagesspiegel*, 28/10/2020; Sara Tor, "Family's fight for cookbook 'aryanised' by the Nazis", *Times*, 1/1/2021.

21 Statement by Ernst Reinhardt Verlag, October 2020. See also Christiane Laudage, "Späte Gerechtigkeit für jüdische Kochbuch-Autorin Alice Urbach – 80 Jahre nach 'Arisierung' wieder als Urheberin anerkannt", *Katholische Nachrichtenagentur KNA*, 21/12/2020.

LIST OF ILLUSTRATIONS

The photographs on the cover and at the beginning of each chapter are of Alice Urbach's "Jewish hands", taken from the original edition of her book, *So kocht man in Wien!*

ARCHIVES AND SOURCES

PRIVATE FAMILY PAPERS

Alice Urbach papers (in the possession of Karina Urbach, Cambridge, and Katrina Urbach, San Francisco)

Karl Urbach papers (in the possession of Katrina Urbach, San Francisco)

Otto Urbach papers (in the possession of Karina Urbach, Cambridge)

Robert and Lola Urbach papers (in the possession of Nina Price, San Francisco)

Mayer family papers (in the possession of Michael Livni, Jerusalem)

Cordelia Dodson papers (in the possession of Sarah Fisher, Maine)

Paula und Peter Sieber papers (in the possession of Vivien Sieber, Oxford)

AUTHOR INTERVIEWS WITH CONTEMPORARY WITNESSES

Lilly Mendelsohn Urbach (wife of Dr Karl Urbach)

Renata Rainer (daughter of Robert Urbach), 2019–20

Clara Fontana (great niece of Cordelia Dodson), 2019

Dr Dorit Whiteman, 2019–20

Ilse Camis (née Gross) and her daughter Susan Camis, 2019–20

Alisa Tennenbaum (née Lisl Scherzer), 2018–21

Elfi Reinert (interview by Vivien Sieber), 2019

ARCHIVES IN GERMANY AND AUSTRIA

Bayerisches Wirtschaftsarchiv, Munich
JHK Aktennotiz zum Ernst Reinhardt Verlag
BWA K1, XXI 16, 91. Akt, Fall 20

Bundesarchiv, Berlin Lichterfelde
Bestand Reichsnährstand (R 16/44 und R 16/58)
Sammlung Berlin Document Center (BDC), NSDAP card index of members (all NSDAP members with the name Rudolf Rösch)

Deutsches Literaturarchiv Marbach
Arthur Schnitzler papers, Sigmund Mayer letter to Arthur Schnitzler, undated (accession number HS.NZ85.0001.04041)

Verlagsarchiv des Ernst Reinhardt Verlags, München
Alice Urbach's publishing contract from 25/1/1935 and declaration of 5/9/1938
18 letters from Alice Urbach to Hermann Jungck, 1950–54

International Tracing Service/Internationaler Suchdienst, Bad Arolsen
Information on Caroline Fleischner, Sidonie Rosenberg, Dr Helene Eissler, Dr Georg Eissler, Leopold Schück and Karl Urbach

Jewish Community of Vienna/Israelitische Kultusgemeinde Wien, Matrikelamt
Birth, marriage and death material on the Mayer family

KZ-Gedenkstätte Dachau, Stiftung Bayerische Gedenkstätten
Prisoner Karl Urbach (Zugangsbuch Nr. 105/28186)

Memento, online database of the Dokumentationsarchivs des österreichischen Widerstandes, Wien
Sammelwohnungen Ebendorferstraße 10, Wien (https://www.memento.wien/address/74/)

Österreichisches Staatsarchiv
Landsturmevidenzblatt Dr Maximilian Urbach (AT-OeStA/KA Pers GB Evidenzen LSt MilKdo Wien Sanität 9)
Archival holdings from the Property Transactions Office and the relief fund for the politically persecuted on Alice Urbach, Felix and Helene Mayer, and Robert and Lola Urbach

Staatsarchiv Freiburg
Dr Herbert Friedberg, restitution file 1957 (F 196/2)

Staatsarchiv Ludwigsburg
Württembergerisches Staatstheater Stuttgart, personnel file for Wera Friedberg (StA Ludw EL221/6, Bü 467)

Stadtarchiv München
Residence registration document EWK 78 I/J/Y225, Hermann Jungck

Stadtarchiv Stuttgart

Reports about the Stuttgart black market, November 1945–December
1946 (StadtA Stgt, 14 – Hauptaktei Gruppe 0, Nr. 49)

Wiener Stadt- und Landesarchiv, WStLA

Registration documents for Alice Urbach and Otto Urbach

Tax register, K2/1 – Zentralgewerberegister, Alice Urbach; cookery
school in 4. Goldeggasse 7

Files relating to the estate of Dr Maximilian Urbach

Files relating to the estate of Sigmund Mayer

Files relating to the estate of Pauline Mayer

US ARCHIVES

CIA, Electronic Reading Room

Diary of Rear Admiral R.H. Hillenkoetter (https://www.cia.gov/library/
readingroom/docs/1947-11-03.pdf)

Ellis Island Foundation, New York

Passenger and arrival data for Alice Urbach, Karl Urbach, Otto Urbach,
Wera Urbach

Holocaust Memorial Museum, Library and Archives, Washington

Alisa Tennenbaum photograph collection

Dorit Whiteman Collection, Kindertransport

Leo Baeck Institute Archives, New York/Berlin

Felix Mayer, poems (LBI MS 102a)

Felix Mayer, *The Mission* (LBI MS 102c)

Leo Baeck Institute, Digital Collections

Mayer Family of Bratislava Collection (LBI AR 370)

Library of Congress, Manuscript Division, Washington

Anna Freud papers (MSS49700), correspondence on Hampstead
Nurseries und Hampstead Child Therapy Clinic 1941, evacuations
1941 and the study "Infants without families: The Case for and against
residential nurseries"

National Archives, Washington (NARA)

Records of the Office of Strategic Services (OSS) 1940–1947

RG 226, Entry 211: Report of Marchese Emilio Pucci, see also Entry 190C, Box 11

RG 243: Records of the US Strategic Bombing Survey

RG 226, Entry 224: OSS File Cordelia Dodson, Box 191, OSS File William Hood, Box 346, OSS File Peter Viertel, Box 804

RG 319, Entry A1134-A: Investigative Records Repository (IRR), Impersonal Files, Box 68, folder "Odessa Organization" ZF 015116.

CIC files, e.g. in RG 59, RG 65, RG 92, RG 107, RG 111, RG 153, RG 159, RG 160, RG 165, RG 226, RG 238, RG 242, RG 260

New York Public Library

Bigelow Papers, Box 9 (correspondence with Emma v. Schirach)

Reed College, Portland, Oregon, Special Collections and Archives

Reed College Bulletin, Vol. 15 (1), January 1936

Reed College Bulletin, Vol. 16 (1), January 1937

File on President Dexter Keezer 28/1/1938

Reed College Quest 1987

Reed Digital Collections (https://rdc.reed.edu/c/reedhisttxt/s?p=1&pp=20&ft=subject&fv=Athletics)

Lecture by Emilio Pucci, 1962 (https://soundcloud.com/reedcollege/pucci-emilio-talk-on-design-at-reed-college-1962)

Seeley G. Mudd Manuscript Library, Princeton University Library

Allen W. Dulles collection, Box 12, Folder 21

ARCHIVES IN GREAT BRITAIN

College Library, Harlaxton College, Grantham

Memoirs of Mrs Van der Elst from relatives and staff at Grantham Castle (uncatalogued)

Manx Museum, Library & Archives, Douglas, Isle of Man

Felix Mayer greeting card, c.1940

National Archives, Kew

Home Office files: HO 396/94 Alice Urbach. Female enemy alien. Exemption from Internment-Refugee; HO 396/113 Felix Israel Mayer

Wiener Holocaust Library, London

Peter Sieber, "The Newcastle-upon-Tyne Hostel for Jewish Refugee girls. In recognition of the Hostel Committee who initiated the hostel and managed it, and of the Newcastle Jewish Community who supported it" (unpublished manuscript, 4184)

Jewish Board of Deputies, *While you are in England. Helpful Information and guidance for every refugee*. Brochure published by the German Jewish Aid Committee/*Für die Zeit ihres Aufenthalts in England: Hilfreiche Informationen und Anleitungen für jeden Flüchtling*. Refugee Pamphlets, London *c*.1938. Reference: S3b 081.

Central Office for Refugees, *Do's and Don't's for Refugees*, London, *c*.1940. Collection 1368 (Kindertransport letters)

World Jewish Relief Archives, London

Card index and detailed files on the children in Newcastle/Windermere (anonymised)

NEWSPAPERS AND PERIODICALS

American Way

ANNO (digitalised newspapers and periodicals, Österreichische Nationalbibliothek)

Aufbau

Badener Curliste

Die Bühne

Die Fackel

Herald Tribune

Illustrierte Kronenzeitung

Jüdische Monatshefte, Zeitschrift für Politik, Wirtschaft und Literatur

Kronenzeitung

Neue Freie Presse

Neues Wiener Journal

New York Times
The Oregonian
Prager Tageblatt
Die Presse
Die Reichspost
San Francisco Examiner
Der Spiegel
Der Standard
Stuttgarter Zeitung
Der Tag
Die Zeit (Austrian weekly paper 1894–1904)

REFERENCE WORKS

Lehmann's Allgemeiner Wohnungs-Anzeiger nebst Handels- und Gewerbe-Adressbuch für die k. k. Reichs-Haupt und Residenzstadt Wien, years 1925–1940

FILM MATERIAL

American programme *Over Easy* with Alice Urbach: episode 5040 (1981), episode 6065 (1982)

FEATURE FILMS

The Third Man (GB, 1949)
Wir Wunderkinder (FRG, 1958)
Professor Mamlock (GDR, 1961)
Der Herr Karl (AT, 1961)
The Odessa File (GB/FRG/USA, 1974)
The Incident (USA, 1990)

DOCUMENTARIES (SELECTED)

The Ritchie Boys (CAN/DE, 2004)
About Face. Jewish refugees in the Allied Forces (USA, 2005)
Menschliches Versagen (DE, 2008)
The Windermere Children (GB, 2020)

RADIO PROGRAMMES (SELECTED)

Franz Marischka, film producer in conversation with Kurt von Daak, "alpha-Forum" on Bayerischer Rundfunk, 2/1/2002

Georg Kreisler, author, composer and cabarettist, in conversation with Christoph Lindenmeyer, "alpha-Forum" on Bayerischer Rundfunk, 28/2/2003

"Poisoned Angel – The Story of Alma Rose", BBC Radio 4, 2004

Philipp Gessler, "Wie deutsche Verlage mit ihrer NS-Geschichte umgehen", Deutschlandfunk Kultur, 19/5/2017 (https://www. deutschlandfunkkultur.de/der-milde-blick-wie-deutsche-verlage-mit-ihrer-ns.976.de.html?dram:article_id=386423)

UNPUBLISHED MANUSCRIPTS

Michael Livni (Max Langer), "An Adolescent Subculture", PhD, 1959, with an autobiographical foreword from 2019, Jerusalem 2019

Felix Mayer, "The Mayer Family, from Pressburg to Vienna", New York 1960, Mayer family papers

Alice Urbach, "Old World – New World. The Personal Life Story of Mrs. Alice Urbach", 1977, Alice Urbach papers

Alice Urbach, "Some Members of the Mayer Family, 1789–1957", told by Alice Urbach, written down by Charles Landstone, London, 1957, Mayer family papers

LITERATURE

Christian Adam, *Lesen unter Hitler. Autoren, Bestseller, Leser im Dritten Reich*, Berlin, 2010

idem, *Der Traum vom Jahre Null. Autoren, Bestseller, Leser: Die Neuordnung der Bücherwelt in Ost und West nach 1945*, Berlin, 2016

Rudolf Agstner, "A Tale of Three Viennese Department Stores in Egypt. The Oriental Adventures of Mayer, Stein and Tiring" in *Aufbau*, Nr. 9, 30/4/1999

Götz Aly/Michael Sontheimer, *Fromms. Wie der jüdische Kondomfabrikant Julius F. unter die Räuber fiel*, Frankfurt am Main, 2007

Leon Askin, *Quietude and Quest. Protagonists and Antagonists in the Theatre, on and off Stage as Seen Through the Eyes of Leon Askin*, Riverside, 1989

David Axmann, *Friedrich Torberg. Die Biographie*, Munich, 2008

Lillian M. Bader, *Ein Leben ist nicht genug. Memoiren einer Wiener Jüdin*, Vienna, 2011

Dorit Bader-Whiteman, *The Uprooted. A Hitler Legacy. Voices of Those Who Escaped before the "Final Solution"*, New York, 1993

Jan-Pieter Barbian, *Die vollendete Ohnmacht? Schriftsteller, Verleger und Buchhändler im NS-Staat, Ausgewählte Aufsätze*, Essen, 2008

idem, *Literaturpolitik im NS-Staat. Von der "Gleichschaltung" bis zum Ruin*, Frankfurt am Main, 2010

Christian Bauer and Rebekka Göpfert, *Die Ritchie Boys. Deutsche Emigranten beim US-Geheimdienst*, Hamburg, 2005

Susanne Belovari, *Wiener Juden und die Wiener Küche vor 1938* (https://experts.illinois.edu/ws/portalfiles/portal/345076995/Wiener_Juden_und_die_Wiener_Kueche_vor_1938.pdf)

Hugo Bettauer, *Die Stadt ohne Juden. Ein Roman von übermorgen*, Vienna, 1922

Heinz Boberach (ed.), *Meldungen aus dem Reich. Die geheimen Lageberichte des Sicherheitsdienstes der SS 1938–1945*, Vol. 2, Herrsching, 1984

Traude Bollauf, *Dienstmädchen – Emigration. Die Flucht jüdischer Frauen aus Österreich und Deutschland nach England 1938/39*, Vienna, 2010

Christian Bommarius, *1949. Das lange deutsche Jahr*, Munich, 2018

Frédéric Bonnesoeur et al. (ed.), *Geschlossene Grenzen. Die Internationale Flüchtlingskonferenz von Évian 1938. Katalog zur Ausstellung des Zentrums für Antisemitismusforschung der Technischen Universität Berlin und der Gedenkstätte Deutscher Widerstand*, Berlin, 2018

Thomas Borghardt, "America's Secret Vanguard: US Army Intelligence Operations in Germany, 1944–47", *Studies in Intelligence 2013*, Vol. 57 (2)

Victor Brombert, *Trains of Thought. Paris to Omaha Beach, Memories of a Stateless Youth*, New York, 2002

Ralph W. Brown III, "Removing 'Nasty Nazi Habits': The CIC and the Denazification of Heidelberg University, 1945–1946", *Journal of Intelligence History 2004*, Vol. 4 (1), pp. 25–56

Lewis Carroll, *Alice's Adventures in Wonderland and Through the Looking Glass*, London, 2003 (first published separately in 1865 and 1871)

David Cesarani and Tony Kushner (eds), *The Internment of Aliens in Twentieth Century Britain*, London, 1993

Connery Chappell, *Island of Barbed Wire. The Remarkable Story of World War Two Internment on the Isle of Man*, London 1984

Lorie Charlesworth and Michael Salter, "Ensuring the after-life of the Ciano diaries: Allen Dulles' provision of Nuremberg trial evidence", *Intelligence and National Security*, 2006, Vol. 21 (4)

Fabrizio Ciano, *Quando Il Nonno Fece Fucilare Papà*, Milan, 1991

Rebecca Clifford, *Survivors. Children's Lives after the Holocaust*, Yale, 2020

Gordon Corera, *The Art of Betrayal. Life and Death in the British Secret Service*, London, 2011

Volker Dahm, *Das jüdische Buch im Dritten Reich*, Munich, 1993

Ruth David, *Child of Our Time: A Young Girl's Flight from the Holocaust*, London, 2003

Rudolf Diels, *Der Fall Otto John. Hintergründe und Lehren*, Göttingen, 1954

Daniel B. Dodson, *The Man Who Ran Away*, London 1961

Martin Doerry, "*Mein verwundetes Herz*". *Das Leben der Lilli Jahn 1900–1944*, Munich, 2002

idem, "Kräftig arisiert", *Der Spiegel*, Nr. 17, 20/4/2019

Wolfgang Dressen (ed.), *Betrifft: "Aktion 3": Deutsche verwerten jüdische Nachbarn – Dokumente zur Arisierung. Katalog zur gleichnamigen Ausstellung im Stadtmuseum* Düsseldorf, 29/10/1998–10/1/1999, Berlin, 1998

Tamara Ehs, *Hochschullager im Austrofaschismus 1935–1937* (https://geschichte.univie.ac.at/de/artikel/hochschullager-im-austrofaschismus)

Violet Van der Elst, *On the Gallows*, London, 1937

Franz Endler, *Wien zwischen den Kriegen*, Vienna, 1983

Günther Fetzer, *Droemer Knaur. Die Verlagsgeschichte 1846–2017*, Munich, 2017

Frederick Forsyth, *The Odessa File*, London, 1972

Norbert Frei, Jose Brunner and Constantin Goschler (eds), *Die Praxis der Wiedergutmachung. Geschichte, Erfahrung und Wirkung in Deutschland und Israel*, Göttingen, 2009

Paul French, *Bloody Saturday. Shanghai's Darkest Day*, London 2018

Anna Freud, *Die Schriften der Anna Freud, Bd. 2, 1939–1945. Kriegskinder. Berichte aus den Kriegskinderheimen "Hampstead Nurseries"*, Frankfurt am Main, 1987

Max Friedlaender, *Lebenserinnerungen des Anwalts Dr. Max Friedlaender* (https://brak.de/w/files/01_ueber_die_brak/friedlaender.pdf)

Charles Neilson Gattey, *The Incredible Mrs. Van der Elst*, London, 1972

Georg Gaugusch, *Wer einmal war. Das jüdische Großbürgertum Wiens 1800–1938 (Jahrbuch der Heraldisch-Genealogischen Gesellschaft Adler, Bd. 17), Bd. 2, L-R*, Vienna, 2016

Peter Gay, *Schnitzler's Century: The Making of Middle-Class Culture 1815–1914*, New York, 2012

Michael Geyer, "The Prague Cookbook of Ruth Bratu, or: How a Historian Came to Feel the Past", *Central European History* 2020 (53), pp. 2–22

Rebekka Göpfert, *Der jüdische Kindertransport von Deutschland nach England 1938/39. Geschichte und Erinnerung*, Frankfurt am Main, 1999

Christian Göschel, *Mussolini and Hitler: The Forging of the Fascist Alliance*, Yale, 2018

Constantin Goschler and Philipp Ther (eds), *Raub und Restitution. "Arisierung" und Rückerstattung des jüdischen Eigentums in Europa*, Frankfurt am Main, 2003

Graham Greene, *The Third Man*, London, 1950

Robert S. Greene, *Blum San! Scholar, Soldier, Gentleman, Spy. The many lives of Paul Blum*, New York, 1998

Eva Haas, "Ein Schild mit Namen und Nummer um den Hals", in Martin Doerry, *"Nirgendwo und überall zu Haus". Gespräche mit Überlebenden des Holocaust*, Munich, 2006

Hans Habe, *Im Jahre Null*, Munich, 1977

Ernst Haeusserman, *Mein Freund Henry*, Vienna and Hamburg, 1983

Murray G. Hall, *Österreichische Verlagsgeschichte 1918–1938. Band 1: Geschichte des österreichischen Verlagswesens*, Vienna, Cologne and Graz, 1985

Murray G. Hall and Christina Köstner, *". . . allerlei für die Nationalbibliothek zu ergattern . . .". Eine österreichische Institution in der NS-Zeit*, Vienna, Cologne and Weimar, 2006

Jonathan Haslam, *The Spectre of War*, Princeton, 2021

Bruce Henderson, *Sons and Soldiers. The Untold Story of the Jews who escaped the Nazis and returned with the US Army to fight Hitler*, New York, 2017

Georg Hermann, *Jettchen Geberts Geschichte/Henriette Jacoby* (novel in two volumes), Berlin, 1919

Raul Hilberg, *Die Vernichtung der europäischen Juden*, Frankfurt, 1990

Ludwig Hirschfeld, *Wien. Was nicht im Baedeker steht*, Munich, 1927 (in 2020 Milena Verlag, Vienna, published a new edition)

Eric Hobsbawm, *The Age of Empire 1875–1915*, London, 1987
idem, *Interesting Times. A Twentieth-Century Life*, London, 2002

Eva Holpfer, "Der Fall Novak. Eichmanns Transportoffizier – der letzte Schuldspruch". Lecture given on 1/12/2005 at Vienna criminal court: (http://www.kreuzstadl.net/downloads/novak_referat_dezember05_holpfer.pdf)

Klaus-Peter Horn, *Pädagogische Zeitschriften im Nationalsozialismus. Selbstbehauptung, Anpassung, Funktionalisierung*, no place given, 1995, Vol. 3

Arnim Höland, *Dr. jur. Viktor Horniger, Reichsgerichtsrat. Aus einem deutschen Richterleben*, Halle, 2020

Jonas Höltig, "Wer war eigentlich Otto Liebmann?", *Legal Tribune Online (LTO)*, 18/12/2017

William Hood, *Mole. The true story of the first Russian intelligence officer recruited by the CIA*, London, 1982

Andrea Hopp and Katja Gosdek, *Die Flüchtlingskonferenz von Évian 1938. Nach dem Roman "Die Mission" von Hans Habe*, Leipzig, 2019

Mona Horncastle, *Margarete Schütte-Lihotzky. Architektin, Widerstandkämpferin, Aktivistin*, Vienna, 2019

Paul Hoser, "Thierschstraße 41. Der Untermieter Hitler, sein jüdischer Hausherr und ein Restitutionsproblem", in *Vierteljahrshefte für Zeitgeschichte*, 2017 (2)
idem, *Die politischen, wirtschaftlichen und sozialen Hintergründe der Münchner Tagespresse zwischen 1914 und 1934: Methoden der Pressebeeinflussung*, 2 Vols, Frankfurt am Main, 1990

Thomas Jahn, "Suche nach 'arisierten' Büchern in den Beständen der Bayerischen Staatsbibliothek. Forschungsstand – Methoden – Ergebnisse" (https://journals.ub.uni-heidelberg.de/index.php/akmb-news/article/view/198/183)

Anne Joseph (ed.), *From the Edge of the World. The Jewish Refugee Experience through Letters and Stories*, London, 2003

Christoph Jungck et al., *100 Jahre Ernst-Reinhardt-Verlag*, Munich, 1999

Hermann Jungck, *75 Jahre Ernst Reinhardt Verlag München Basel. Verlagsgeschichte*, Munich, 1974

Ela Kaczmarska, "Kindertransport: Britain's rescue plan": (https://media.nationalarchives.gov.uk/index.php/kindertransport-britains-rescue-plan/)

Stephen Kinzer, *The Brothers. John Foster Dulles, Allen Dulles and Their Secret World War*, New York, 2013

Egon Erwin Kisch, *Marktplatz der Sensationen* (new edition with 33 reportages), 2019

Victor Klemperer, *Ich will Zeugnis ablegen bis zum letzten. Tagebücher 1933–1941*, Vol. 1, Berlin, 1995

Marie Kolkenbrock, *Stereotype and Destiny in Arthur Schnitzler's Prose*, London, 2018

Hubert Kolling, "Riederer von Paar, Viola", *Journal für Pflegewissenschaft und Pflegepraxis*, 2004, Vol. 3

Angelika Königseder, *Walter de Gruyter. Ein Wissenschaftsverlag im Nationalsozialismus*, Tübingen, 2016

Karl Kraus, "Reaktion auf Sigmund Mayers Vortrag vom 5. Februar 1903 über 'Die Schaffung großer Vermögen und die ökonomische Wissenschaft'", *Die Fackel*, Nr. 131, February 1903, pp. 15–16

Hiroaki Kuromiya, "Stalin's Great Terror and the Asian Nexus", *Europe-Asia Studies*, 2014, Vol. 66 (5), pp. 775–93

Tony Kushner, "Politics and Race, Gender and Class: Refugees, Fascists and Domestic Service in Britain, 1933–40", in Tony Kushner and Kenneth Lunn, *The Politics of Marginality. Race, the Radical Right and Minorities in Twentieth Century Britain*, Oxford, 1990

Kurt Landsberger, *Prisoners of War at Camp Trinidad, Colorado 1943–1946. Internment, Intimidation, Incompetence and Country Club Living*, Wisconsin, 2007

Charles Landstone, *I Gate-Crashed*, London, 1976

Eran Laor, *Vergangen und ausgelöscht. Erinnerungen an das slowakisch-ungarische Judentum*, Stuttgart, 1972

Joe Lederer, *Blatt im Wind*, Munich 1951 (first edition Vienna, 1936)

Deborah E. Lipstadt, *Beyond Belief. The American Press and the Coming of the Holocaust 1933–1945*, New York, 1986

Michael Löffelsender, *Kölner Rechtsanwälte im Nationalsozialismus. Eine Berufsgruppe zwischen Gleichschaltung und Kriegseinsatz*, Tübingen, 2015

Ernst Lothar, *Die Rückkehr. Roman*, Vienna 2018 (first published 1949)

Robert Mackay, *The Test of War. Inside Britain 1939–45*, London, 1999

Kurt Salomon Maier, *Unerwünscht. Kindheits- und Jugenderinnerungen eines jüdischen Kippenheimers*, Heidelberg, 2018

Stephan Malinowski, *Vom König zum Führer. Sozialer Niedergang und politische Radikalisierung im deutschen Adel zwischen Kaiserreich und NS-Staat*, Berlin, 2003

idem, *Die Hohenzollern und die Nazis. Geschichte einer Kollaboration*, Berlin, 2021

Julian Marcuse and Bernardine Woerner, *Die fleischlose Küche*, Munich, 1909

Franz Marischka, *Immer nur lächeln. Geschichten und Anekdoten von Theater und Film*, Munich, 2001

Christof Mauch, *Schattenkrieg gegen Hitler. Das Dritte Reich im Visier der amerikanischen Geheimdienste 1941–1945*, Stuttgart, 1999

Adelheid Mayer and Elmar Samsinger, *Fast wie Geschichten aus 1001 Nacht. Die jüdischen Textilkaufleute Mayer zwischen Europa und dem Orient*, Vienna, 2015

F. Arnold Mayer and Heinrich Rietsch, *Die Mondsee-Wiener Liederhandschrift und der Mönch von Salzburg. Eine Untersuchung von Literatur- und Musikgeschichte nebst den zugehörigen Texten aus der Handschrift mit Anmerkungen*, 2 Vols, Berlin, 1894–96

Sigmund Mayer, *Ein jüdischer Kaufmann 1831–1911. Lebenserinnerungen*, Berlin and Vienna, 1926. (The English translation by Karl Urbach – expanded and updated – appeared in a revised version by Michael Livni in 2021)

idem, *Die Wiener Juden 1700–1900*, Vienna and Berlin, 1917

idem, *Die soziale Frage in Wien. Studie eines Arbeitgebers*, Vienna, 1871

idem, "Die Aufhebung der Gewerbefreiheit", *Neue Freie Presse*, 8–10/2/1882

idem, "Der Reichtum der Juden", *Die Neuzeit*, 2/4/1886

idem, *Die Aufhebung der Gewerbefreiheit. Streit- und Fehdeschrift gegen die Wiederherstellung der Zunft in Österreich*, Vienna, 1883

Thomas Mayer, "My Background", in Roger Backhouse and Roger Middleton (eds), *Exemplary Economists. North America*, Vol. 1, Aldershot, 2000

Elizabeth P. McIntosh, *Sisterhood of Spies. The Women of the OSS*,
   Maryland, 1998
Andrew Meier, *The Lost Spy. An American in Stalin's Secret Service*,
   New York, 2008
Ib Melchior, *Case by Case. A U.S. Army Counterintelligence Agent in
   World War II*, Novato, 1993
George Mikes, *How to Be a Brit*, London, 1984
James V. Milano and Patrick Brogan, *Soldiers, Spies, and the Rat Line.
   America's Undeclared War Against the Soviets*, Washington, 2000

Norman Ohler, *Blitzed: Drugs in Nazi Germany*, London, 2016
Sandra Oster, *Das Autorenfoto in Buch und Buchwerbung. Autorinszenierung
   und Kanonisierung mit Bildern*, Berlin, 2014

Eugen Felix Pagast and Viola Riederer von Paar, *Zoologie für Studierende
   und zum Selbstunterricht*, Munich, 1938
   idem, *Botanik für Studierende und zum Selbstunterricht*, Munich, 1938
Iris Pawlitschko, "Jüdische Buchhandlungen in Wien. Arisierung und
   Liquidierung in den Jahren 1938–1945", dissertation, University of
   Vienna, 1996
Hella Pick, *Simon Wiesenthal. A Life in Search of Justice*, London, 1996
Alfred Polgar, *Im Lauf der Zeit*, Hamburg, 1954
Daniela Punkl, "Verlag Moritz Perles", dissertation, University of
   Vienna, 2002

Emma Quenzer, *Das süddeutsche Koch- und Haushaltsbuch. Mit Beiträgen
   von Prof. Rud. Hecker und Dr. Julian Marcuse*, Munich, 1933

Heidi Reuschel, *Tradition oder Plagiat? Die 'Stilkunst' von Ludwig Reiners
   und die 'Stilkunst' von Eduard Engel im Vergleich*, Bamberg, 2014
Viola Riederer von Paar, *Vererbungslehre für Studierende und zum
   Selbstunterricht. Grundriß, Kurzes Repertorium, Prüfungsfragen und
   Antworten, Reinhardts naturwissenschaftliche Kompendien*, Vol. 9,
   Munich, 1937 (editions printed until 1946)
Curt Riess, *The Nazis Go Underground*, New York, 1944

idem, *Total Espionage. Germany's Information and Disinformation Apparatus 1932–40*, New York, 1941

idem, *Das war ein Leben! Erinnerungen*, Munich, 1977

Felix Römer, *Kameraden. Die Wehrmacht von innen*, Munich, 2014

Rudolf Rösch, *So kocht man in Wien!* (German and Austrian editions from 1939–66)

idem, *Wiener Mehlspeisen*, Munich, 1954

idem, *Fleischlose Kost. Bewährte Rezepte für die fleischlose Küche*, Munich, 1939 and 1954

Sidonie Rosenberg and Alice Urbach, *Das Kochbuch für Feinschmecker*, Vienna and Leipzig, 1925

Sidonie Rosenberg and Emma Schreiber, *Das Kochbuch des Junggesellen*, Vienna and Leipzig, 1926

Anders Rydell, *The Book Thieves. The Nazi Looting of Europe's Libraries and the Race to Return a Literary Inheritance*, London, 2017

Anja Salewsky, *"Der olle Hitler soll sterben!" Erinnerungen an den jüdischen Kindertransport nach England*, Munich, 2001

Roman Sandgruber, *Traumzeit für Millionäre. Die 929 reichsten Wienerinnen und Wiener im Jahr 1910*, Vienna, Graz and Klagenfurt, 2013

Philippe Sands, *The Ratline: Love, Lies and Justice on the Trail of a Nazi Fugitive*, London 2021

Klaus G. Saur (ed.), *Verlage im "Dritten Reich"*, Frankfurt am Main, 2013

Ian Sayer and Douglas Botting, *America's Secret Army. The Untold Story of the Counter Intelligence Corps*, New York, 1989

Frederik Steven Louis Schouten, "Ernst Toller. An Intellectual Youth Biography, 1893–1918", European University Institute, PhD, Florence, 2007

Günther Schwarberg, *Dein ist mein ganzes Herz: Die Geschichte von Fritz Löhner-Beda, der die schönsten Lieder der Welt schrieb, und warum Hitler ihn ermorden ließ*, Göttingen, 2000

Tom Segev, *Simon Wiesenthal. Die Biographie*, Munich, 2010

Peter M.F. Sichel, *The Secrets of My Life. Vintner, Prisoner, Soldier, Spy*, Bloomington, 2016

Stefan Stirnemann, "Das gestohlene Buch" in *Schweizer Monat*, 2003, No. 927

Franziska Tausig, *Shanghai Passage. Emigration ins Ghetto*, Vienna, 2007

Toni Tipton-Martin, *The Jemima Code: Two Centuries of African American Cookbooks*, Austin, 2015

Friedrich Torberg, *Die Tante Jolesch oder der Untergang des Abendlandes in Anekdoten*, Parts 1 and 2, Vienna, 1986 (first published 1975)
idem, *Eine tolle, tolle Zeit. Briefe und Dokumente aus den Jahren der Flucht 1938 bis 1941*, Munich, 1989

Florian Traussnig, *Militärischer Widerstand von außen. Österreicher in US-Armee und Kriegsgeheimdienst im Zweiten Weltkrieg*, Vienna, 2016

Fred Uhlman, *The Making of an Englishman. Erinnerungen eines deutschen Juden*, Zürich 1998

Alice Urbach, *So kocht man in Wien!* (various editions, 1935–38)
idem and Sidonie Rosenberg, *Das Kochbuch für Feinschmecker*, Vienna and Leipzig, 1925

Karina Urbach, *Go-Betweens for Hitler*, Oxford, 2015
idem, "Nützliche Idioten. Die Hohenzollern und Hitler", in Thomas Biskup, Jürgen Luh and Truc Vu Minh (eds), *Preußendämmerung. Die Abdankung der Hohenzollern und das Ende Preußens*, Heidelberg, 2019
idem, "'England is pro-Hitler'. German opinion during the Czechoslovakian Crisis 1938", in Julie Gottlieb, Daniel Hucker and Richard Toye (eds), *The Munich Crisis, Politics and the People*, Manchester, 2021.
idem, "Geraubte Bücher", *Die Zeit*, No. 52, 10/12/2020, p. 21

Peter Viertel, *Dangerous Friends. At Large with Huston and Hemingway in the Fifties*, London, 1992

Peter Voswinckel, "Um das Lebenswerk betrogen: Walter Guttmann (1873–1941) und seine Medizinische Terminologie", *Medizinhistorisches Journal*, 32 (1997), pp. 321–54
idem, *Dr. Josef Löbel. Botschafter eines heiteren deutschen Medizin-Feuilletons in Wien-Berlin-Prag*, Berlin 2018

Frederic Wakeman, *Policing Shanghai 1927–1937*, Berkeley, 1995

Guy Walters, *Hunting Evil. The Nazi War Criminals Who Escaped and the Quest to Bring Them to Justice*, London, 2010

John R. Watt, *Saving Lives in Wartime China: How Medical Reformers Built Modern Healthcare Systems Amid War and Epidemics, 1928–1945 (China Studies)*, Leiden, 2014

Rüdiger von Wechmar, *Akteur in der Loge. Weltläufige Erinnerungen*, Munich, 2000

Pablo Wessel and Viola Riederer von Paar, *Curso general di Fisica*, Madrid, 1942

Paul Wessel, *Physik, Teil I, Mechanik, Wellenlehre, Akustik, Kalorik, Optik, Physik. Teil II, Magnetik, Elektrik, Elektronik, Atomistik. Atomistik. Teil III, Kurzes Repertorium und Formelsammlung, Prüfungsfragen und Antworten, Tabellen und Zahlenwerte*, Munich, 1937

    idem and Viola Riederer von Paar, *Physik für das Studium an technischen Hochschulen und zum Gebrauch in der Praxis*, Munich, 1938–46

Simon Wiesenthal, *Ich jagte Eichmann*, Gütersloh, 1961

    idem, *Doch die Mörder leben*, Munich, 1967

Elisabeth Young-Bruehl, *Anna Freud: a biography*, New York, 1988.

Stefan Zweig, *Die Welt von gestern. Erinnerungen eines Europäers*, Frankfurt am Main, 1978 (first published 1942)

Veronika Zwerger and Ursula Seeber, *Küche der Erinnerung. Essen und Exil*, Vienna, 2018

INDEX OF PEOPLE

KARINA URBACH is a Senior Research Fellow at the University of London. She received her doctorate from the University of Cambridge and has taken part in several BBC, PBS and ZDF documentaries. In 2015 her book *Go-Betweens for Hitler* (OUP) triggered a debate in the UK about the Royal family's links to Nazi Germany. For her historical novel *Cambridge 5* (written under the pseudonym Hannah Coler) she was shortlisted for three literary prizes and won the Crime Cologne Award in 2018. The story of her grandmother Alice Urbach and the fate of her cookbook is currently being made into a TV documentary by arte/ZDF. Karina Urbach lives with her family in Cambridge, UK.

JAMIE BULLOCH is the translator of Timur Vermes' *Look Who's Back*, Birgit Vanderbeke's *The Mussel Feast*, which won him the Schlegel-Tieck Prize, *Kingdom of Twilight* by Steven Uhly, Robert Menasse's *The Capital* and *Love in Five Acts* by Daniela Krien, amongst other works. He is also the author of *Karl Renner: Austria*.

A *SPECTATOR* AND *PROSPECT MAGAZINE* BOOK OF THE YEAR 2022

"An unputdownable narrative"
A.N. WILSON

What happened to the books that were too valuable to burn?

Alice Urbach had her own cooking school in Vienna, but in 1938 she was forced to flee to England. Returning to the ruins of Vienna in the late 1940s, she discovers that her bestselling cookbook has been published under someone else's name.

Eighty years later, the historian Karina Urbach – Alice's granddaughter – uncovers the truth behind the stolen cookbook, and tells the extraordinary story of a family torn apart by the Nazi regime, of imprisonment and escape, persecution and fraud, and ultimately of a woman who, with her unwavering passion for cooking, survived the horror and losses of the Holocaust to begin a new life in America.

Impeccably researched and incredibly moving, *Alice's Book* sheds light on an untold chapter in the history of Nazi crimes against Jewish authors.

"A gripping piece of 20th-century family history . . .
moving and clear-eyed" *FINANCIAL TIMES*

"Brilliant . . . the material is stunningly interesting . . .
It is a triumph" DANIEL FINKELSTEIN

"Engaging, elegant and moving"
LITERARY REVIEW

Translated from the German by Jamie Bulloch

MACLEHOSE PRESS NON-FICTION | HISTORICAL

ISBN 978-1-52941-632-9

9 781529 416329

FSC

e Also available in ebook

An imprint of QUERCUS UK £10.99

Design by Andrew Smith, with an original photograph from *So kocht man in Wien!*
Photograph of Karina Urbach © Dan Komoda, Princeton